WAS JUSTICE SERVED?

For the Brutal Murder of Former TIME
Magazine Writer/Reporter Julie R. Grace

TOLD BY RUTH GRACE AND WRITTEN BY NANCY HOFFMAN

iUniverse, Inc.
New York   Bloomington

Was Justice Served?
For the Brutal Murder of Former TIME Magazine Writer/Reporter Julie R. Grace

iUniverse books may be ordered through booksellers or by contacting:

iUniverse
1663 Liberty Drive
Bloomington, IN 47403
www.iuniverse.com
1-800-Authors (1-800-288-4677)

ISBN: 978-1-4502-5670-4 (pbk)
ISBN: 978-1-4502-5672-8 (cloth)
ISBN: 978-1-4502-5671-1 (ebk)

Printed in the United States of America

iUniverse rev. date: 11/1/2010

I dedicate this poem to my best friend and beautiful daughter.
Although you are gone from this earth, you will always be
very close to me in my heart and in my thoughts.

The angels brought you home today
To a place of peace so far away.
A place where there will be no pain,
A place where you are safe from suffering in vain.
A place where you are free to feel
Love, joy and happiness so surreal.
A paradise from this place on earth,
A place of new beginnings,
A place of your rebirth.
A place full of angels watching over you
To protect, to guide, to see your journey through.
When once again, one day we will meet
Where we feel soft clouds of white beauty beneath our feet.
Where we can fly with the angels or take a walk with God;
Nothing is off limits, this paradise abroad.
Although I may miss you and think of you each day,
My heart is at peace knowing you're in heaven,
No longer in harm's way.
You were my angel here on earth, always by my side.
Now an angel in heaven
You no longer have to hide.
I look forward to the day when I will see my Julie Grace.
In Heaven's paradise that's **nothing** like this place.

—*Heidi Thomas*

Contents

Preface

Since May 20, 2003, Ruth Grace has been living a nightmare. Under no circumstances do parents ever want to get a call telling them that their child is dead. But to get a call and then know that your daughter has been murdered by an abusive partner is more than most parents can handle. Although Ruth and her husband both knew their daughter Julie was living in an abusive relationship, their numerous attempts to get her to leave had failed.

Unfortunately, domestic violence claims the lives of innocent victims every year, but many of the deaths could be prevented if the judicial system did a better job of locking up those who commit these crimes. Julie's case was not unique in that there were many episodes prior to Julie's death where the abuse got to the point that police were called, her abuser was taken to jail, and restraining orders were issued. But like many restraining orders, they are worth no more than the paper they are written on. Julie's abuser, George Thompson, ignored restraining orders, and he continued to pursue Julie until he ultimately killed her.

Over the last seven years, Ruth has endured the pain of losing her daughter and then her husband. However, the final blow came when she and her son, Glenn, faced Julie's accuser in a courtroom for his first-degree murder trial. They saw how the judicial system managed to twist the facts to make it appear that Julie caused her death, and not George Thompson, even though George had previously confessed to murdering her. It turned out that the judge felt George had done nothing more than fail to get medical treatment for Julie in a timely manner. Because of this, he tossed out the first-degree murder charge and handed George a much lesser verdict of involuntary manslaughter. As a result, George served a light sentence and was released from prison in May 2007.

Ruth is haunted every day by the fact that her daughter's body was badly beaten, and she suffered miserably for three days before she died while George did nothing more than sit by and watch. Ruth will always wonder what she could have done to have prevented Julie's untimely death.

Domestic violence is nondiscriminatory. It is prevalent in all races, ages, and socioeconomic income levels. Julie's story is an example of how an intelligent and financially successful career woman with a vibrant personality fell for someone who told her he loved her while all he wanted was to take advantage of her generous, kindhearted ways and totally control and run her life. When she failed to do exactly what he wanted, he physically and mentally abused her until her body could no longer take it and then waited while she died a slow, painful death.

Was Justice Served was written because Ruth wants to share Julie's tragic story with others, especially those who may currently be in an abusive relationship. She wants to warn them to leave while they can before it's too late, and they end up like Julie. The second reason for writing this book is to show how the judicial system fails to treat crimes of domestic violence seriously enough and put abusers behind bars forever. Ruth strongly believes that laws need to be changed to severely punish those who take pleasure in abusing innocent women. No woman should ever be subjected to the horrible abuses that Julie was subjected to. Laws must be changed so that Ruth will find solace in knowing that Julie did not die in vain and that other women's lives will be saved.

CHAPTER 1
WHY DID THIS HAPPEN TO JULIE?

No matter how long I live, I'll always be haunted and tormented by the horrible news I received at approximately 7:45 the morning of Tuesday, May 20th, 2003. Hearing the phone ring, I quickly went over, picked it up and said, "Hello," confident that I would be hearing my daughter Julie respond back with, "Hi, Mom." It had been a few days since I had spoken with her, and I was very excited that she had finally called, as I was beginning to really worry. She and I typically spoke one or more times a day, and even though I had tried numerous times to reach her, she never answered her phone. I thought, finally, she's calling to let me know why I hadn't heard from her since last week. I believed my worries were over. I could now relax, knowing everything was okay.

However, that was not the case, and my excitement soon turned into horror and shock. Instead of hearing Julie's voice, what I heard was the voice of Edward Heerdt, a detective from the Chicago Police Department. My heart sank and my body went numb as he told me the news that Julie was dead, and the cause of her death was under investigation. He went on to say that George Thompson had been arrested and taken into custody.

"What? No way! Julie cannot be dead! You've made a mistake. It can't be my Julie!" These phrases kept running rampantly through my head.

What the detective said to me after that fell on deaf ears. I was confident I was having a very bad nightmare, and as soon as I woke up everything would be fine. Julie would call me and let me know what she had been doing. We'd discuss her plans for the day, just as we had always done.

My husband of forty-six years, Duard, was standing beside me watching my reaction as Detective Heerdt relayed the dreadful news. Soon after hearing that Julie was dead, I became speechless. Sensing my severe state of shock, the detective asked to speak to my husband. I handed the phone to Duard. Detective Heedt relayed the news of Julie's death to him. Duard asked some questions, and then the detective proceeded to explain what procedures had to be followed in the handling of Julie's remains.

After hanging up the phone, Duard and I stood motionless, still in disbelief that our Julie was gone. Why? What happened? In those long, agonizing moments, no matter what the detective had told us, we knew. Julie had become a victim of domestic violence. An investigation wasn't necessary. There was no question in our minds that George had killed her.

The loss of Julie was almost more than either of us could handle, but life goes on, and that's what we knew we had to do. Duard and I had been through a lot during our life together, but we'd never experienced anything as devastating as Julie's death. We knew we had to lean on each other and remain strong in order to accomplish our goal of seeing Julie's killer convicted of murder. It was going to happen. We weren't sure when, but we knew it would happen, and we were both committed to seeing that it did because that was the only way justice for Julie's murder could be served.

Although we were deeply grieved by the detective's phone call, Duard and I asked each other why this had happened to our daughter and searched for answers, hoping that would somehow ease our pain. We questioned, "Where did we go wrong? What should we have done to protect Julie? Could we have kept this from happening if we had just made her move out of Chicago?" Over and over again we continued to blame ourselves for Julie's untimely death. We had thoughts that if we had raised her differently she would still be alive, well, and happy. After all, how could someone with such an outgoing personality be the victim of this horrible tragic death?

Looking for answers, both Duard and I continued to focus more and more of our attention on Julie's life, trying to determine how we had failed her. We had moments where we believed that if we had been better parents, Julie would not have been so trusting of people but rather would have been more cautious of everyone she met, especially those with whom she developed close relationships. Over and over again we mentally researched Julie's and our past to try and determine what we did wrong. Even though we knew we couldn't bring our Julie back, we thought that perhaps by retracing our past we would learn what we should have done to have prevented her death. We were both so disturbed and distraught, and we desperately searched for answers to help us understand what led to Julie's untimely death.

I thought maybe it was my fault, as Duard was always a very good husband and a wonderful father to our children. Duard had been raised in a very poor household; however, his father always stressed to his children that they needed to set high goals for themselves and work very hard to attain them. As a result, Duard and his siblings did just that, and each grew up to be a very successful and productive adult. Because of the way he was raised, Duard impressed these same beliefs and convictions upon our children. His drive and determination to succeed were things I always admired about him. Yes, Duard was a good man who loved his family very much. He always did everything possible to be a good provider and role model for his children.

I'll never forget the day I met Duard. There was no doubt in my mind the moment I saw him that he was someone I really wanted to get to know. I was nineteen years old, and he was twenty-seven. It was summer, and I had just graduated from Scottsboro High School, a small school in northern Alabama, and was spending a few weeks with my aunt in Homewood, Illinois, before starting nursing school in the fall. However, my career plans soon changed after I met the love of my life.

It was on a Sunday afternoon after church when a girlfriend talked me into going to one of our local restaurant hangouts in Harvey, Illinois, a small suburb of Chicago. While having lunch, I noticed a very handsome man seated at another table. We exchanged glances, and soon after, he came over and introduced himself. He told me he had recently graduated from David Lipson College in Tennessee with his bachelor's degree in psychology and business administration. He had been teaching two years in Tinley Park, Illinois. He went on to say that he had been in the army two years and attended college under the GI bill.

Well, it was love at first sight when I met this handsome, six-foot-three, slender built man with black curly hair and dark brown eyes. We talked awhile, and then he said he was going to the movies and asked me to come along. Although I wanted to, I told him I could not go because I had just met him. Instead, I invited him to come to my aunt's house the following weekend. Without hesitation he graciously accepted my invitation. I was so excited. I couldn't wait to see him again.

Well, that was the beginning of our whirlwind courtship. Duard came over the following Saturday, met my aunt, and we started dating. After a couple of dates I knew he was the man I wanted to marry. But how could this be, I wondered? I thought I was in love with my high school boyfriend, who I had been dating for four years.

Teddy was a basketball player. He was a few years older than me, so we weren't able to see much of each other, as he was off at college. However, when he came home to Scottsboro we always got together. Prior to meeting Duard, I believed Teddy and I would one day get married, even though we had never discussed marriage and had made no plans.

I loved spending time with Duard. He liked to party, smoke, and drink, something I was never allowed to do growing up in a religious household. My dad was a Christian minister, so he did not look at smoking and drinking in a favorable way.

Duard had one favorite hangout, a bowling alley that had a small bar. Musical entertainment was provided by a coin-operated jukebox. There was never a live band. Because we had no car, everywhere we went was on foot. The bowling alley was close, so that's the main reason we picked it for our usual hangout place.

Being raised as a minister's daughter, my exposure to any activities outside the church was limited, so I had never met anyone like Duard. We loved going out, and he labeled me as a cheap date because I only ordered one drink all night. When I introduced Duard to my dad, he immediately liked him even though my dad would have preferred he was someone who didn't smoke or drink. However, Mom and Dad were very happy we had found each other and never discouraged us from being together.

On November 25, 1956, three months after we met, Duard and I were married by the justice of the peace in a small town in Indiana. We had no money, so we could not afford a big wedding. Duard and I asked two of our close friends to stand up with us. After we got married, the four of us went to the corner café in Harvey, Illinois, to celebrate. Duard called his parents to tell them the news, and I called mine. All were very happy and excited for us.

Our first home was a one-bedroom apartment in Harvey. Duard continued teaching at Tinley Park, and I stayed home. Approximately one year after we were married I became pregnant, and on August 12, 1958, I gave birth to a cute bouncing baby boy, Glenn Duard Grace.

CHAPTER 2
RAISING GLENN AND JULIE

Since we now had three people living in a one-bedroom apartment, Duard said it was time to find a bigger place, so we packed up and moved into a small three-bedroom house in Harvey. A few months after Glenn was born, Duard realized he needed to make more money to support his family. That is when he returned to college and began working on his master's degree. While continuing to work full time as a teacher, he attended night school at the University of Chicago.

Upon receiving his master's degree in psychology, Duard was promoted to principal at Tinley Park School. Soon after being promoted, construction began on our new home in Country Club Hills, a small suburb of Chicago, which was near Tinley Park. Within a few months the house was finished, and Duard, Glenn, and I moved once again. It was so nice to be able to move into a new home all our very own. Even better yet, within a short time I became pregnant with our second child. Things were good for us, and we were very happy.

On March 30, 1962, at 3:15 AM, Julie Ruth Grace entered this world weighing in at a whopping eight pounds nine ounces. Taking after her dad's tall, slender build, she measured twenty-two inches long. Julie was born at Ingalls Memorial Hospital in Harvey, Illinois. I was twenty-four years old, and Duard was thirty-two.

Born almost three weeks late, I experienced a difficult childbirth, and both Julie and I almost died. Fortunately, we both survived, and Duard was very thankful Mom and daughter suffered no ill effects. He and I were so thrilled and proud to have a healthy, beautiful baby girl to join her very active four-year-old big brother Glenn. Although I was told I could not have any more children, I didn't care. We had the perfect family—one boy and one girl—and that was good enough for Duard and me.

The effects of the difficult childbirth left me very weak and tired for a few days afterward. I was so bad that I was in no condition to even see, let alone hold, my daughter. However, I'll never forget how wonderful it felt when I was finally able to cuddle my Julie in my arms. Her tiny little body, her big brown eyes, and her black hair were all so beautiful. From the moment she was born she was always very special to her dad, brother, and me, and she was loved and adored by everyone she met.

Julie was always a very busy little girl, even as a baby. Of course, she had big brother Glenn, who was more than willing to teach her a thing or two. Thanks to him, she learned how to climb out of her playpen before she could even walk. Glenn loved his baby sister and couldn't wait until she was big enough to play with him. Julie worshiped her big brother Glenn, and, in order to keep up with him, she became a tomboy at a very early age. The two of them were always great friends, and both were very good kids. They seldom created any problems for Duard and me, except for the usual sibling rivalry that comes along with the raising of children in any normal family.

As a mother of two, I spent most of my time caring for my family, as Duard never wanted me to work outside the home. He always believed I should be home to raise and take care of our family. I loved being a mom and taking care of Glenn and Julie, so that was never a problem for me.

Once we became a family of four, Duard knew it was time to set another goal. He could see that a bigger income was needed to support our growing family. To accomplish this goal, he decided that once again he would return to college and get his PhD in psychology. He told me that the family would have to move close to Bloomington, Illinois, for a couple of years. He asked me if that would be okay. Because I was confident Duard knew what was best for our family, I never questioned his decision to return to college even though it would result in a temporary move for us. For that reason I told him it was fine, even though I knew I would miss living in Tinley Park. I understood Duard's reason for making this decision and was willing to do whatever he felt was necessary for our family.

Our moving meant we had to do something with the house where we were living. We decided to rent it to another family for the two years while Duard was attending school. When finished with college, our plan was to move back into our house in Country Club Hills, and Duard would complete his one-year internship at Tinley Park. Well, it just so happened that the high school coach of Tinley Park and his family were in need of a place to live, so they were happy to rent our home.

When Duard finished college and we were anticipating our move back to our home in Country Club Hills, the coach and his family didn't want to move and asked if we would sell our house to them. Duard and I discussed the coach's offer and decided that once Duard had completed his internship we wanted to move to the small rural town of Taylorville, Illinois. Duard and I agreed to sell and then rented another house in Country Club Hills for one year.

Upon completion of his internship, Duard accepted a job as psychologist for Mid State Special Education. This was the perfect job for him, as he loved working with kids starting with preschool age and going up through high school. Covering several counties in Illinois, Duard was able to play an integral role in the educational development of many children. Duard was always good with kids, and he wanted all of them to live a prosperous and successful life. Just as he was with his own children, he was always willing to do whatever he could to help other kids achieve their goals and expectations.

When we made the move to Taylorville, Julie was four years old and Glenn was eight. At first we rented a house while we were looking for a place to buy. Approximately one year later, we found and purchased a nice, older, two-story home that was in need of much renovation. Duard and I decided it would be the perfect place to raise our family and were ready to take on the task of completely renovating both floors and the basement. Once all our hard work was completed, our finished home was perfect for us. It had a huge master bedroom, living room, dining room, kitchen and bathroom downstairs. Upstairs was a loft with a bathroom and two bedrooms for Julie and Glenn. The laundry room was located in the finished basement along with a workout room for Glenn's weight-lifting equipment. A pool table and a Ping-Pong table were situated in the basement and were used when Glenn's friends came to visit.

It was a very comfortable home, and Duard, Glenn, Julie, and I all loved living there. Even after Glenn and Julie were grown and had moved away, Duard and I continued to reside there until we moved to Tallahassee, Florida, in 1989. For more than twenty-four years this house was home. All four of us had very fond memories of our life in our home at 805 West Poplar Street. Julie's childhood and teenage memories always held a special place in her heart, and she wanted those memories preserved forever. Today I have a watercolor painting of our Taylorville home hanging on my dining room wall. Julie had it painted for her dad, and she presented it to him on his seventieth birthday.

Not only was our home a very comfortable place to live, the Taylorville area was filled with lots of good, friendly people who, like us, enjoyed the rural community life. It was a great place to raise Glenn and Julie, and they were both involved in many school and community activities.

When it came to school, Glenn always did very well. In high school he was a straight-A student and was focused on getting a college scholarship when he graduated.

Even though Glenn liked school, he wasn't interested in socializing a lot, nor was he anxious to participate in many of the school's sports and extracurricular activities. Duard coaxed him to try different things but always told him he could quit if he found it wasn't for him. So Glenn did as his dad asked and finally settled on weight lifting and swimming. After a short time, he became a competitive swimmer on his high school swim team. This enabled him to become a lifeguard at the community pool during the summer months before he reached the age of sixteen. Typically no one under age sixteen was permitted to work as a lifeguard, but Glenn personally went down to the courthouse and asked for an exception. Due to his excellent swimming ability, he was granted permission to become a lifeguard each summer until he graduated from high school.

While Glenn was the quiet, studious type, Julie was more of a social butterfly and wasn't nearly as serious about getting straight As as Glenn. She adored her brother and wanted to do everything he did. She loved life so much and loved to socialize with everyone she met that sometimes her school work suffered. Julie had a big heart and was always busy trying to take care of anyone she felt needed her help. While in high school she enjoyed working at the hospital as a candy striper. All the patients loved her too because she was always very friendly, caring, outgoing, and energetic. She had lots of friends both young and old, and I never thought she would ever have an enemy or anyone who would dislike her and treat her badly.

I recall that while living in Taylorville we had a next-door neighbor named Vivian. She was a bedridden older lady who lived alone. Julie felt sorry for Vivian and would pick lilacs and take them to her to make her feel better. Julie would frequently stop by Vivian's house to just sit and talk with her and keep her company. Vivian especially loved it when Julie came over and read stories to her. Even after Julie moved away from Taylorville, she never forgot Vivian and kept in close contact with her. She always visited Vivian whenever she was in Taylorville.

Julie wasn't an A student except for one subject. That was English. She loved this class and always got As in it because she loved to write. Her goal at a very early age was to become a news reporter. Julie would frequently watch the daily news on television and was fascinated with the young, attractive reporters she would see and hear. She was always confident she would achieve her dream career goal and be the best reporter no matter what it took to get there.

Now don't get me wrong. Julie made nothing below a C in school, but she was usually too busy socializing with friends and participating in sporting events and school and community activities to devote as much time to studying as she should have. However, in order to keep her on track, there was a standing rule at our house. No grade could be lower than a C or she would lose a privilege. Also, Duard would give her "the talk," which went on for hours, or so it seemed. Julie couldn't stand to have a privilege of any kind taken away, and, worse yet, she could not stand being subjected to "the talk," so there was never a problem with her getting at least a C in her classes.

Julie tried ballet when she was in the elementary grades but soon gave it up, as she wanted to be outside. She later decided to try piano lessons, as we had a piano on the back porch where she could practice and be close to the outdoors. In high school she sang in the choir, acted in school plays, played basketball and softball, and ran in track meets for the Taylorville Tornadoes. Although she wasn't very good in many sports, that didn't matter to her. She was very competitive and loved to try everything. Mr. Hicksonball, her high school coach, always said Julie was one of his favorite students. Her winning personality as well as her spunk and enthusiasm for any sport she played made her a star, and she was very effective in creating a winning attitude among teammates. And just like big brother Glenn, one sport where she excelled and won many awards was swimming. She too was a member of the high school's swim team. And just like Glenn, she became a lifeguard at the Taylorville community pool at the age of fifteen.

Even though Julie loved swimming, when she was older we used to laugh and talk about the days when she took swimming lessons. She used to tell me, "Mom, I am so mad at you. You made me go out into the cold water to take swimming lessons." Yes, I guess I did, but in our discussions I always knew she wasn't mad at me. She may have hated the cold water, but she was never mad at me, especially when it came to my coaxing her to be a competitive swimmer.

As a teenager, Julie was very popular. She had several boyfriends but no steady, serious one. Many boys had crushes on her, and she went out on a lot of dates, but she was never interested in developing a serious relationship. She was more interested in attaining her career goals. She always planned to attend college after graduating from high school and did not want any unnecessary distractions to keep her from becoming a well-known reporter.

Julie in second grade

Julie her senior year in her basketball uniform

Julie's high school senior photo

Julie during her college years at Southern Illinois University

CHAPTER 3
JULIE BEGINS HER CAREER

On May 27, 1980, Julie graduated from Taylorville High School. She spent the summer working as a lifeguard and then went off to Southern Illinois University in Carbondale in the fall. In addition to the courses she took in Carbondale, Julie completed course work at both the University of Maryland and DePaul University. Just as in high school, Julie was a social butterfly. She kept busy socializing with her fellow students and participating in activities that would further her career in news reporting. She loved the world of politics, and while in college Julie moved to Washington, D.C., attended night school, and worked as an intern with Senator Alan J. Dixon. She also spent two years as staff assistant for Congressman Paul Simon and then, in 1984, served on the national advance team, where she campaigned for Walter Mondale for president.

After taking the required courses and working as a legislative intern, Julie graduated in 1985 with a bachelor of science degree with a major in communications and minors in journalism and political science. Coincidentally, big brother Glenn also graduated from Southern Illinois University on the same day with a PhD in psychology. Julie worked hard to get her career up and running while she was still in college. Prior to graduation and after, she moved to Chicago to pursue her writing career in the political world by working as an account executive for Jascula/Terman & Associates, an independent strategic communications firm specializing in public affairs, event management, and creative and interactive services. In this position, Julie conceived and implemented public relations strategies, wrote press materials, and helped coordinate and advance national media tours, including Jimmy Carter's book tour and Habitat for Humanity. Julie loved being an active participant in government and politics. In order to pursue this love, she volunteered to work on campaigns of candidates she supported in upcoming elections.

In 1986 she became even more involved in Illinois' governmental affairs when she was hired as editor and press advance for the Office of the Attorney General. As editor, she researched, wrote, and designed newsletters for advocacy divisions. As press advance, she coordinated on-site media at public appearances and represented the attorney general at community events.

In continuing her career goal of becoming a reporter, in 1988 she accepted a position with the Illinois Department of Commerce and Community Affairs, where she served as editor and spokesperson for the Bureau of Tourism. She was responsible for writing, editing, and layout of monthly tourism newsletters. Julie also represented the bureau on weekly radio and television shows. She spent much time away from her home in Chicago, traveling back and forth to Springfield.

Soon after going to work for the Bureau of Tourism, Julie decided to move and found a beautiful one-bedroom condo in the Gold Coast area of downtown Chicago. Located in an upscale neighborhood, her condo was on the twentieth floor of a high-rise residential building. It had a couple of big floor-to-ceiling windows in her living room, which provided her with a beautiful view of Lake Michigan. It didn't take Julie long to turn her new place into a beautiful, comfortable home. She had a flair for decorating and spared no expense when it came to choosing just the right décor to make her home complete.

Julie rented her condo for approximately one year, and then she told her landlord that she was interested in buying it if he ever decided to sell. A short time later he notified her that he was putting her condo on the market. Julie got into a bidding war with another buyer; but, in the end, Julie won, and the landlord sold it to her. She was so excited to become a homeowner, and the condo was perfect for her.

Oh, I almost forgot to mention that Julie did not live alone. She had a pet dog named Bronte. Prior to moving in with Julie, Bronte had been a stray dog that she rescued one day when a neighbor saw her wandering the streets and called Julie over to show her. It was obvious Bronte had been tortured and badly beaten. Julie felt sorry for Bronte, so she took her in, nursed her back to health, and invited Bronte to permanently live with her. That's just the way Julie was. She couldn't stand to see anyone suffer, whether it was a person or an animal. She was always there for them. She felt it was her responsibility to take care of them, as no one else would. Because Julie took such good care of her, Bronte paid Julie back by being a very protective dog. When Julie came to visit, she would bring Bronte. Bronte would sleep with Julie, and if anyone came around Julie they had to go through Bronte to get to her.

Also living in the same condo building was a very good friend from Taylorville that Julie had known for many years. Mark Williams was very close to Julie. They had even taken a trip to Europe together. Mark was an attorney in Chicago, and he would often ask Julie to accompany him on various business functions. I don't know if there was ever any talk of marriage between the two of them, but I do know that Mark was good for Julie, and they enjoyed each other's company very much.

While Julie was busy with her career in Chicago and Glenn with his in Wisconsin, Duard retired from the school district in 1989, and the two of us sold our house and moved to Tallahassee, Florida. Approximately two years before Duard retired, the two of us visited Tallahassee and fell in love with the area. We knew we wanted to get away from the cold winters, and Florida was where we wanted to live. So we found a house, purchased it, and rented it for two years until we were ready to move to Florida. After Duard retired we moved into our house in Tallahassee.

At this point we were so thrilled that Julie and Glenn were both happy and doing very well. Glenn was working in a hospital in Louisiana, and Julie was on the fast track to achieving her career goal as a reporter. Her next job change occurred in 1989, when she was offered the position of press secretary with a well-known communications firm in Chicago named Serafin & Associates. As press secretary, Julie coordinated political strategies and press operations for the Illinois lieutenant governor's race, the Cook County Board president's race, and judicial candidates. Not only was Julie an employee of the company, she was a longtime friend of its owner, Thom Serafin. Julie and Thom originally met while she was doing volunteer work for Mayor Daley's election campaign. While working for Mr. Serafin, I frequently came to visit Julie on weekends, so she introduced me to him on one of my visits. Julie always spoke very highly of Thom and enjoyed working in his firm very much. And the feeling was mutual. Thom told me he had a lot of respect and admiration for Julie due to the professionalism she displayed and the way she handled issues in the world of both journalism and politics. Because he felt so strongly about Julie's talents, he played a very important role in helping her to attain her ultimate career goal and secure her dream job.

Graduation day at Southern Illinois University in 1985

Julie with her bachelor of science degree with a major in communications and minors in journalism and political science and Glenn with his PhD in psychology

Julie on graduation day with her proud parents

Julie with her mom

Julie and Bronte

Julie and Sen. Alan Dixon

Julie with the late Senator Paul Simon

Julie with Mrs. Paul Simon

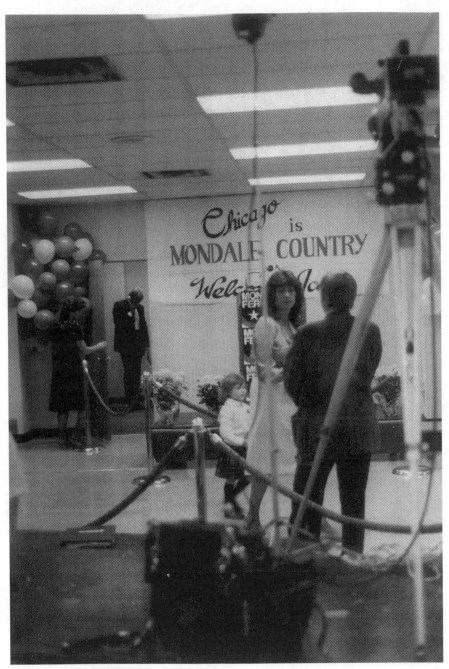

Julie at a campaign rally for Walter Mondale

Julie at a campaign rally for Walter Mondale in 1984

Julie campaigning for Joe Kennedy in his run for Congress

Julie with Chicago Mayor Richard M. Daley

CHIGAGO MARATHON
October 19, 1997
MARATHON**FOTO**

Julie when she ran in the Chicago Marathon

CHAPTER 4
JULIE LANDS HER DREAM JOB

In 1991 Julie received a call from *TIME* magazine asking her if she would like to come in for an interview. She was very surprised and honored to get the call and was convinced there was no way she could possibly meet their hiring requirements. However, she graciously accepted their invitation without hesitation. She then called me and told me the news. She was so excited, and I was very happy for her. But after she described the job, I told her she didn't want to work for *TIME*, as the job she was to interview for sounded too boring for her. It was a clerical position and not the reporting job she had always dreamed about. Although Julie was ready to accept almost any type of job she could get at *TIME*, she was confident there was no way they would hire her, as she was not good enough. She was just so thrilled that she had been called for an interview.

Well, to make a long story short, she went in, interviewed, and was immediately offered a job. Julie was so shocked! No, it wasn't her dream reporter job, but it was a start. She was hired to answer phones, sort newspapers, and manage assignments of freelance reporters.

However, this did not last long. Soon after starting her job, Julie was anxious to do more than just administrative work, and she didn't sit around quietly waiting for something to happen. Instead, she convinced the bureau chief that she was ready to be a reporter who was capable of getting the story. He finally allowed her to pursue her reporting career, and she soon proved she was a natural. Her kind, warm-hearted ways opened doors for interviews with people that other reporters were unable to get. As an example, when *TIME* was writing a book about the Unabomber they sent Julie, as they knew she was one of very few reporters that could get an interview with Ted

Kaczynski's mother. She didn't let them down, either. She got the interview just as predicted.

Once Julie moved into her dream job, she was so excited, and Duard and I were both very happy for her. For the next ten years Julie worked for *TIME* magazine. During that time she wrote over one hundred bylines. She covered beat and national breaking stories, including five school shootings, the Cunanan murders, Jack Kevorkian, pilots of the B-2 Stealth bombers at Whiteman Air Force Base, Sammy Sosa, and Michael Jordan. She worked on award-winning issues such as *The Gun in America* and received individual reporting honors. She specialized in social issues and was touted as one of *TIME's* "best human drama reporters" during the Columbine School shooting. In addition, Julie coordinated and reported on *TIME* special issues, *Life on the Mississippi* and *Backbone of America*. She also facilitated news desk coverage during the Oklahoma City bombing and at the 1996 Democratic Convention in Chicago.

Although Duard and I were no longer living close to her in Illinois, Julie and I continued to remain very close. We phoned each other daily, just as we had done in the past. No number of miles between us ever changed that. Because she was so busy and it was tough for her to get away, I made frequent trips to Chicago to visit her, both when we lived in Taylorville and after we moved to Tallahassee. Julie would come and visit Duard and me whenever she had the time. Although she was working her dream job, Julie soon found out a reporter's life was not quite as she had imagined. It was far from glamorous. It was a lot of hard work and a lot of mental and emotional stress. She would take long flights, go on assignments, do interviews, report and write stories, all with very little time to eat, sleep, or relax. Before she was even done with one story, she was already on her way to the next one. Julie knew it was going to take someone really tough to be able to handle the situations she would be facing in the upcoming years, but she was confident she was up to it. She felt that because she got along well with everyone she met, her ability to be an excellent reporter and her love for life were bound to make her successful.

Just like her dad, Julie loved to party and have a good time. She also loved the attention that comes along with being in the limelight. Prior to working for *TIME*, she did a lot of socializing and drinking. She became associated with a lot of politicians and started drinking at campaign functions. Although she drank, it wasn't a real problem, but unfortunately this changed soon after she went to work for *TIME*. Julie started frequenting bars, where she would meet with others as her job required her to take people out for interviews, and that too often meant drinking was involved. In a short time, Duard and I became very concerned that Julie was drinking much more than she should, and we began to worry about her. One weekend she and a friend came to visit us in Tallahassee, and after their visit Duard told me Julie was drinking too much. I then went to her and told her that her dad and I were worried about her excessive drinking and partying. Unfortunately, Julie did not share our same concern, as she was confident she did not have a problem.

Also, as time went on it was obvious she was suffering from anxiety and depression due to the types of stories she was required to cover. They were about very violent crimes and oftentimes involved massive killings. Soon after she covered the story about Yummy in 1994, signs of anxiety were evident to Duard and me. This tragic story was tough for those who covered it, and it especially took a real emotional toll on Julie. She soon realized just how tough reporters have to be when dealing with tragic deaths such as the death eleven-year-old Robert Sandifer (Yummy) experienced. In the interviews Julie conducted with family and friends of Robert's, reality hit, and she had trouble dealing with the fact that there are neighborhoods throughout the United States where it's the normal way of life for juveniles to live in constant fear of being beaten or, worse yet, killed by a gunshot wound, often without provocation. She was shocked and horrified when she heard the many stories of young people who were exposed to constant fear as a result of the violent living environment they were forced to cope with on a daily basis.

Julie became extremely distraught with what she discovered in her interviews. She empathized and felt very sorry for the individuals she talked with. She let the horrifying situations play on her heartstrings and ultimately consume her every thought. Even though she constantly reminded herself that she was only a reporter doing her job and nothing more, she had great difficulty separating the responsibilities of her job from her personal emotional anguish, which was tearing her apart. It was almost more than she could handle.

It became more and more apparent to Duard and me that Julie's dream job was beginning to totally consume her and become a very stressful and agonizing way of life. We were concerned, but, as parents, there was only so much we could say or do. After all, she was a grown woman. It was her life, and she was doing what she wanted. All we could do was hope and pray that one day the stresses of her job would ease, and Julie would be able to once again truly enjoy life. But that was not meant to be. The stories she covered continued to be more and more difficult for her to handle.

In April 1999, Julie was sent to Littleton, Colorado, to cover the Columbine school massacre. While in Colorado interviewing, reporting, and writing about the massacre, Julie became so distraught and upset she couldn't sleep. She empathized and felt very badly for the families, teachers, and students she interviewed. Julie had great difficulty coping with the emotional scars of those who were affected by the horrible incident. She would call Duard and me in the middle of the night, and it was obvious to both of us just how distraught she was and that it was extremely difficult for her to handle the stress of the job. She would tell us that people would look at her as if she were their friend. They were expecting her to help them. Because of her personality, she truly wanted to help but knew there was nothing she could do. Teenage girls would call her crying and looking to Julie to provide comfort in their time of grief. Julie kept telling herself that she was just a reporter that had been asked to cover a tragic story. She was not there to counsel and comfort anyone. But no matter how hard she tried to convince herself that her only responsibility was to do her job as a reporter, she still was tormented by the fact that people were suffering, and she desperately wanted to help ease their pain.

Duard and I believed that Julie felt she had the burdens of the world on her shoulders, and no matter what she did, there was no way to get them off. She spent weeks living in Colorado with daily exposure to this disturbing environment. Close to the breaking point, we encouraged Julie to call her doctor and let him know how she was feeling. Dr. Footy, her personal doctor and good friend of many years, prescribed anxiety medication. Dr. Footy was always very fond of Julie, and he went out of his way to ensure she got the best medical care possible no matter what was ailing her. Although it helped some, she continued to rely on alcohol to calm her nerves and help her cope with the emotional stresses of her job.

Even though life as a reporter was not what she had dreamed it would be, Julie still made it her goal to be the best reporter possible. It was no secret at *TIME* that if there was a difficult story that needed to be covered, send Julie Grace. This sometimes bothered her, as she felt she was able to get interviews because people viewed her as their friend. Naturally, this was not the case. Because they trusted her, Julie felt she was being dishonest with them but didn't know how to correct this misconception.

Julie covering a story for *TIME* magazine

CHAPTER 5
JULIE MEETS GEORGE

As time went on, it was obvious Julie's job with *TIME* was in jeopardy because of her alcohol and anxiety problems. She started having great difficulty writing and reporting stories by their required deadlines. Although she had been an outstanding, commendable reporter, the decision was made by *TIME* that the stress was more than she could handle, so in 2001 she separated her employment from *TIME*. She left the dog-eat-dog world of a high-profile reporter for a very prestigious magazine. At that time she wasn't real sure what she wanted to do. She just knew that she could no longer handle the stresses of being a reporter and was ready to take on a new, less stressful challenge.

As it became more and more apparent that Julie's drinking had gotten out of control, Duard and I finally convinced her to seek professional help. After much prompting, Julie sought help at an alcohol rehab center. Her dad and I were both very pleased that she was willing to go even though she still would not admit she had a problem. Duard and I were confident that if Julie continued down the path she was going, alcohol would eventually ruin her career and, worse yet, destroy her life. We could see signs where this was already happening. Julie was a good person and an accomplished woman, and we wanted only the best for our daughter.

Julie's rehab experience appeared to go well in the beginning, as she was learning to live without using alcohol to cope with everyday stresses. She met others at the substance abuse rehabilitation program at Chicago Lake Shore Hospital who had experienced similar situations, and they helped her through difficult times. But even though she was attending rehab for her addiction, she soon became focused on befriending and helping others at the center, whether it was for alcohol, drug addiction, or any other personal problems they were having. One such individual she met and soon developed a close relationship with was a man named George Kenneth Thompson.

George, who was eight years younger than Julie, lived in Chicago and worked various jobs in the construction-related industry. That is, whenever he worked. Soon after meeting George, she came to visit Duard and me for the weekend and brought George along with her.

When we met George, our first impression of him was good, primarily because he was not drinking and neither was Julie. He appeared to be a very nice, well-mannered, good-looking, well-built man. I remember that he was wearing shorts and a short-sleeved shirt. His hair was brown and I believe he was around five feet ten inches tall. He told me that he had been in rehab for an anger management problem, but later I discovered it was for both anger management and drug addiction.

On their visit, Julie appeared to be happy with George, even though he would become angry and short with her for very insignificant things. I recall on one occasion Julie mentioned she was cold, and George actually scolded her for making such a statement. It was typical for George to show his displeasure with Julie through his body language, even if he didn't say anything, and it was quite obvious that he had a lot of pent-up anger, which he had no problem taking out on Julie.

Duard and I became skeptical by the time the weekend was over, as we soon realized that George was a very deceiving person and a pathological liar. During their visit, Julie and George spent time reading Bible scriptures and discussing religion with both Duard and me as well as our next-door neighbor. Previous to meeting George, Julie was not one to either bring up the subject of religion or discuss her religious beliefs. Duard and I were not sure what prompted her to start talking about religion; however, I'm sure it had something to do with her rehab counseling, her relationship with George, and his pretending to be a religious person. I say pretending because Duard and I soon found out that he was far from religious, and he definitely was not the God-fearing Christian he wanted us to think he was. In fact, after their weekend visit, Duard told me that if Julie had brought George around the house while she was a kid and still living at home, he would have run him off. Both Duard and I knew something was just not right, and George was definitely not the person he tried to portray himself as.

Duard and I never knew a lot about George or his background, but from what Julie told us, he was a good person that had come up against some bad luck, and he needed help in order to recover. It is my understanding that George and his sister were children of a broken home. His parents divorced when George was young, and his biological dad, who lives in South Carolina, never had much to do with him. Both parents remarried, and George grew up living with his mom and stepdad. When Julie met George, he was living with his parents somewhere in the Chicago suburbs, where his stepdad was a construction worker and his mom, I believe, worked in a bank.

As time went on, it became more and more obvious to her dad and me that Julie had opened her heart and home to someone who was not a good person. Although Julie was oblivious to what was going on around her, Duard and I, as well as her close friends, tried to convince her that George was taking advantage of her. She believed everyone was wrong, and she argued that she was there to help him turn his life around. She frequently commented, "If I don't help him, who will?"

In a very short time after meeting George, Julie and he started drinking again. George worked very little because he was able to get Julie to support him. He stayed in her condo living a good life, not worrying about making money to survive. Julie provided a roof over his head, clothes for him to wear, cigarettes for him to smoke, and food for him to eat. Due to the constant pressuring from George's dad, Julie even made his monthly truck payments. Whenever possible, George stole from her, sold the stolen goods, and used the money to support his drug addiction.

It became obvious to Duard and me that Julie's life with George was growing more and more miserable each day. It wasn't long before both Julie and George were drinking heavily again. George took advantage of her and became physically abusive if he did not get his way. On more than one occasion she called her dad and me and told us about George hitting and hurting her. She would come to visit, and I would see bruises on her body that were the result of the violent, abusive treatment imposed upon her by George.

One such trip she made to our house was right after George tried to strangle her to death. Fortunately, she managed to escape and run away. She immediately went to Chicago's O'Hare Airport. Because she was so scared of George, she took the first flight available just to get out of Chicago and away from George before he found her. Julie ended up in Michigan and then booked a flight to Florida. Duard and I picked her up at the Orlando airport and brought her home. We were relieved she was out of harm's way, since George was still in Chicago.

Julie stayed with us for a couple of weeks. Things went pretty well the first week. She had no contact with George. Duard and I were beginning to convince her that she needed to get away from George. We even agreed to help her move from Chicago to Florida.

However, during the second week things changed. George's stepdad started calling and begging her to make George's truck payment. Since George was not working, his stepdad said he was paying George's bills and really needed her to help him out. After a few conversations, Julie started feeling sorry for George and sent money to his stepdad. She then decided things were okay with her and George, and she should go back to her home in Chicago, so that's what she did.

After Julie and George had been together approximately five months, I recall another incident that occurred while Julie and Bronte were riding with George in his truck. George got upset with Julie and pushed her and Bronte out while they were moving. In this incident, Julie broke her nose, and Bronte was seriously injured.

Then there was another time when Julie called in a panic, saying George was in a violent rage because he was so mad at her. While we were talking, he threw a bar stool through her living room plate-glass window. Fortunately, she was able to call the police and have him arrested before he managed to do any serious bodily harm to her. When the detective came to arrest George, he told Julie to get rid of George. He said he could tell that George was a very bad person, and it was unsafe for her to associate with him. The detective further advised her that if she continued to be with George, he would eventually kill her.

On each occasion, Julie got restraining orders, but somehow, after a few days, she would manage to either see or talk to George. He had a way of making her feel guilty and of convincing her that it was her fault for causing his outrageous behavior. Duard and I always wondered how anyone as brilliant and intelligent as Julie could let someone as evil and devious as George con and deceive her so badly. As long as I live, I will never understand how he was able to physically abuse my daughter time and time again and then make her believe she was a bad person, and she deserved the abusive treatment he subjected her to.

Fearing each day for her life, Duard and I tried to do everything possible to help Julie understand the horrible negative impact George was having on her. Although she was not as convinced as we that she had serious problems, Duard and I finally got her to agree to see a psychologist in the hopes that he would be able to make her understand the critical nature of her situation and get away from George before he killed her.

Although she continued to remain in denial, Julie scheduled an appointment with a psychologist in Chicago, and she and I went to see him together. After hearing her story, he responded the same as everyone else who knew and cared about her. He advised Julie to move out of the area and get far away from George. He understood the behaviors of individuals like George, and he knew that his abusive ways were not going to end but would continue to get worse, and, if left unrestrained, the end result would not be good for Julie. But no matter what anyone told her, Julie remained insistent that she was fine and felt she did not need to move out of her condo and away from George. She loved living in Chicago, and she believed that the problems she had previously experienced with George had been resolved and were no longer an issue.

However, she was wrong, as this was not the case. George's abusive ways never improved. Instead, just like the psychologist and everyone else warned her, they got worse. He continued to frequently hit and beat her. Duard and I, as well as her friends, continued to warn Julie she needed to get away from him.

In November 2002, George got into one of his rages, and he went after Julie again. This time she almost didn't get away. She was so scared and thought she was going to die. Julie had George arrested and convicted of domestic battery, and he was sentenced to eighteen months of probation. Julie also got a restraining order against him, and he was not to come near her until June 2004. Unfortunately, the restraining order did not keep him away.

On March 7, 2003, George saw Julie and beat her up again. George was arrested one more time, but, soon afterward, Julie felt sorry for him because it was his birthday on March 10, and she went and bailed him out of jail. She continued to say George wasn't a bad guy, and she would be able to eventually help him overcome his problems.

No amount of sentences, restraining orders, or anything else against George kept him away from Julie. Finally, Julie was beginning to realize that maybe he was a big threat to her life and that just maybe it was time for her to get away from him permanently. Duard and I begged her to come and stay with us for a while. She finally agreed and decided she would sell her condo, buy a house in Florida, and start a new life for herself. We were so happy and relieved Julie had finally come to the conclusion that George was not going to change, and she had to get away from him if she was going to survive. Furthermore, she realized she had a drinking problem, and the best place for her to be was with her parents.

George and Julie at a dog show

CHAPTER 6
JULIE'S FAILED ATTEMPT TO ESCAPE

Around the first of May, Julie gave us the news that she was going to move to Florida. Fearing that George would go after Julie again if he heard she was moving, Duard and I told her to tell none of her friends or neighbors. Understanding the type of person he was, we knew that if George heard that he would no longer have Julie and her home to run to it would send him into a violent rage.

Julie agreed to tell no one; however, for some reason, and I'll never know why, Julie told a neighbor approximately four days before her death. Somehow George heard she was moving. Once he heard the news, he did just as predicted. On May 17th, he appeared at Julie's door. Whether she invited him in or he forced his way in is unknown to me, but one thing I do believe is that he had come to murder my daughter. I'm pretty confident there was no way he was going to let her move away from him. He especially did not want her to go to Florida and be anywhere close to her parents. He hated Duard and me and did not want Julie to have any contact with us at all. He needed to control her, and our influence on Julie was a constant distraction; he wanted her to have no part of us.

According to public records, which are documented in the prosecutor's report, Illinois Assistant State's Attorney Patricia Sudendorf told the judge at a bond hearing that "Thompson had hit Grace many times and pushed her, causing her to strike her head on a dresser. He allegedly then watched her slip in and out of consciousness, convulsing with seizures and vomiting blood, for three days. Thompson finally called paramedics."

Initially, George confessed that he was guilty of murdering Julie, and, as a result, he was arrested. However, soon after going to jail, he reversed his guilty plea to innocent. He said the prosecutor's account was an "exaggeration" and what had happened to Julie was an accident. He implied that she was drunk and as a result fell and hit her head and that he did not harm her. He went on to say that he loved her and that he was not responsible for her falling and hitting her head.

So what really happened between May 17 and May 20, 2003? I had called Julie on numerous occasions, and she never answered her phone. Sometimes George would answer but never Julie. I never talked to George, as I knew he would not tell me the truth about what was going on even though I was very concerned that Julie never answered the phone. After all, Julie knew we talked every day, and she had to know I would be worried when I didn't hear from her. My mother's intuition told me something was terribly wrong, but I didn't know what to do.

When Duard and I heard the details of Julie's death, this confirmed our worst nightmare, that our daughter's life had been abruptly ended by a cold-blooded murderer. He beat her and then watched her die a slow death. For three days he did nothing to help save her badly bruised and broken body. On the third day he finally called a friend of Julie's to tell her that he thought Julie needed medical attention. He told Julie's friend that he had been reluctant to call anyone because of the order of protection, and he thought he would be arrested and put in jail. The friend finally convinced him to call 911, but it was already too late. Julie was beyond saving.

The news of Julie's death spread rapidly throughout the media. The many people who had known or worked with Julie were shocked and deeply saddened. They questioned how such a beautiful, warm-hearted, vibrant, and talented woman could have succumbed to such a violent death. Julie would never have harmed anyone, so why would someone brutally take her life? No one had answers, only tears.

Although we had tried and tried to prevent this horrible crime, Duard and I were defenseless, and there was nothing more we could do now but mourn our daughter's passing and wait a very long three years for her killer to be brought to trial.

Julie at Mrs. Serafin's 40th birthday party
(Photo was on the front of Julie's Memorial Service program)

CHAPTER 7
Julie's Memorial Service

On May 31, 2003, a very emotional memorial service was held at the Immaculate Conception Church in Chicago. Over thirteen hundred of Julie's family, friends, and colleagues came to the service, and there wasn't a dry eye in the place. One of her previous employers, and a very close friend, Thom Serafin, gave a heartwarming, emotional tribute to Julie.

"The picture on the front of your program was taken in our backyard on my wife's fortieth birthday, a few years ago. You might wonder what Julie is wearing around her neck. It looks like it might be a necklace, but it happens to be a rubber dog nose, the kind you can wear over your own nose with an elastic band to hold it on.

"The birthday coincided with the annual La Grange Pet Parade, and Julie was just getting into the spirit and fun of the party. She was really terrific at that. She had a mischievous sense of humor. Her laughter was infectious, and she was generous in sharing it.

"I'd like to think about her in the sunshine of that day. I don't want to lose sight of that image of her, in the darkness of losing her. The heart-wrenching, violent way Julie died should not let us forget how we knew her.

"These are not traits typically mentioned together, but those who knew Julie Ruth Grace knew of Julie's sweetness, compassion, and toughness.

"Julie did what very few have been able to accomplish—bridge the oceans between the professional worlds of journalism and politics. There's only one way to make that happen; you have to be a pro in both worlds. Julie Grace was a pro, but she never made anyone feel less than a pro themselves. She made it look easy.

37

"Julie was warm and caring. She tended to look out for all of us. Julie always had an eye for matchmaking between friends. And she wasn't hesitant to suggest what her friends should wear to present themselves better.

"Julie loved to hear a good story, the inside details, because she loved people, foibles and all. She had an amazing number of friends, including people she encountered as a journalist.

"When it came to politics, she had the instincts of someone much older because she observed carefully and schmoozed effortlessly with veterans twice her age, while keeping her eyes open for some revelation.

"She was observant without being cynical. Good-hearted to a fault; passionate about life, her friends, her work. She looked to learn from those of us who were older and more experienced, but we often learned from her in the process because she had her eyes open, a quick mind, and the soul of a lion.

"I will always remember the laugh, so full of life and good humor. We need to remember that on this very difficult day for people who loved her, Julie's fabulous sense of humor.

"A very gutsy young lady from Taylorville, I first thought on meeting her some eighteen years ago. Julie wasn't hesitant in telling me her views of life and politics, and of me, and we had just met! I immediately knew Julie was special and that our paths would cross again. It was the end of the '86 Dixon campaign, but the beginning of a long and loving friendship.

"Julie attacked this town, Chicago, with verve, energy, and gusto! There were few dull moments when Julie was around. I introduced her to Gavin Scott, *TIME*'s bureau chief in 1991, who hired Julie. He told me last week, 'Julie seemed to know lots of people, was bursting with energy, and just full of sparkle. I thought of her as Ms. Chicago.'

"Naturally inquisitive. Naturally outgoing. Naturally beautiful, with that bursting smile, and blessed as a gifted writer, insisting we share the intimacies of our human condition that only Julie could see.

"She was quite serious about her profession. She considered it a privilege to be a journalist, maybe because she worked harder than most to get there.

"When my wife taught journalism at Columbia College, she invited Julie to speak to her class about magazine writing. Julie told the students about the excitement of covering Michael Jordan on the road but also about the hours of research, attention to accuracy, need for detail, and meeting deadlines that her job demanded. She connected so well with the students that at the end of the semester most of them chose her lecture to write about in their final essays.

"I always thought of Julie as a kid sister, an innocent, a butterfly of life landing where her heart sent her. Always vulnerable and always giving. This morning at Immaculate Conception Church we have gathered to celebrate Julie's life. Julie's pain is gone. Julie's peace is at hand."

Julie as a bridesmaid at a friend's wedding

CHAPTER 8

HEARTWARMING REMEMBRANCES
AND RESOLUTIONS

D uard and I received many beautiful remembrances from Julie's friends around the world. One special tribute came from James Graff, who runs *TIME* magazine's bureau in Paris. He wrote the following:

"The really sad thing is that in some ways and alas, not in others, Julie had a stronger sense of purpose than anyone I've known. By sheer force of will, she moved from being the bureau manager when I got to Chicago in 1995, to becoming a reporter with a singular gift.

"She pleaded for the stories the rest of us shied away from; the ones with grief and pain all over them. She succeeded at them because her empathy opened doors that couldn't be opened any other way."

Mr. Graff said he recalled the efforts and the trips Julie made to Evergreen Park after Ted Kasczynski was arrested as the Unabomber.

Mr. Graff further wrote, "Julie managed to talk to Ted Kasczynski's mother, Wanda, who was talking to no one at the time. She was always the one who could do it if no one else could, and she was always game.

"She managed to get interviews that no one else could because there was nothing false about the concern Julie felt for people in pain. She took it on as it came, all of it, though she had plenty of her own.

"Her enthusiasm, her complicated energy, made her a force to be reckoned with. Ignoring Julie was impossible. I would have thought harming her would be, too."

In June 2003, Duard and I received a letter from Sam Gwynne, executive editor of *Texas Monthly Magazine*. Hearing of Julie death, he wrote:

"I am writing to tell you how sorry I was to hear about Julie's passing. I got to know her [Julie] when I was Detroit Bureau Chief for *TIME* and she was working Chicago Bureau (of which Detroit was a satellite). The last time I saw her was when we worked together on the Columbine High School story. Her work on that story was brilliant. By the time the Columbine shootings happened, she had already gotten a reputation as someone who could go into the mass chaos of one of these mega-stories and come out with the critical interviews that literally thousands of other journalists were after. *TIME* was never very good at this, and they knew it. It was one of the reasons they pretty much had to make Julie a correspondent. At Littleton our paths crossed several times. I always enjoyed her company; I got to see how she worked, too. It was a process of street-level networking, and she had networked her way into two or three different groups who were already treating her as an insider. She was one of the best street reporters I have ever seen."

Then, on June 16, 2003, Alderman Edward M. Burke presented to Duard and me a resolution adopted by the City Council of the City of Chicago, Illinois. It was signed by Mayor Richard M. Daley. Along with the resolution, Mr. Burke included a letter addressed to "The Family of Julie R. Grace" that read:

"Please accept my condolences on the loss of Julie R. Grace. I also extend my sympathy to all those who knew and admired her. As a token of our admiration and esteem, the Chicago City Council has adopted a resolution in memory of Julie. It is my pleasure to enclose with this letter a parchment copy of this resolution. Although this kind of commemoration can never replace your personal loss, I hope, in some small way, it demonstrates our respect for her memory."

A resolution

adopted by The City Council

of the City of Chicago, Illinois

Presented by ___Alderman Edward M. Burke___ on ___June 4, 2003___

Whereas, Julie R. Grace has been called to her eternal reward at the age of forty-one; and

WHEREAS, The Chicago City Council has been informed of her passing by Alderman Edward M. Burke; and

WHEREAS, Born in Harvey and raised in downstate Taylorville, Julie R. Grace was a talented journalist and a former Congressional campaign aide; and

WHEREAS, A 1985 graduate of Southern Illinois University, Julie R. Grace earned a degree in communications and worked on the campaigns of former United States Senator Alan Dixon (D-ILL) and a number of other high-profile politicians; and

WHEREAS, After a successful stint writing press releases for political campaigns, Julie R. Grace joined *Time* magazine's Chicago Bureau as an assistant in 1991 and worked her way up to reporter; and

WHEREAS, Julie R. Grace's news coverage included a 1994 piece on the murder of eleven-year-old Robert "Yummy" Sandifer of Chicago's Roseland neighborhood, the dropping of charges in 1998 against two Chicago children who had been arrested for the murder of young Ryan Harris, the 1999 shootings at Columbine High School in Colorado, and a number of other stories of national interest; and

WHEREAS, Julie R. Grace most recently ably served as a freelance writer for a number of clients; and

WHEREAS, Julie R. Grace was an individual of great integrity and professional accomplishment who will also be remembered by her many friends and relatives for her kindness and generosity to others; and

WHEREAS, To her parents, Duard and Ruth Grace, her brother, Glenn, and a nephew, Julie R. Grace imparts a legacy of faithfulness, service and dignity; now, therefore

BE IT RESOLVED, That we, the Mayor and the members of the Chicago City Council, assembled this fourth day of June, 2003, do hereby commemorate Julie R. Grace for her grace-filled life and do hereby express our condolences to her family; and

BE IT FURTHER RESOLVED, That a suitable copy of this resolution be presented to the family of Julie R. Grace.

Mayor

City Clerk

Resolution presented to the family by Alderman Edward
M. Burke and signed by Richard M. Daley

HR0401
May 30, 2003

WHEREAS, The *members* of the *House of* Representatives of the State of Illinois were shocked and deeply saddened to learn of the untimely death of Julie R. Grace of Chicago on Tuesday, May 20, 2003; and

WHEREAS, Ms. Grace was born in Harvey to Durard and Ruth Grace; she was raised in Taylorville; she graduated from Southern Illinois University with a bachelor's degree in communications; and

WHEREAS, Ms. Grace had worked as an intern for U.S. Senator Alan Dixon; she went on to work as a writer and public relations coordinator on political campaigns for Walter Mondale, Senator Dixon, Senator Paul Simon, Cook County Commissioner Ted Lechowicz, and for public relations consultant, Thom Serafin; and

WHEREAS, In 1991, Ms. Grace was hired by Time Magazine's Chicago Bureau; she covered some of the most difficult and tragic stories for the Chicago Bureau, including the 1994 shocking death of 11-year old Robert "Yummy" Sandifer, the Columbine High School shootings, the Unabomber, the Andrew Cunanan murders, *five* school shootings nationwide, and the 1999 murder verdict in a Michigan courtroom against Dr. Jack Kevorkian; and

WHEREAS, In 2001, Ms. Grace became a free-lance writer for various clients; her life exemplified great kindness, empathy, and generosity; and

WHEREAS, The passing of Julie R. Grace has been deeply felt by her parents, Durard and Ruth Grace; her brother, Glenn; her nephew; and her beloved street dog, Bronte; therefore, be it

RESOLVED, BY THE HOUSE OF REPRESENTATIVES OF THE NINETYTHIRD GENERAL ASSEMBLY OF THE STATE OF ILLINOIS, that we mourn the passing of Julie R. Grace and extend to her friends, family, and all who knew and loved her, our deepest sympathy during their time of bereavement; and be it further

RESOLVED, That a suitable copy of this resolution be presented to the family of Julie R. Grace as an expression of our sincere condolences and profound sadness at the death of an excellent writer and caring individual.

Adopted by the House of Representatives on May 28, 2003.

Anthony D. Rossi, Clerk of the House

Michael J. Madigan, Speaker of the House

Resolution adopted by the House of Representatives

CHAPTER 9
TRAGEDY STRIKES AGAIN

Although the memorial service was over and Julie was laid to rest, the mourning continued. In our time of grief, Duard and I did a lot of research on domestic violence. We decided that even though Julie was no longer with us, perhaps there was something we could do to help ensure other women were not abused and killed in such a violent manner. That's when we became involved in the Chicago Abused Women Coalition (CAWC). The Julie R. Grace Memorial Fund was set up, and the money collected was used to provide abused women and their children with support services. We chose CAWC because of its mission statement:

> CAWC is committed to ending domestic violence. Using a self-help, empowerment approach, we provide counseling, advocacy, and a 24-hour hotline for people affected by domestic violence, including a shelter for women and children. We work for social change through education, service collaboration, and institutional advocacy.

For eighteen months Duard and I were involved in fundraisers for Julie's memorial fund. On August 28, 2004, CAWC sponsored a 5k walk/run fundraiser that they called "Step Out to Stop Abuse." All proceeds and pledges went directly to the Julie R. Grace Memorial Fund. Our participation in this organization brought great satisfaction to Duard and me, as this was one way we could help preserve Julie's memory. Furthermore, the money raised was used to increase the level of awareness of domestic violence and help prevent other women from becoming innocent victims.

Unfortunately, Duard's and my work for CAWC was abruptly interrupted on November 4th, 2004, when tragedy struck again. Duard and I had just finished breakfast when he decided to do some research on the Internet. He wasn't feeling real well but wasn't concerned there was anything seriously wrong and told me not to worry, as he was okay and didn't need to go to the doctor. I was in the bedroom when he decided to make a phone call. He went into the living room to get the phone and then sat down on the couch. Soon after, I came out of the bedroom and saw him slumped over with the phone in his hand. The love of my life was gone.

I was devastated! First Julie and now Duard! What was I going to do, I wondered? The nightmare continued. When was it ever going to end? How could I go on without him?

I'm confident Duard died of a broken heart. He was in excellent health, but Julie's death was just too much for him to handle. Even though George Thompson had never laid a hand on Duard, there is no doubt in my mind that Duard became George's second victim. The toll that Julie's brutal death took on Duard was more than he could physically and emotionally handle, and that's how George ultimately killed him too.

Now that Duard was gone too, the world around me seemed to be caving in. Not only had I lost my daughter by the hands of George Thompson, I now had lost my husband, best friend, and partner of forty-seven years. To help ease some of the pain from our losses, my son Glenn and I decided the two of us would continue working with CAWC to ensure Julie and Duard did not die in vain. We knew we had to do it, as that's what Duard would have wanted. As a result of our efforts, we were quite pleased that from May 2003 through the summer of 2005, over $10,000 was raised for the Julie R. Grace Memorial Fund.

CHAPTER 10
DAY ONE OF GEORGE'S TRIAL

Without Duard by our side, Glenn and I knew it was going to take everything we had to remain strong throughout George's trial, scheduled to begin on May 11, 2006. Naturally we were concerned about the potential outcome, but our attorney, Daniel Groth, assistant state's attorney, assured us that we had a very good case and that George would be found guilty and face a stiff sentence. That was our only hope as court commenced and the proceedings began.

Glenn and I walked into the courtroom. It was filled with spectators, friends of Julie's, and several members of the media. I was told there were reporters from the *Chicago Tribune, Chicago Sun Times, Chicago Magazine,* Fox News and the local Chicago TV station. Glenn, Julie's friends, and I were wearing lapel pins with a picture of Julie on them, and we were all asked to remove them because we were told that they might have an influence on the outcome of the trial. We were deeply disappointed that we could not even bring a picture of Julie into the courtroom. This was when we started to wonder whether the trial's end result would be a conviction of first-degree murder for her killer. We were worried that the judge would not be fair and that justice for Julie would not be served.

Judge Gaughan was a dark-haired, stern-looking man who appeared to be sixty-something. It was obvious he was thrilled to be the judge in a high-profile case that was well attended by members of the media. Throughout the trial he spent a lot of time primping so that he would look his best for media cameras.

Also, the judge made it very clear to all who attended the trial that no talking to anyone at any time and no outbursts of any kind would be allowed in his courtroom. He even implied that smiling was prohibited; and if anyone did not abide by his rules, they would be immediately removed from his courtroom and could possibly even end up in jail.

Because I was a witness and the court had ordered that no witnesses be allowed in the courtroom until after they had testified, I was not present when the opening statements were made; but according to the public records of the courtroom documents, this is how the session began.

"Be it remembered that on the 11th day of May, 2006, this cause came on for hearing before the Honorable Vincent M. Gaughan, Judge of said Court, upon the indictment herein, the defendant having entered a plea of not guilty."

The judge stated, "Mr. Thompson is charged with first degree murder. Is this going to be a bench or jury, Mr. Breen?" Thomas M. Breen was George's attorney.

Mr. Breen replied, "This will be a bench trial, Your Honor."

Judge Gaughan went on to say, "State, this is a seven-count indictment. What counts are you going to trial on?"

Mr. Groth advised the judge that George Thompson was being tried for first-degree murder, felony domestic battery, and a violation of the order of protection.

The judge then asked everyone to state their name for the record. The defendant's attorney responded by saying, "Good afternoon, Your Honor. My name is Thomas Breen. I, along with Todd Pugh, represent George Thompson, the gentleman to my right."

The judge then said, "Mr. Groth has already stated his name, his position and he'll be representing the People of the State of Illinois."

Mr. Groth then advised the judge that Assistant State's Attorney, Michele Popielewski, would be there soon.

"All right," said the judge. "Mr. Thompson, it is my understanding through your attorney that you are going to give up your absolute right to jury trial and have me hear your case, is that correct?"

"Yes, Your Honor," answered George.

"All right. I know your attorneys have explained to you what a jury trial is. I have to make sure in my mind you understand what a jury trial is before I make a decision that you knowingly and voluntarily are giving up your right to that particular type of trial. You understand that?"

"Yes, Sir," replied George.

"Basically, a jury trial would be twelve people gathered from a cross section of Cook County. What they would do is hear your evidence, determine the facts and determine your innocence or guilt. In the event you were found guilty, the jury would not have anything to do with your punishment, do you understand that?"

"Yes."

"Only you can give up your absolute right to jury trial. Your attorneys can't give that right up. In fact, I can't even order you to give up that right to jury trial. Do you understand that?"

"Yes, Sir."

Having gone through the legal formalities regarding a trial by jury, Judge Gaughan asked George to sign a jury waiver. He then proceeded by asking, "Any pretrial motions?"

Mr. Breen responded, "Your Honor, there will be a motion to exclude witnesses."

Mr. Groth followed by saying, "We join in that motion."

The judge ruled, "Mutual motion to exclude witnesses will be sustained as to both sides."

The judge then instructed Mr. Groth to make his opening statements.

Dan Groth was a younger, good-looking man, I'd say in his thirties, with an average height and build. He had always been very nice to Glenn and me and was supportive of the fundraisers we did on Julie's behalf. He even participated in walks for the Chicago Abused Women Coalition. Mr. Groth made it a point to stay in close contact with me during the three years prior to George's trial.

"Counsel, Your Honor. May 20th, 2003, the relationship between Julie Grace and this defendant, George Thompson, ended the only way he would allow it to end, which is with her dying on the floor of her own bedroom from the wounds that he inflicted on her a few days before.

"Judge, you're going to hear evidence that the relationship between these two, which starts in a rehabilitation facility, was punctuated by episodes of violence on the part of this defendant towards the victim, Julie Grace.

"November 27th, 2002, going into November 28th, the defendant committed a battery against Julie Grace. Police were called, photographs taken. That became the underlying source for an order of protection in this case which is the subject of count seven.

"In addition, Judge, March 7th, 2003, this defendant again beat Julie Grace. Only this time, it was so unfortunate he had to do it in the full view of two witnesses; one of them is going to testify, who were watching this horror unfold from their apartment building looking into Julie Grace's building where she lived with this defendant.

"You will hear how on the 7th of March he punched her, kicked her, smothered her, strangled her; did everything he could but kill her on that day. Again, police were called; photographs were taken, which Your Honor will see.

"On the 22nd of April, 2003, again this defendant expressed his displeasure at Julie Grace's actions and was arrested for an assault at that occasion. Again he was in the apartment with her that they shared.

"Subsequent to that Judge, the victim, Julie Grace, received an order of protection against this defendant; an order of protection that allowed him to live in that apartment, but commit no further unlawful act against her.

"Well on May 17th Julie Grace ran afoul of this defendant again. For whatever real or imagined plight she committed against him, he inflicted yet another brutal and heinous beating upon her. And after the 17th of May, she started to die slowly, slowly.

"She was kept incommunicado from her family. She wasn't able to call for any help. This defendant was in control of that crime scene for the next three days until approximately 4:00 in the morning on Tuesday, which would be the 20th of May.

"At that point when Julie Grace was turning purple, that's when this defendant decided to call for assistance for the injuries he inflicted upon her.

"When he called, paramedics arrived. They saw Julie naked on the floor of her own bedroom. They saw the area was covered with human waste. They did their attempt to try to save Julie Grace. But it was all for naught, because she was not breathing at the time the paramedics got there. She was dead when she got to Northwestern Hospital.

"Dr. An performed an autopsy and found that the cause of death was bronchopneumonia due to cerebral trauma brought on by blunt force trauma and the manner and cause of death was homicide.

"This defendant committed that crime, Judge. He caused her death. He's the one that set these events in motion. He's the one who was the cause of her death that day.

"When this case is over, we're going to ask you to find him guilty of first degree murder, felony domestic battery and felony violation of an order of protection."

"Thank you, State. Defendant." directed the judge.

Mr. Breen stood up and began his opening remarks. "Your Honor," began Defense Counsel Thomas Breen, "I'm going to ask the court to take note if I may, so that the court, as the trial progresses can figure out the timeframe we're referring to.

"There are four or five specific dates. Saturday, May 17th, 2003, is the date alleged in the indictment. And it is alleged that the incident that eventually caused the death of Julie Grace took place Saturday in the evening, May 17th.

"We then have Sunday, May 18th, 2003. We have Monday, May 19th, 2003, and Tuesday, May 20th, 2003. May 17th, on Saturday in the evening hours, is when the incident occurred. On Tuesday, May 20th after 4:00 in the morning, between four and four-thirty in the morning, 911 was called by George Thompson. I believe you will hear those tapes.

"Now the prosecution's theory is somehow he set something in motion that caused her to die of bronchopneumonia. That will not be the case, Your Honor, that he set anything in motion that would cause her to die of bronchopneumonia."

Mr. Breen was a knowledgeable, experienced attorney who had the experience and expertise to do a good job of defending his client. When he spoke of Julie, he always showed no emotion. He was determined to show that George was not responsible for Julie's death. Mr. Breen had a reputation for taking on cases just for the publicity and so I'm sure, that's why he took George's case.

Mr. Breen went on to say, "The tragic life of Julie Grace that ended on May 20th, 2003 had begun to show, at least we think the evidence will show through the pathologist, had begun years in the past when Julie Grace was an uncontradicted alcoholic who on certain days, would drink two to three, excuse me, during a 48-hour period would drink two to three fifths of vodka.

"She had sought treatment, unsuccessfully. She had embraced the people of AA. She didn't get recovery from that. She met George Thompson in 2002 at Lake Shore Hospital. George Thompson was there for treatment in rehab himself. He was there for approximately two weeks and his insurance ran out.

"Upon his departure from there, he was invited by Julie Grace to spend the evening with him, excuse me, with her in her Sandburg Village apartment. That began a long, what one doctor refers to as a mutually abusive relationship, that went on until May 20th of 2003.

"The indictment in this case alleges, among other things, that without lawful justification, George Thompson intentionally or knowingly performed acts which caused the death of Julie Grace. Your Honor, the evidence is going to show that Julie Grace would become a verbally and physically abusive person under the influence of alcohol.

"The evidence is going to show that she has in the past physically attacked George Thompson. The evidence is going to show, through the State's own evidence, that on May 17th, 2003, the date of this incident, Julie Grace attacked George Thompson. That was not unusual. She attacked him. He pushed her away. She attacked him. He hit her in the chest.

"As a result of hitting her in the chest, the following unintended events occurred. She fell. She hit her forehead. Excuse me. She hit her temple area on the left side of the head.

"The reason I want to emphasize on the left side of the head, is because the autopsy will be perfectly consistent with what George Thompson's recollection of the events are. The striking of the temple area caused, in the next two or three day period, a black eye.

"When a lay person looks at the black eye, we immediately think that she was punched in the eye. That is not the case. She struck herself according to the State's own evidence, on something sharp, to wit, the dresser or a drawer in the dresser, on the left side of her head. As a result of that, she was, she had a black eye.

"She also had bruises about her, a couple of which are identified by George Thompson as being bruises that would have resulted from that struggle.

"Now the State tells you that what he did was, under the law, not justifiable. I submit to the court, under the circumstances it was, and that what occurred after he defended himself was not intentional. It was not a knowing act. It was a push to safeguard his own personal safety. And the result was, quite simply, an accident that occurred after she fell.

"Also, Your Honor, the State theorizes in count two that again, without lawful justification, which I respectfully submit they will not be able to prove, inflicted blunt trauma injuries that killed Julie Grace knowing that such acts created a strong probability of death or great bodily harm.

"We take severe issue and plead not guilty, as well, Your Honor, to that count there was nothing he did under the circumstances that was unlawful. There is nothing he did that would cause him to knowingly know what would occur when he struck her in the chest to get her away.

"But again, the State theorizes that on May 17th an incident occurred and that George Thompson somehow waited patiently for her ultimate death. That is absolute nonsense.

"After the event on May 17th, they went to bed. On May 18th, that Sunday at 7:46 at night, Julie Grace, the one that Mr. Groth says was being held incommunicado from her family, which is also nonsense, called the Pottash grocery store across the street from her apartment in the Sandburg Village.

"Judge, I've driven by it many times. Perhaps the court knows that there is a small grocery store in the Sandburg Village area. And at 7:46 on May 19th, Julie, she doesn't call 911, she doesn't call a cab to take her to a hospital, she doesn't call her mother. She calls the Pottash grocery store and requests of the manager that a delivery be made of a liter of vodka, cigarettes and some food items. And those things that she requests in a state of drunkenness I might add, are delivered to her apartment. The truth of the matter is, Your Honor, whether people wish to believe it or not, and we all including George, suffered a loss when Julie Grace died on May 20th. It is a huge stretch to charge him with any kind of theory under first degree murder and I suggest to the court that it is a huge stretch to come up with anything he did that would have caused bronchopneumonia, which the court may, or soon will learn, is caused by a bacteria or a virus.

"The truth of the matter is, Your Honor, Julie Grace was a very sick individual. The alcoholism had taken a horrible physical toll on her. She was infected with a virus and bacteria. She was on antibiotics and I think, Your Honor, the evidence is going to suggest that she succumbed to an infection that she already had long before May 20th, 2003.

"So Your Honor, we have issues here of lawful justification. We have issues here of cause of death. And also, Your Honor, we have issues of perception. Julie Grace was well educated, comes from a nice family, part of a cultured community. George Thompson got a GED, worked as an iron worker and comes from a broken home.

"But the two of them enjoyed each other's company, physically and emotionally. Whether they were made for each other or should never have been with each other is not for us to decide. The point is, it was a mutually abusive relationship. She would strike and hurt him. He would, from time to time, respond.

"He never intended to do great bodily harm to Julie. He was remorseful and is remorseful that he would have had anything to do with it. But the most important thing, Your Honor, is for the court's consideration is that this is not a first degree murder case. Thank you."

As the trial proceedings moved on, Mr. Groth was asked to call his first witness. "Judge, I'll call Ruth Grace."

Since witnesses were not allowed in the courtroom prior to testifying, I was instructed that it was time for me to enter the courtroom. I was escorted from the witness room and into the courtroom. When I walked in, I saw Judge Gaughan in the front of the room with the attorneys sitting across from the bench, facing him. In front of the judge and directly to his right, was the witness stand. There was no jury, but the jury box was to the right of the witness stand. Although I had never been in a courtroom before, it was much like I had imagined it would be. The courthouse was in downtown Chicago in a very old building. There was nothing that particularly stood out about this courtroom, as it closely resembled those I had seen on TV.

Although I was nervous as I walked to the witness stand, I was anxious to get the trial started. I knew my testimony was not going to take a long time, but Mr. Groth felt that what I had to say was important and would be beneficial to our case.

After I was sworn in and stated my name, Mr. Groth asked, "Do you have any children?"

"I have one daughter that's deceased and a son, Glenn Grace."

"Were you married at one time?"

"I was married."

"What was your husband's name?"

"My husband's name is Duard A. Grace, Jr."

"Did he pass away recently?"

"Yes."

"Ma'am, you said you had a daughter named Julie, deceased."

"I have a daughter named Julie."

"I'm going to show you what has been marked People's Exhibit number 1 for identification. Do you recognize who that is?" he asked.

"I do."

"Who is that?"

"That's my Julie."

"Thank you. Where do you normally live?"

"I live in Florida."

"Okay. Back in 2002, 2003, where was Julie living?"

"She was living in Chicago on North LaSalle."

"Would that be 1540 North LaSalle?"

"1540 North LaSalle."

"The top floor."

"20th floor."

"Had you ever been in that apartment?"

"Many a time."

Mr. Groth then asked, "In 2002 and 2003, did you meet a young man that Julie was dating?"

"Yes," I answered.

"I want you to take a look around the courtroom and see if you recognize that person."

Because I didn't have a clear view of George from where I was sitting, I stood up to seek him out. When I spotted him, I noticed he had a crew cut and was wearing the Department of Corrections khaki shirt and pant suit.

After a brief moment, I said "Yes." I then pointed to the defendant, George Thompson.

Mr. Groth followed up by asking, "Where had you first met the defendant, George Thompson?"

"Julie brought him home."

"Back in Florida?"

"Back to Florida."

"Okay. Did you ever have conversations with Mr. Thompson on the telephone?"

"Yes."

"Were you able to recognize his voice?"

"Yes."

"Ma'am," said Mr. Groth, "I want to draw your attention to the weekend of May 17th, 2003. Did you ever try and get in contact with your daughter, Julie?"

"Yes."

"Okay. How did you try to do that?"

"By phone."

"Okay. At that time, did Julie have phone number 312-751-1698?"

"That's correct."

"Okay. Did you use your cell phone to try and make contact with her?"

"I sure did. I used my cell phone. I bought the cell phone just purposely to call my daughter."

"That weekend of May 17th, 18th, 19th going into Tuesday the 20th, were you able to get in contact with your daughter, Julie?"

"No."

"When you phoned over to her apartment on those occasions, did anyone ever answer the phone?"

"Yes."

"Who did?"

"George Thompson. We called him Kenneth."

"You knew him by Kenneth?"

"We knew him by Kenneth. George Kenneth Thompson."

"Can you describe for the court, if you could, what it was the defendant said to you when you tried to speak on the phone?"

"I was looking for my daughter. I was searching. I called his parents. They told me they had not heard"

Mr. Groth interrupted, "Without going into what anybody said except for this defendant, tell the court what it was the defendant said to you."

"He told me, he said you hang up this telephone right now."

"Okay. What kind of voice did he say it in?"

"Meanest voice I ever heard in my life," I said.

"Did you attempt to call Julie when somebody didn't answer?"

"Yes."

"Did you try to leave messages?"

"Yes."

"Now on May 20th, 2003, did you eventually get a phone call from the Chicago Police Department?"

"I did."

"Okay. And as a result of that phone call, did you have to come into Chicago?"

"I did."

"Okay. What was the condition of your daughter at that time?"

"She was dead. She had been murdered."

Mr. Groth ended his cross-examination and Mr. Breen was asked to cross-examine me. "Mrs. Grace, did Julie have a cell phone?" he asked.

"Yes."

"Did you call her on the cell phone?"

"No, I called her on her home phone."

"Did you ever call her on the cell phone?"

"I called her lots of times on her cell phone."

"How about that weekend?"

"That weekend, I don't think I did, but I could have."

"When Julie went on a bender or a binge, she didn't want to talk to you, did she?"

"Objection," responded Mr. Groth. "Calls for speculation."

"Overruled," replied the judge.

"Julie never refused to talk to her mother," I said.

Mr. Breen then asked, "Was she ever unable to talk to you?"

"She was unable to talk to me when he murdered her; when she was lying there dying. I couldn't reach her. He tells me to hang up the telephone. I couldn't reach her."

"Did you call her cell phone then?"

"I called her home number."

"Did you ever call her cell phone that weekend?"

"Yes, I called her cell. If I did, I'm sure I did. I was calling everywhere."

"Were you able to talk to anybody?"

"George Thompson answered the phone. I did talk to his parents."

"Okay."

"I talked to the mother and then I talked to the father, which was his stepfather. They told me that they had not heard from Julie for two days. That was very unusual."

"Did you ever call the police?"

"No, I didn't call the police. I wished I had."

"Nothing further, Your Honor," responded Mr. Breen.

The judge instructed me to step down and then announced the court would take a short recess.

As I walked away from the witness stand, I kept wondering to myself why didn't Mr. Groth ask me more about Julie's life and the many times George physically abused her. Why didn't he let me tell about all those times Julie had told me about the bruises George had inflicted upon her just because she didn't do exactly what he wanted. There was so much I wanted to say but was not given the opportunity. I was very disappointed by the way Mr. Groth handled my testimony.

When court reconvened, Judge Gaughan instructed Mr. Groth to call his next witness.

"Call Corazon Cruz," said Mr. Groth.

Ms. Cruz came forward and was sworn in. After stating and spelling her name, Mr. Groth asked, "Ma'am, where do you live?"

"1540 North LaSalle."

"Did you live there back in 2002 and 2003?"

"Yes."

"Did you know a young lady by the name of Julie Grace?"

"Yes."

"How did you know her?"

"My next door neighbor," answered Ms. Cruz.

"I'll show you a photograph that's been marked People's Exhibit number 1 for identification. May I approach the witness?" asked Mr. Groth.

The judge instructed him to go ahead.

"You recognize that?"

"Yes."

"Who is in that photograph?"

"My neighbor, Julie Grace."

"Okay. Now at the time you knew Julie Grace, about 2002, 2003, did she have a boyfriend that lived with her?"

"Yes."

"You see him in court today?"

"Yes."

"Would you identify him by something he's wearing?"

"Beige shirt and white sweater down at the bottom," Ms. Cruz replied.

"May the record reflect this witness identified this defendant in open court," instructed Mr. Groth.

"Record so reflect, Counsel," stated the judge.

"Mr. Groth continued. "Before the 17th of May, 2003, when was the last time you saw Julie Grace in person?"

"Two weeks before she died."

"On the evening, the Sunday before she died, the 18th, did you hear anything unusual?"

"A big thump in the bedroom."

"You say the bedroom. Whose bedroom?"

"Julie's bedroom, because her bedroom was across from my bedroom."

"You had separate apartments but you shared a common wall."

"Yes."

"Okay. Did you hear anything else?"

"No."

"Did you hear any voices?"

"No."

"After you heard that thump, that was Sunday evening, is that correct?"

"Yes."

"The 18th?"

"Yes."

"Now on Tuesday morning, the 20th, approximately 4:00 in the morning, did you hear anything else unusual?"

"Yes."

"What did you hear?"

"A scream saying that she couldn't breathe."

"Okay, and did you recognize the voice?" asked Mr. Groth.

"Yes."

"Who was it?"

"Ken."

"Is that the person you identified?"

"Yes."

"You knew him as Kenneth?"

"Yes."

"After that, did anything else unusual happen in regards to Julie's apartment?"

Ms. Cruz replied, "I heard an ambulance pulling up in the driveway and I was awakened."

"Did you ever see or hear emergency personnel responding to that apartment?"

"I heard noises. I did open my door."

"What did you see?"

"I saw the paramedics, Chicago Fire Department and police and I closed my door."

"I have nothing further for this witness at this time," stated Mr. Groth.

Judge Gaughan asked, "Cross examination, defense?"

"No cross, Judge," answered Mr. Breen.

The judge instructed Ms. Cruz to step down. He then said, "State, call your next witness."

Mr. Groth asked the judge if he could stipulate copies of phone records showing that I had tried to call Julie just as I had testified. The judge ordered the stipulation of these documents, and they were moved into evidence.

Mr. Groth then said, "There is a further stipulation regarding the next piece of evidence," stated Mr. Groth. "It is hereby stipulated by and between the parties that if called to testify, Sam Low would state he is employed by the city of Chicago, Office of Emergency Communications and that the Office of Emergency Communications is in the business of providing emergency services to citizens of Chicago; that the Office of Emergency Communications maintains records of emergency calls in the ordinary course of business.

"That Sam Low's duties include maintaining and keeping these audio tape records for the Office of Emergency Communications, that exhibit number 5 is a true and accurate copy of the 911 call made by defendant George Thompson to the Office of Emergency Communications on May 20th, 2003, at approximately 4:00 AM, that this record was maintained in the ordinary course of business. So stipulated?"

"So stipulated," replied Mr. Pugh.

Judge Gaughan said, "That stipulation is allowed and moved into evidence."

Mr. Groth advised the court that he had a transcript of the tape. After a brief discussion between the judge, Mr. Breen, Mr. Pugh, and Mr. Groth, Judge Gaughan instructed Mr. Groth to go ahead and play the tape.

As I sat listening to the tape and George's voice, it was obvious to me that he was just putting on an act, pretending to be upset. The tone in his voice was not of someone who was sincerely concerned about Julie's well-being. Even though he said things like, "Get over here right now, you're taking too long," anyone who had ever talked to George would know he was merely putting on an act. I could tell that all he was trying to do was avoid being arrested for the murder of my daughter. He knew he had killed her and didn't want to go to jail.

At the conclusion of the tape, Mr. Groth stated, "Judge, I'd like to call Paramedic Greer."

Mr. Greer proceeded to take the stand and was sworn in.

After stating his name, Mr. Groth asked Mr. Greer, "How are you employed?"

"City of Chicago Fire Department, paramedic."

"How long have you been a paramedic?"

"Eleven years with the city of Chicago."

"What did you do before that?"

"EMT and paramedic in the private sector."

"On May 20th, 2003, approximately 4:00 in the morning, were you working and on duty as a paramedic for the Chicago Fire Department?"

"Yes."

"Did you have a partner?"

"Yes, I do."

"Who is that?"

"Norman Meske."

"Did you and your partner receive a dispatch to go to the area of 1540 North LaSalle, apartment 2004?"

"Yes."

"And what did you do when you got there?"

"It was for a person down, and to do ALS care on the person we were there for."

"What is ALS care?" asked Mr. Groth.

"Advanced life support. Consists of incubation, maybe monitoring, oxygen, certain drugs."

"Okay. When you got to that apartment 2004, where did you go?"

"Straight to the bedroom."

"What did you see when you got to the bedroom?"

"Female down on the ground; appeared to be lifeless; breathless."

"Did you check to see what her signs were?"

"Yes."

"What were they?"

"She was not breathing. She was pulseless."

"She had no pulse." stated Mr. Groth.

"No pulse," answered Mr. Greer.

"Did you notice anything about her appearance?"

"Very bruised."

"Okay. What did you notice about the appearance of the bedroom she was in?"

"Very messy, junky, strong smell of urine, fecal material, alcohol."

"Was there any other type of body emissions in that room?"

"Appeared to be urine on the floor."

"Did you notice any vomit?"

"I did not, no," answered Mr. Greer.

"You said that the body of the young lady was bruised. What was her state of clothing?"

"She was unclothed."

"Do you see anyone in this courtroom that you saw in that building at that time, that apartment at that time?"

"The gentleman sitting to the left, to the right of me."

"Describe something that he's wearing."

"Wearing 3XL tan jersey shirt."

"May the record reflect this witness identified this defendant in open court." stated Mr. Groth.

"Describe for the court, if you could, the way this defendant was acting as you and your partner tried to perform life support services on Julie Grace."

"The gentleman was very belligerent, screaming and yelling at us, mostly in the way"

"What type of words did he use?"

"I don't know if I can say those in court."

"Yes, you can," said the judge.

"Hey motherfucker; do something, hurry up. What the fuck? Do something. Things like that."

"Okay," stated Mr. Groth. "Now, as part of your job as a paramedic you have to make assessment or diagnosis of the person you are treating."

"Not generally a diagnosis," replied Mr. Greer. "We assess our findings and act on those findings."

"Based on the bruising and Julie Grace's condition, what did you think had been going on there at that time to render her to that condition?"

"Appeared she had been beaten."

"Okay," said Mr. Groth. He then showed the witness several photos of Julie's apartment as it appeared to him on May 20th and asked Detective Greer to comment on each one. "I'm going to show you People's Exhibits 6 through 19. Take a look at those and see if you recognize what those are."

"This is the bedroom."

"And with the exception of some of the police evidence markers, do those exhibits truly and accurately depict the bedroom where you were rendering life saving services at 1540 North LaSalle, apartment 2004, on May 20th, 2003?"

"Yes, Sir."

"Is there any remnants of your life saving treatment on the floor there?" Hearing no response from Mr. Greer, Mr. Groth asked again, "Any signs that you saw in that picture?"

"Looks like one of our tourniquets on the floor there," answered Mr. Greer.

"What is the next Exhibit, number 11, what does that show?"

"The tourniquet and looks like some blood maybe."

"You think that may have come from the IV you administered?"

"Possible."

"People's Exhibit number 13."

"That's the closet of the bedroom, with some stain of some pillows and such."

"People's Exhibit number 17."

"Again, stained carpet and pillow case and pillows."

"People's Exhibit number 18."

"Looks like a pillow behind the bed."

"People's Exhibit number 19."

"More pillows on the bed with stains."

"I'm going to show you People's Exhibits 2, 20, 21 and 22," said Mr. Groth. "See if you recognize what those are photographs of."

"The first one is the victim we were treating."

"Okay."

"Head shot."

"The next one; that's number 2. What is the next one, number 20?"

"Side view of the same patient."

"All right, number 21."

"Bruising on her torso and arms."

"Number 22."

"Looks like the right side of the same."

"Aside from the Medical Examiner's tags positioned on the young lady's body, do these photographs depict the condition she was in when you and your brother paramedics are trying to treat her as far as bruising goes?"

"Yes, Sir."

"Thank you," replied Mr. Groth. "Nothing, Judge. Tender this witness."

The judge asked Mr. Breen if he wanted to cross-examine the witness. Replying that he did not, Judge Gaughan instructed Mr. Groth to call his next witness. He called Dr. Arangelovich to the stand.

The witness came forward and was sworn in. After stating her name, Mr. Groth began questioning her. "Do you have a profession?" he asked.

"Yes, I do."

"What is that profession?"

"I am a deputy medical examiner."

"Are you licensed to practice medicine in the State of Illinois?"

"Yes, I am."

"How long have you been a deputy medical examiner?"

"Since July 2004."

"Doctor, as a deputy medical examiner your duties include performing autopsies."

"Yes."

"Do your duties include testifying regarding autopsies performed by other medical examiners?"

"Yes, it does."

"Is that why you are here today?"

"Yes."

"Did you review Cook County Medical Examiner office file number 332 for May 2003?"

"Yes."

"Do you have a copy of that file with you?"

"Yes, I do."

"Would it assist you today in testifying to use that file?"

"Yes, it would."

Turning to Mr. Breen, Mr. Groth asked, "Any objection?"

"Not at all," answered Mr. Breen.

Mr. Groth continued, "We'd ask the witness be allowed to use the file to testify in this case."

"Certainly," said the judge. "Proceed."

Mr. Groth asked Dr. Arangelovich, "What's an autopsy?"

She replied, "Autopsy is an examination of the body performed after death. And to begin with, it starts with an external examination where we examine the external surfaces of the body. This examination can be supplemented with x-rays, photography. After that, the body is opened. We take various bodily fluids, test for certain poisons or drugs. Subsequently the internal organs are removed and examined for any pathology."

"Was an autopsy performed on the remains of Julie Grace on May 20th, 2003 by Dr. An?" asked Mr. Groth.

"Yes."

"Was it recorded under 332 May 2003?"

"Yes."

"You indicated earlier that you had reviewed that. I'm going to show you People's Exhibits number 2, 20 through 22 and 24 through 38. Take a look at those photographs and see if you recognize them as being relevant to this."

"Yes, they are."

"Okay. Describe for us if you could, what the external examination regarding this autopsy revealed."

"To begin with," said the doctor, "the external examination, we start at the head and neck. On the face, there was bruising about the left eyelid, upper and lower eyelid, which extended towards the lower left side of the forehead. And this bruise was purple, dark purple color."

She continued, "Also, we look at the chin. She had two bruises on the right side of the chin. These were kind of pinkish. There was one bruise, also, on the left side of the chin."

"Okay," stated Mr. Groth. "Now, the bruise on the eye, did it contain any lacerations?"

"No, it did not."

"Okay. You indicated the external examination of the head also revealed two others on the chin."

"Yes."

"What did the chest examination show?"

"The chest examination showed several irregular dark pinkish areas that were seen in the middle of the chest and extending towards the sides of the right and left breasts. The largest bruise there was documented as being seven by five centimeters.

"Also, on the left lateral chest, almost beneath the outer margin of the left breast, there was a bruise, also two dark pink bruises. The largest of that measured ten by ten centimeters."

"What did the examination of the abdomen show?" asked Mr. Groth.

"On the abdomen, on the right lower side, there were two yellow-bluish areas consistent with bruises and each of these measured about two by two centimeters."

"What did the back show, if anything?"

"The back showed on the left upper back, a dark purple bruise that measured five by five centimeters."

"How about the upper extremities?"

"To begin with, starting with the left upper extremity on the left arm, the medial aspect which is closest to the chest, there were several dark pinkish areas consistent with bruises."

"May the record reflect the witness is using her fingers on the interior part of her left arm," instructed Mr. Groth.

The witness then stated, "And the largest one here was seven by five centimeters, and then as we go down, we go to the elbow which is the posterior part of the arm. There was also another bruise which was five by five centimeters. This is dark pink.

"If we go down further onto the left hand posterior aspect, there was also a bruise here which was two by two centimeters.

"Now if we go to the right extremity on the right shoulder, there were two dark pinkish areas. The larger bruise measured three by three centimeters.

"Then there was a medial aspect on the arm. There was also a dark pinkish area and this was seven by five centimeters. If we go down further to the right upper extremity, down to the forearm on the interior aspect, there were several dark pinkish areas here as well as on the right hand, the posterior aspect. The largest bruise was three by three centimeters."

"When you said here, what part of the wrist was that?" asked Mr. Groth.

"It was the anterior right forearm as well as the back of the right hand."

"The anterior would be?"

"The part facing everyone. The posterior is behind. Then as we continue down with the lower extremities, we have on the right hip area on the outside, a dark pinkish bruise. This was about seven by seven centimeters. If we go down to the left side, on this side, on the lateral aspect which is the side of the thigh, there were also two yellow- blue bruises there. The largest one measured ten by ten centimeters.

"Then if we go down the left thigh, the left leg, the anterior part, there was yellow-bluish area. If we go down even further going onto the right leg, the same location but on the right leg, the anterior, there were several yellow-bluish areas. And the largest one measured about seven by seven centimeters."

"Could you tell the age of all these various bruises?" asked Mr. Groth.

"All these bruises were relatively recent, within a few days. Generally, by the end of a week, bruises generally look more kind of a greenish because the blood is breaking down. Generally, bruises that are purple, red, bluish, those are relatively more recent. They can begin to develop a yellow margin, recent bruises as they are aging."

"When you examined the body of Julie Grace, did you find anything to show she'd been treated medically?"

"Yes, I did."

"What did you find?"

"I found in the right elbow crease there were some needle marks. There was also needle maximum in the right groin area, as well as an identification band about the left wrist."

"And then was there an internal examination?" questioned Mr. Groth.

"Yes, there was," answered the witness.

"Would you tell us about that please?"

"The internal examination was most prominent for the central nervous system or the brain. Generally, we reflect the scalp backwards and forward in order to look into the skull and subsequently into the brain. And underneath the scalp on both sides, the right and left, there was hemorrhage, mainly predominantly on the left side of the scalp once it was reflected. And then we looked at the skull. There were no fractures."

"What is a hemorrhage?" asked the attorney.

"A hemorrhage is basically an area where blood has seeped into the tissue from general injury," replied Dr. Arangelovich.

"Could you tell where this hemorrhage originated?"

"Because usually you see subgaleal hemorrhage where there is force or blunt trauma, most likely it originated from the trauma that was inflicted that we saw on the left eyelid and the lower left side of the forehead."

"What else did the interior examination of the head show?"

"Okay," responded the witness, "continuing now, we opened the skull. And we see underneath the dura, which is covering of the brain, we saw a subdural hematoma. And this was mainly on the left side—left side of the brain. And this extended all the way from the side, backwards and forwards. This was actually the hematoma, relatively easily separated from the covering of the brain. That suggests to us this was an acute or more recent hematoma."

Mr. Groth then asked the witness, "What else did you find as you examined the skull area?"

"Once we took off the skull," answered Dr. Arangelovich, "we took off the dura, we see the subdural hematoma. We also saw, once we looked at the surface of the brain, we saw subarachnoid hemorrhage. This was mainly on the right side as well as on the left side of the brain. That subarachnoid hemorrhage you can see because it is bright red. Usually the brain is kind of pale."

The judge interrupted, "I'm sorry, Doctor. Just for clarification, that would be hemorrhages, not one big hemorrhage on both sides of the brain."

"That would be discrete multiple hemorrhages predominantly on the right but also on the left," replied the witness. "Then if we just continue into the examination, once we actually looked at the brain and we section it to look for hemorrhages and so forth, he did so in the corpus callosum, which is the part of the brain that connects the right and the left, some hemorrhages, as well. These were focal pinpoint hemorrhages, very tiny."

"Okay. And after the corpus callosum, what was the next finding?"

"The next finding there we basically looked at the cerebral hemispheres. They showed no hemorrhage. They took out the spinal cord. No evidence of hemorrhage there. Then we continued with the neck."

"That part of the brain that had the hemorrhage, what functions of the body does that control?" asked Mr. Groth.

"In the corpus callosum?" questioned the witness.

"No, I'm sorry. The left part of the brain you were talking about earlier."

"You have the skull. Then you have the dura, the covering. Then underneath here, we saw the subdural hematoma. That subdural hematoma that's underneath here is now pressing against the brain, which is here. And the subdural hematoma will press on the brain because it is occupying space. The skull is a relatively rigid chamber of the body. It is not going to expand. The subdural hematoma is going to press on the brain, compressing the brain, which therefore leads to the little hemorrhages that I talked about in the corpus callosum. Eventually, that compression of the brain is going to affect the respiratory and cardiac centers of the brain stem, thus leading to complications."

"Was the neck examined, as well?" asked Mr. Groth.

"Yes."

"What happened there?"

"In the neck organs, there was some hemorrhage and subcutaneous tissue in the right chin. Previously, I spoke that there were two bruises. Otherwise, there was also a note of some hemorrhages in the larynx, the throat, which most likely is from resuscitation when you put in an endotracheal tube."

"The respiratory system itself, was that examined?"

"Yes."

"What were the findings there?"

"Lungs weighed five hundred fifty grams each. That's a bit heavy. They appeared pale and pinkish. And they were somewhat edematous, which means they had a lot of fluid in them. Sometimes that happens from the death process. Otherwise, there can be some pathology in the lungs. You just can't see grossly; but otherwise the pulmonary arteries were patent without any emboli."

"How about the cardiovascular system?"

"The cardiovascular system was fine. The heart weighed two hundred forty-five grams, which is consistent for someone of her height and weight. The walls of the heart looked fine. There were no congenital anomalies noted, either. The aorta was smooth internal surface. There was no atherosclerosis."

"Now the system that the liver is part of; that has a special name. What is that?"

"The hepatobiliary system, meaning liver and bile system."

"That system, was that examined?"

"Yes, it was."

"What did Dr. An find?"

"Dr. An found a rather enlarged liver. It was two thousand four hundred ninety-seven grams. It showed a prominent yellow discoloration throughout. Generally, a healthy liver is supposed to be red, brown. Here it is yellow. Generally, that's from accumulation of fat. This occurs in infants due to congenital problems. It could occur in adults due to morbid obesity or alcohol use. Here we have a prominent yellow discoloration which Dr. An stated indicated a fatty liver. Otherwise, there was nothing else wrong with the bile system."

"How about the hemolymphatic system?"

"The hemolymphatic system, which makes up the spleen, the blood and lymph nodes, that was fine."

"And the endocrine system."

"The endocrine system that deals with the hormones of the body, the pituitary gland, thyroid gland, the adrenal gland; they were all within normal appearance."

"Now, the genitourinary system."

"Yes. In the genitourinary system this includes the kidneys; the urethras; the bladder; in women, the ovaries, the uterus, the fallopian tubes; in men, the prostate, the testes. With her, the kidneys were fine. The uterus was fine. No evidence of any pregnancy. The ovaries, the fallopian tubes and the vagina were all of normal appearance."

"How about the gastrointestinal system?"

"The gastrointestinal system was fine. The stomach only contained a small amount of brownish fluid. Just fecal material, as expected, was present in the small and large intestine."

"The brownish fluid in the stomach, are you able to assess from there when it was the last time Julie may have had a meal?"

"No."

"What was Dr. An's diagnosis regarding Julie Grace?"

"Dr. An stated the cause of death of Julie Grace was bronchopneumonia due to cerebral injuries due to blunt trauma. And the fatty liver due to chronic alcoholism was considered to be a contributing factor in her death."

"Did he have an opinion to the manner of death?"

"Yes, he did."

"Doctor, to a reasonable degree of scientific and forensic certainty, do you have an opinion as to the cause of death of Julie Grace?"

"Yes, I do."

"What is that?"

"And it is bronchopneumonia due to cerebral injuries due to blunt trauma."

"Do you have an opinion to the same standard regarding the manner of death?"

"Yes," answered Dr. Arangelovich.

"What signs or symptoms does somebody who has had this blunt trauma begin to exhibit?" asked Mr. Groth.

"They would most likely begin to exhibit some mental confusion, some decreased alertness. Perhaps they might even start vomiting due to the brain swelling. That's going to affect the vomiting centers. They then could also experience seizure activity, as well."

"Okay. Now the person's thinking, what happens to that?"

"It becomes altered. They become confused. The brain is not getting profused right. There is pressure on it. It is an ultra confused state."

"You stated earlier about the autopsy, there were toxicology reports. Was one done in this case?"

"Yes."

"And what were the results for toxicology in this case?"

"In this particular case, we tested for a multitude of drugs. And I'll go through each of them. We tested for Benzoylecgonine, which is a metabolite of cocaine, which was negative. We tested for alcohol. That was negative. We tested for opiates, which concerns morphine and heroin and so forth. That was negative. All of this was done on blood specimens. We also did tests for prescription medications. Haloperidol, which is an anti-psychotic—that was tested for. That was negative. We tested for Lorazepam or Ativan which is an anti-anxiety agent. That was negative.

"We tested for Olanzapine or Zyprexa, which is an anti-psychotic. That was none detected or negative. We tested for Paxil or Paroxetine which is an anti-depressant and that was positive as two hundred nanograms per mill. We also tested for Trazodone, which is a sleep aid as well as an anti-depressant, and that was negative, as well."

Mr. Groth then handed the witness a pen and several photos and asked Dr. Arangelovich to circle specific items on each. After this process was complete, Mr. Groth continued his examination by asking the witness, "Dr. An examined Julie Grace. He also examined the hands as part of the upper extremities, is that correct?"

"Yes."

"All right. Were there any other injuries to Julie Grace's hands?"

"She had injuries to the right and left hands."

"On the back part?"

"Back part of the palm, yes."

"Is that consistent with an offensive or defensive wound?"

"Most likely these are defensive wounds."

"Thank you," said Mr. Groth. "Judge, nothing further. Tender the witness."

Mr. Breen began his cross-examination of Dr. Arangelovich. "Doctor, you did not do the autopsy, correct?"

"Correct."

"Dr. An did the autopsy."

"Yes."

69

"And where is Dr. An today?"

"Dr. An is in Columbus, Ohio."

"Is he retired?"

"No, he's working there as a deputy medical examiner."

"Did you speak to him at any time prior to your testifying today?"

"No, I didn't."

"So you never had a conference or anything like that with Dr. An, and Dr. An is actually the one who did the hands-on autopsy."

"No, I didn't."

"But you are familiar with the fact, are you not, that the autopsy was done by Dr. An on May 20th, 2003?"

"Correct."

"And you are familiar with the fact that the cause of death was not pronounced by Dr. An until September 5th, 2003, is that correct?"

"That is correct. Actually that's July 7th."

"July 7th, I'm sorry, July 7th of 03."

"Yes."

"Now during the course of June, July, that two month period or two and a half month period, Dr. An and people from the medical examiner's office reviewed the extensive medical history of Julie Grace, did they not?"

"They did, yes."

"And you have reviewed that file, have you not?"

"Yes, I have."

"Let me talk about the effects of alcoholism for a moment. Julie Grace was, at the time of the autopsy, the time of her death, how old was she?"

"She was 41."

"How tall was she and what did she weigh?"

"She was sixty-eight inches in length, one hundred forty-seven pounds."

"You do have an opinion that Julie Grace, after reviewing all these matters as well as her prior record or prior medical record, was an alcoholic, correct?"

"She had alcohol dependency issues."

"When you say alcohol dependency issues, does that mean that she drank too much and could not stop?"

"Yes."

"And she drank so much and could not stop that she was doing physical harm to her own body, was she not?"

"I don't know that."

"Well you looked at the liver, did you not, or photos of the liver?"

"I did look at photos of the liver."

"You determined, did you not, that she was an acute alcoholic?"

"Yes."

"Okay. So as an acute alcoholic, she was doing damage to her body, her organs, specifically for this moment, her liver, isn't that right?"

"Yes."

"So she was damaging herself, correct?"

"Internally."

"I'm going to ask you, based on your review of the records, can you tell me for what period of time Julie Grace was or would be defined as an alcoholic?"

"I have looked at records from 2001 to 2003," answered the witness.

"Okay. During that time there were hospitalizations for alcohol dependency issues. And that played a role, did it not, in determining the cause of death as well as the manner of death in this matter?"

"It played a role in the cause of death."

"You reviewed records, you indicated, and some of the records that you reviewed and I will try to go in chronological order," said Mr. Breen. "In January, on January 21st, 2001, did your records reflect that she was hospitalized at Northwestern Hospital for vomiting and diarrhea?"

"My records begin on March 2nd, 2001."

"March 2nd, 2001."

"Yes. I have her date of admission March 2nd, 2001 at Chicago Lake Shore Hospital."

"You have not seen January 21st, 01 at Northwestern that indicates she had been suffering from vomiting and diarrhea and that they diagnosed her as an alcoholic who needed treatment?"

"I have not seen these."

"What is Ativan?"

"Ativan is an anti-anxiety agent. It helps relax people if they have, for example, panic attacks."

"Did you know, Ma'am, she was diagnosed in February of 2001 by Northwestern as having, what you referred to, as a fatty liver?"

"I did not know that. I didn't look at those records. I didn't have those."

"So the first records you looked at were from March 2nd, 2001."

"Yes."

"And those records reflect that in March of 01 she was admitted to Chicago Lake Shore Hospital up at 4840 North Marine Drive, is that correct?"

"Correct."

"And what was her history of illness at the time she was checked in to Lake Shore Hospital?"

"Her history was alcohol dependence by Benzodiazepine dependence and panic attacks without acrophobia. Also, in her diagnosis, job loss."

"And did it indicate how much she was drinking at that time?"

"When I reviewed the records, it did indicate when the last drink was, which was the night prior to admission. Then they go forth asking her and she reports drinking on a daily basis."

"Does she report how much she drinks?"

"Yes, she does."

"And how much was she reportedly drinking back in March of 01?"

"According to the records from the Chicago Lake Shore Hospital, it states six to seven glasses of wine on a daily basis."

"Now is that consistent with the resident of the Lake Shore reports?"

"Yes, it is."

"Did it also indicate she needed to be placed in detox?"

"Yes, it did."

"Now, in your opinion, Ma'am, does six glasses of wine make you eligible for a detox program or would it be more alcohol consumption than that?"

"I believe it would."

"In March of 01, what was the recommendation of Chicago Lake Shore Hospital to their patient, Julie Grace?"

"They put her on new medication and they did want her to return to Lake Shore Hospital for further evaluation and treatment."

"Do you know how long it was she was in a detox unit at Lake Shore Hospital?"

"I believe the date of discharge for her was March 8th. She was in there about six days."

"In a detox unit, correct?"

"Yes."

"And detox means that your body has to be detoxed from the effects and dependence of alcohol, is that correct?"

"Correct."

"Did you review a March 12th, 2001, report from Lake Shore Hospital?"

"I do have the laboratory. I have up until March 8th. Yes."

"You don't have anything from March 12th, 01?"

"No, I don't."

"Are you aware of the fact that, once again, she was diagnosed as being alcohol dependent?"

"I did not review those records so I would not know."

"Have you seen in your records, that the patient, Julie Grace, had a history of using chemicals to escape feelings?"

"Yes."

"Did you read in those records that she was depressed and anxious?"

"Yes."

"Did you read in those reports that she drank up to two fifths in a 48-hour period?"

"Yes, Sir, I remember reading that."

"Did you look and see an October 11th, 01 report from Chicago Lake Shore Hospital?"

"I do not have that."

"Did you read reports that indicated that in October of 01 Julie Grace was still drinking?"

"I don't have those records."

"Did you review reports of March 10th, 2002, some fourteen months prior to this autopsy, from Northwestern Hospital where Julie Grace was taken in because she was having DTs?"

"That, I do not have a record of. The next medical record that I do have a record of is October 13th, 2002."

"So you did not see any records from March of 02 from Northwestern Hospital."

"Correct."

"Have you seen any reports that indicate that she was diagnosed as being in a mutually abusive relationship with a boyfriend?"

"Yes."

"Do you remember on what report you saw the admission by her or the diagnosis that she was in a mutually abusive relationship?"

"I went back to March 2nd, 2001 and it states there the history of domestic violence."

"Back in March of what year?"

"March 2001 at Chicago Lake Shore Hospital," answered Dr. Arangelovich.

"That was prior to meeting George Thompson, was it not?" asked Mr. Breen.

"I don't know when she met George Thompson."

"Did you see a July 10th, 02 report from Northwestern Memorial Hospital where she was admitted in the emergency room for alcohol abuse?"

"That report I do not have."

"And did you see a report where it indicated that she was violent and aggressive and hit one of the doctors in the emergency room?"

"I don't have that report."

"Did you see, Ma'am, a Northwestern Memorial Hospital report indicating that on September 3rd, 02 she was taken into the emergency room for alcohol detoxification?"

"I do not have that report. The report that I have begins on October 13th, 2002."

"Well, this would be September 3rd, 2002."

"Yes. I don't have that."

"Did you see a report from Northwestern Hospital on October 21st, 2002 that indicates she was admitted, she, being Julie, was admitted to the emergency room at Northwestern Hospital?"

"I don't have that admit, no."

"Where she had cut herself with a knife, you haven't seen that?"

"No, I haven't."

"Did you see a Northwestern report where on December 4th, 2002, she was admitted to the emergency room at Northwestern again for detoxification from alcohol?"

"I do not have that report."

"Do you have a report that indicates she drank a fifth of vodka on or about December 4th, 02?"

"I don't have that."

"Do you have a report or did you review a report, Ma'am, from December 19th, 2002 where Julie Grace was admitted to an emergency room for detoxification and alcohol abuse?"

"I don't have that."

"Have you seen or reviewed a December 21st, 2002, some three days later, an emergency room report from Northwestern Hospital where Julie Grace was admitted again for detoxification of alcohol?"

"I do have from Northwestern Memorial Hospital with the admittance day of December 21st, 2002. I have her laboratory values."

"Do you have the 12-21-02 report that indicates she was admitted for detoxification?"

"No."

"Does it indicate why she was at Northwestern on December 21st?"

"No, it doesn't."

"But you have lab reports from December 21st, correct?"

"Yes, I do."

"Did you review reports from December 22nd, 02 where she was again at Northwestern Hospital for detoxification?"

"I just have the laboratory values from that admittance."

"Do you have a report from Northwestern Hospital where again and again, but also on December 22nd, 02, she is advised by medical people not to drink alcohol?"

"I do not have that."

"How is detoxification linked to alcohol?"

"What happens is once you start drinking alcohol, your body is trying to flush it out. You are losing a lot of fluids with that alcohol as it goes to your urine and is excreted. So your body's water content is being decreased. The alcohol is essentially a dehydrator."

"What are the symptoms of dehydration?"

"Generally, you have an increased thirst. You can tremble due to dehydration. You can also have altered thinking, as well."

"Wouldn't the simple solution then be just to drink water?"

"What happens is sometimes you get so far along that you are not thinking clearly enough that that's what you should do."

"So you are indicating that if a person were dehydrated as a result of alcohol use, that that person's thinking could be so altered that they wouldn't even think of drinking water?"

"It could be, yes."

"Did you see a report of October 10th, 2002, where Julie Grace was again admitted to Northwestern Hospital for alcohol withdrawal symptoms?"

"I just have the laboratory values of that admittance."

"Well, if you received the lab reports, is there some reason you didn't receive the narrative reports, the reason for the admission, the reason for the lab reports?"

"That I can't tell you. I don't know."

Judge Gaughan interrupted, "Just a point of clarification. Did you seek out these reports or were these reports, to your knowledge, used by Dr. An?"

"These reports, I believe Dr. An examined," replied the witness.

By this time I'm really getting uneasy about the doctor's testimony. I keep wondering again and again why Mr. Groth called Dr. Arangelovich to testify and not Dr. An. After all, Dr. An was the medical examiner on Julie's case and not Dr. Arangelovich. In my eyes, Mr. Breen was doing an excellent job of discrediting Dr. Arangelovich's testimony, and that was certainly not helping our case.

Mr. Breen continued, "Did you see an April 7th, 2003 report from Northwestern Memorial Hospital?"

"Yes, I did."

"What was the diagnosis on April 7th, 03, some forty days or so before the autopsy?"

"The diagnosis was pyelonephritis."

"And what is pyelonephritis?"

"That is an infection of the kidneys."

"What type of drugs was she placed on or should have been taking at that time?"

"She was placed on antibiotics. I believe the first one they gave her was Leviquin."

"Did they give a second type of antibiotics to her?"

"Yes, they did."

"What was that?"

"I believe they switched it to Bactrim."

"When did they do that, Doctor, if you know?"

"I believe on the morning of April 9th, which is two days after admitted she was having some hallucinations and they thought perhaps that could be from the antibiotic."

"So they switched it. She was having a reaction to that antibiotic."

"Yes."

"What else did they place her on?"

"She was placed on Haldol, as well."

"What is that?"

"That's mainly an anti-psychotic."

"Okay, what else?"

"They also put her on Ativan which is again, an anti-anxiety pill. They put her, I believe, on Zyprexa, which is an anti-psychotic agent."

"Now is it recommended that one drink while on those medications?"

"No, it is not."

"In fact, Northwestern recommended that she avoid any alcohol, correct?"

"Correct."

"And how does the alcohol interact if you know?" asked Mr. Breen. "I may be getting far afield here and I don't want to put you on the spot, but if you know, how does alcohol interact with antibiotics?"

Dr. Arangelovich replied, "What happens when the antibiotic is given to a person there are enzymes in the liver that actually degrade that antibiotic so that you excrete it. Alcohol uses these same enzymes that the antibiotic uses. So the alcohol can either increase the amount of antibiotic in the body or decrease the amount. Sometimes alcohol can increase those enzymes. They are very hyperactive and they are degrading the antibiotic too quickly or it can slow down those enzymes and the antibiotic level will rise."

"So in any event, whether it moves it faster or moves it slower, the antibiotic is not being given a chance, for lack of a better expression, to fight the infection."

"It is making it more difficult."

"Now she had a urinary tract infection, correct?"

"Yes."

"That a bacterial or viral based urinary tract infection?"

"Bacterial."

"Bacterial. Bronchopneumonia is a bacterial infection, is it not?"

"Generally, it can be viral. More likely it is bacterial."

"If someone were on antibiotics, that should kill the bacteria, kill the infection and make them better, correct?"

"It depends if that antibiotic will kill that certain organism that's been isolated. Some antibiotics won't work."

"Well as it relates to bronchopneumonia, you have a much higher risk of getting bronchopneumonia if you don't pay attention to an infection somewhere else in your body, isn't that right?"

"Generally you can get increased risk if there is another infection. It is kind of like if you have a boat. There's a hole in a boat and you put another one in there, your chances of sinking are going to increase. So if you already have an infection in your body, it is going to increase the risk that you can get another one."

"What Julie Grace died of was a bacterial infection in the form of bronchopneumonia, is that correct?"

"It was a bronchopneumonia. I don't have bacterial cultures to let me know if it was bacterial or viral."

"Isn't it a fact that the medical position is that a susceptible group in society to contracting bronchopneumonia are the elderly and children?"

"Yes."

"But among others, the high risk area is vagrants and alcoholics, correct?"

"Yes."

"Why are alcoholics more susceptible to bronchopneumonia than people who did not drink or drink very lightly?"

"Generally an alcoholic, sometimes they can aspirate their gastric contents if they drink too much and throw up. Some of that gastric content can go into the trachea and start an infection. That's one way of how it happens."

"Would you please tell the court and all of us what the relationship is between bruising, if any, and alcohol abuse?"

"In alcohol abuse, the liver begins to get damaged. The liver doesn't make clotting factors. Without the clotting factors you can bruise easily. You know, minor trauma can bruise the body."

"So an alcoholic would be more susceptible to at least showing signs of trauma than someone else might be."

"Yes."

"All right, and an alcoholic's body or organs would be less able to defend against trauma than someone who is not an alcoholic."

"Yes."

"They would hemorrhage faster."

"Yes."

"A bump in the night could cause a big bruise."

"It could."

"And an alcoholic, and I certainly mean no disrespect to those who suffer from the disease, but an alcoholic just by the nature of the intake of alcohol, their mind is altered when they are under the influence of alcohol, are they not?"

"What happens with a chronic alcoholic, they can handle higher levels of alcohol versus somebody who is naïve to alcohol and drinks the same amount."

"Yes, but once they are intoxicated as a result of their alcohol intake, their thinking and judgment is altered, is it not?"

"Yes."

"And their balance and ability to walk around and do things is, in fact, impaired, is it not?"

"It could be."

"And you certainly have seen and know of alcoholics who fall, don't you?"

"I have seen cases, yes."

"If a doctor were to tell you to stay on the antibiotics and not drink alcohol, is it an alteration of your mind that causes you to drink the alcohol."

"It most likely is part of the dependency issue."

"Ma'am, just as an example if I may, I have a face sheet, kind of a narrative form regarding an admission to the emergency room on January 21st, 01. This is for Julie Grace indicating vomiting and diarrhea. Is that what it says?"

"Yes."

"And then, you are probably much better at reading all of this; what is the diagnosis on this report?"

"Here they are giving the history as well as her medications. They don't have a diagnosis on this page."

"Okay. Anything on the next page?"

"This page they have a diagnosis, vomiting, dehydration."

"Now attached to this, I believe, are some additional reports. Would you just kind of look through those, if you will, and tell me what we're able to determine from those reports and I'll clear up my question."

"We can determine her history of illness, what medications she was on at that time, the examination, what the doctor found as well as her vital signs. We have a consent form that she signed."

"What is her history of illness as of January 21st, 01 on that Northwestern report?"

"She has a three-day history of nausea, vomiting, I believe diarrhea with fever and chills."

"Okay. Now there are lab reports attached to that, correct?"

"Let me see. Yes, there are."

"Are those lab reports that are attached to Defendant's Exhibit 1? Did you review those lab reports or did Dr. An?"

"These were not included in the file."

"I'm going to do maybe one more here, Doctor. I'm going to show you what purports to be a 2-7-01 Northwestern Memorial report. I'll ask you to take a look at this, if you will."

"Yes."

"Ma'am, does that purport to be a Northwestern report of Julie Grace?"

"Yes."

"Date of entry please, to the emergency room."

"I believe date admitted, February 7th, 2001."

"What does it tell us about her illness and the diagnosis?"

"They give a diagnosis of vomiting."

"Okay. Does it say what may have caused this or caused her illness?"

"Not on the first page. They don't say what is causing this."

"Does it mention her alcohol abuse?"

"Yes, under her history."

"And what does it say about her history of alcohol abuse?"

"It says just positive which means she does have alcohol, chronic."

"Attached to that report, that February 7th report, are there lab results?"

"Yes, there are."

"Are those lab results contained in the file that you reviewed or Dr. An reviewed?"

"No."

"When you say your office issues subpoenas for medical records and believe me, Ma'am, I know how the system works and I'm not being critical of you, can you tell us why it is you may not have received those reports per the subpoena?"

"I cannot tell you."

The judge asked Dr. Arangelovich, "Just a point of clarification. If the medical examiner's office issues subpoenas, are they kept in the regular course of business?"

"Generally they are."

"Thank you," replied the judge.

Mr. Breen turned back to the witness and said, "I'm going to do one last one, Ma'am. I'll mark this Defendant's Exhibit number 3 for identification. Ma'am, I'm going to show you what purports"

"Mr. Breen," interrupted Judge Gaughan, "I know you mean no disrespect. You need to call her Doctor, okay?"

"I apologize," said Mr. Breen. "I have a great deal of respect for her."

"I know that," replied the judge.

"Doctor, I apologize. I've been called a lot worse than even Ma'am," said Mr. Breen. He continued by asking, "Doctor, I'm going to show you what purports to be a March 10th, 2002 report from Northwestern Hospital, okay?"

"Okay."

"Would you take a look at that, Ma'am, and does that indicate that she was taken in at Northwestern because of some kind of alcohol withdrawals syndrome?"

"It does state under diagnosis, I'm having withdrawals syndrome."

"Would you take a look at that report please, and the pages that are attached to it?"

"Okay."

"What is the diagnosis or profile of her illness as of that March? First of all, let me ask you this. Was that record included in the ones you reviewed?"

"No, it was not."

"Would you tell us what that report indicates about Julie Grace?"

"Regarding?"

"Her illness."

"Her illness. Under the management plan it states alcohol abuse withdrawal. It gives a history of alcohol abuse."

"Does it mention any medications given to her?"

"Her history of meds, I believe it says Trazodone."

"What is that?"

"That is a sleeping aid as well as an anti-depressant."

"Okay."

"They do state the medicines given in the emergency room."

"What are those?"

"Ativan, multivitamin, thiamine and folic acid."

"I think I know what folic acid is. For the record, what is that one before that?"

"Ativan is an anti-anxiety agent. Multivitamins, one a day. Thiamine is part of the vitamin B complex, which is just another vitamin, as well."

"Was she also placed inpatient for the purposes of detoxification?"

"It says previous inpatient, something detoxification efforts."

"Does it say whether or not it was successful or not?"

"It does not state that."

"Okay. It mentions her previous mental illness, does it not, and she has two previous DUIs, correct?"

"Two previous DUIs."

"Does it describe her relationship with her boyfriend?"

"Yes, it does."

"How does it describe it?"

"It says, in a mutually abusive relationship with boyfriend while drinking."

"I'm sorry, Ma'am. Does it indicate that she had been drinking two fifths of vodka over the past three days?"

"Yes."

"Are the injuries you noted in reviewing the file of Julie Grace consistent with a mutually abusive relationship?"

"No."

"Did you look at any photographs of George Thompson?"

"No, I did not."

"So, you do not know what injuries George Thompson may have sustained on May 17th, 2003, correct?"

"Correct."

"And you don't know if those injuries were the result of some kind of mutual combat."

"That I don't know."

"I have nothing further," said Mr. Breen. "Thank you, Doctor."

"Redirect?" asked Judge Gaughan.

"Mr. Groth answered, "Just a couple questions, Judge."

"Mr. Groth asked the witness, "Doctor, based on the examination of Julie Grace's liver, it was apparent she had alcohol problems, is that correct?"

"Yes."

"What is an alcoholic?"

"An alcoholic is somebody who has a desire to drink that supersedes any other desires. They generally need an eye-opener in the morning. They drink multiple glasses of wine or beer, hard liquor per day. Generally, even though friends tell them they have a problem, they still don't seek treatment."

"Okay. Is there a relationship or correlation between alcohol abuse and domestic abuse?"

"Yes, there is."

"Counsel asked you about your review of the injuries of Julie Grace regarding whether or not they are consistent with mutual combat."

"Yes."

"You said they were not."

"They were not."

"What are they consistent with?"

"They are consistent with blunt trauma, which is quite severe. She has quite large bruises and they are on multiple areas of the body as well as internally. The subdural hematoma is consistent with blunt trauma, which is severe enough to cause that hemorrhage."

"You talked about that before on direct, about the blunt trauma. How much force is required to inflict that kind of blunt trauma?"

Mr. Breen interrupted, "Objection, Judge, as to which alleged blunt trauma."

"Sustained and particularize your question," responded Judge Gaughan.

Mr. Groth rephrased his question. "How much force would be needed to inflict the blunt trauma that was found in Julie Grace's brain area?"

"Now with her and her fatty liver which would contribute, it would require a lot of force. Generally she's at high risk to bleed though due to her fatty liver. That's why it is a contributing factor. But regarding what we see on the face as well as the hemorrhages we see outside of the brain, inside of the brain, it was an extensive amount of trauma."

"Okay. Now Counsel asked you about, I think, seven or eight different times where Julie went to the hospital. Is that correct?"

"Yes."

"Based on your experience as a doctor, somebody who has gone to the hospital seven or eight times for alcohol withdrawal certainly knows how to get there, right?"

"Yes."

"And they know when their body is telling them to get yourself to the hospital?"

"Yes."

Mr. Groth showed the witness several photos of George Thompson's face and hands and asked Dr. Arangelovich if she saw any type of injuries.

"It appears to be just a few scratches," the witness replied.

"Which one?"

"For example, if you look at the face there are a few scratches on the left nostril, the right side of the cheek, also on the chin."

"The one on the chin, is that a pimple or a scratch?"

Mr. Breen interrupted, "Objection to leading the doctor."

"Sustained. Rephrase," directed the judge.

Dr. Arangelovich continued, "Kind of hard to tell right now. It is a reddened area. I'll go with that but we definitely have a few scratches on the face, maybe a small red area underneath the left lower eyelid."

"Three, possibly four injuries." said Mr. Groth.

"Yes."

"How about the hands, what do they show?"

"The hands, we have what appears to be blood, blood on the fingernails, maybe one or two scratches."

"Thank you. In comparison to the injuries found on Julie Grace, which are worse?"

"Julie Grace."

"You were aware, Doctor, when you reviewed the autopsy and the protocol and the photos of Julie Grace having higher elevated liver levels, right?"

"Yes, I was."

"From the lab reports?"

"Yes."

"That would be consistent with somebody going to seek the alcohol detoxification process on the different occasions that Mr. Breen asked about in his cross-examination, is that correct?"

"Yes."

"Thank you," said Mr. Groth.

Mr. Breen said, "Just a few, if I may. Your definition of an alcoholic is someone who has a desire to drink. Would you kind of complete that? I didn't hear the last part."

"And that desire supersedes all other activities of their life."

"Including their health, isn't that correct?"

"Generally, yes."

"And an alcoholic with the experience that Julie Grace has, would not necessarily be looking forward to a detoxification unit, would such an alcoholic?"

"The only problem is she kept going for them."

"Well how many times should she have gone for them and didn't go? You have no idea."

"I have no idea."

"And you talked about the trauma that caused, at least, the head hemorrhaging. I think you said it had to be significant trauma."

"It was significant."

"Well a person of Julie's size, a hundred forty-seven pounds falling and hitting her head on the corner of a piece of furniture, that would cause significant trauma, wouldn't it?"

"It would cause some trauma, yes."

"Well some or significant depending on how badly she fell."

"It depends what type of furniture it is whether the furniture has a very sharp, jagged edge versus a blunt edge."

Mr. Breen ended his questioning and Judge Gaughan dismissed the witness.

"State, call your next witness," instructed the judge.

The State called Peter Goldsmith. Although I don't remember much about Mr. Goldsmith, I recall he was a younger man, and I had heard Julie speak of him before.

Mr. Goldsmith was sworn in and Mr. Groth began his direct examination of the witness.

"I'd like to draw your attention, if I could, back to March 7th, 2003 at approximately 9:00 in the evening. Did you live in the Old Town area then?"

"I did."

"What was your address?"

"1560 North Sandburg. Also, 1560 Clark."

"What floor did you live on?"

"Twenty-eighth floor."

"From your apartment, could you see the apartment of the 20th floor at 1540 North LaSalle?"

"Yes."

"About 9:00 PM on March 7th, 2003, did you see anything that drew your attention?"

"I saw a man and a woman, a man with his arm around the woman like this, a head lock, and striking her."

"Okay, and describe for the court what you observed as far as the force involved."

"Enough to see from across the way. It was punching in the face. It was holding the arm and swinging it; swinging it across the room; banging into the furniture. While she was on the floor he did a running kick a couple of times into her and also had a pillow over her face for a long duration of time, what looked to be, when she was lying on like a sofa. This went on for several minutes."

"When you say several minutes, how many minutes?"

"Probably anywhere from fifteen to twenty minutes."

"Okay. At any time did you contact anybody to assist this young lady?"

"A few minutes in, when we realized the severity of it, we called the police."

"When you say we, was somebody else with you?"

"Yes, it was a friend of mine, Tom Bretberg."

"Okay. Now you said you called the police and the beating lasted about fifteen to twenty minutes. Did you see the police arrive in that apartment?"

"I did."

"Okay. And how many people were occupying that apartment?"

"Two."

"You said a man and a woman."

"Yes."

"Okay. Now from 1560 North Sandburg looking on over on 1540 North LaSalle, did you see faces?"

"No."

"Could you see the police take anybody into custody?"

"The man."

"You saw them take the man."

"Yes."

"When you said that the person took a running kick into the woman, the man took a running kick, could you see where the man kicked her?"

"Looked to be like the torso."

"Did you talk to the police afterwards?"

"No."

"Were you ever contacted by anybody from the State's Attorney's Office regarding this case at the misdemeanor level?"

"Yes."

"Thank you."

"Anything further?" asked the judge.

"Nothing further," answered Mr. Groth.

"Just a couple questions, if I may," said Mr. Breen.

"Sure," replied the judge.

Mr. Breen asked, "Do I have it correct, you are across the street?"

"Yes."

"About how many feet would you say that is?"

"Probably a hundred feet."

"About a hundred feet and it is March and it is about what time of day?"

"Night time."

"Okay. So, but there's probably light on in the apartment you were looking at."

"Yes."

"And there were no drapes or anything, were there?"

"Everything was pulled aside."

"You never see any drapes in those windows, do you?"

Mr. Groth interrupted, "Objection to the form of the question, Judge."

Mr. Breen continued, "Well, you looked in that apartment before March of 03 and after March of 03, have you not?"

"Probably."

"And did you see Julie Grace walking around the apartment?"

"No. I actually have a friend who lives a couple down from Julie and that's why I look over, usually."

"Well do you see her in her apartment or did you see her in the apartment?"

"Not that I noticed before."

"This was the only time you ever saw anybody in that apartment on March 7th?"

"The only time I noticed."

"You were not able to hear what was going on."

"No."

"You don't know what precipitated it."

"No."

"You did not. You are only talking about seeing a man with a headlock and hitting a woman, is that correct?"

"Yes."

"And then I think you said he kicked her and you called the police."

"Yes."

"I have nothing further," stated Mr. Breen.

Mr. Groth began his redirect examination of the witness by asking, "Mr. Goldsmith, the twenty minutes you saw this incident occur, who was inflicting injuries?"

"The male."

"What was the female doing?"

"Really nothing, looked like a rag doll."

"For the whole twenty minutes."

"She would sit. She'd be on the ground motionless for a few minutes. He would walk away then come back and start again."

"So from what you were seeing, the female was no threat to the male and he would just come back and start abusing her again."

"Absolutely."

"Objection, Judge," interjected Mr. Breen. I don't think we can lay a proper foundation."

"Overruled," replied Judge Gaughan. "I'll allow you wide latitude on re-cross."

"I have nothing further," said Mr. Groth.

"I have nothing," said Mr. Breen.

"Thank you," said the judge and the witness stepped down.

The judge asked both attorneys to approach the bench. After a brief discussion, Judge Gaughan said, "Okay, thank you. This trial is going to be commenced and continued until tomorrow. We're going to begin at 11:00 AM. Thank you."

Glenn and I left the courtroom and went back to our hotel. Later that evening we had dinner with some of Julie's friends. All of us strongly agreed that nothing but the maximum sentence of first-degree murder should be given to George Thompson but after hearing the day's testimony, we were concerned it may not happen. The judge had been very critical, intolerant, and argumentative with Mr. Groth while at the same time, appeared cordial and receptive of whatever Mr. Breen had to say.

CHAPTER 11
DAY TWO OF GEORGE'S TRIAL

G lenn and I walked into the courtroom as day two of the trial began. We were both very anxious to hear the rest of the testimonies of the witnesses. However, the trial was already starting to wear me down. For many months prior to the trial, I had great difficulty sleeping and as a result, was mentally, physically and emotionally exhausted by day one. Because of this, much of the testimony in the remaining days of the trial and details about the witnesses are all a big blur to me. However, according to the court transcripts, the following occurred on day two.

"Be it remembered that on the 12th day of May, 2006, this cause came on for hearing before the Honorable Vincent M. Gaughan, Judge of said Court, upon the indictment herein, the defendant having entered a plea of not guilty."

The judge and attorneys exchanged greetings and then Ms. Michele Popielewski (instead of Mr. Groth), assistant state's attorneys on behalf of the people, called her first witness. Christopher Pinzine was sworn in and the direct examination began.

Ms. Popielewski asked the witness to state his name and spell it, give his star number, and current unit of assignment, in which Mr. Pinzine complied.

Ms. Popielewski was an attractive middle-aged woman who came across as being very knowledgeable and an experienced attorney, much more knowledgeable than Mr. Groth appeared. She stood confident and composed as she began questioning the witness.

"Officer, how long have you been a Chicago Police Department officer?"

"Seven years."

"I want to draw your attention back to the 7th of March of 2003. Were you working and on duty at that time?"

"Yes, Ma'am."

"And where were you assigned at that time?"

"In the area of 15 and15 hundred LaSalle."

"Were you working in the 18th District?"

"Yes, Ma'am."

"And specifically, at approximately 9:00 PM did you receive a call to go anywhere specific?"

"Yes, Ma'am."

"And is that to 1540 North LaSalle?"

"Yes, Ma'am, that was."

"In Chicago?"

"Yes."

"Were you assigned to go to any specific apartment?"

"Yes."

"And was that 2004?"

"Yes."

"Why was it that you were called to that location on that date and time?"

"It was a call of domestic disturbance."

"Did you arrive alone or with a partner?"

"With a partner."

"Who was your partner that day?"

"Officer Mueller."

"Is his star 7919?"

"Yes."

"Once you arrived at that location and that apartment did you hear or notice anything before entering?"

"Yes, Ma'am."

"What did you notice?"

"We, I heard a female voice coming from the apartment yelling help."

"Once you heard that, what did you do?"

"We knocked on the door and"

"Did you gain access to that apartment?"

"Yes, Ma'am."

"And how was it that you gained access to the apartment?"

"The victim opened the door."

"Do you know the name of the person who opened the door for you?"

"It was Julie."

"When you arrived and you saw Julie at the door, can you describe the physical condition at that time?"

"Yes. She had a bruise. Her face was red with like contusions and scratches. She had a bloody lip. She had contusions and scratches on her neck."

"Okay. Were you allowed access to that apartment?"

"Yes, Ma'am."

"Once you entered, did you see anyone else inside the apartment at that time?"

"Yes, Ma'am."

"Do you see that person here in court today?"

"Yes, Ma'am."

"Can you point to that person and describe something he or she is wearing right now?"

"The individual to my right wearing the khaki outfit."

"Ask the record to reflect the in-court identification of Mr. Thompson, Your Honor," requested Ms. Popielewski.

"The record will so reflect," replied the judge.

"Where was the defendant in the apartment when you arrived?" Ms. Popielewski asked Officer Pinzine.

"The bedroom."

"Once you went inside the apartment, did you speak with Julie Grace at that time?"

"Yes, Ma'am."

"And what, if anything, did she tell you at that time?"

"Objection, hearsay," interrupted Mr. Pugh, attorney for the defendant.

"Your response?" asked the judge.

Ms. Popielewski replied, "My response, Your Honor, would be that obviously, at that point, Miss Grace is not available, is an unavailable witness to be able to testify as to what occurred. It would be an excited utterance to the police and that, at this point, it is presumed by the State that Miss Grace is not available due"

Judge Gaughan interrupted, "I'm sorry. Hearsay doesn't pertain to whether there is availability of the witness or not. As far as the excited utterance, lay your foundation for that."

Ms. Popielewski replied, "I will, Your Honor," and continued her questioning of the witness.

"Officer, did you speak with Miss Grace on the scene?"

"Yes, Ma'am."

"And at that point you were called in regards to a domestic disturbance."

"Yes, Ma'am."

"Did you have the opportunity to view her?"

"Yes."

"You're repeating what is in evidence, move forward," instructed the Judge.

"I understand," replied Ms. Popielewski.

"Who else was present at the time?" asked Ms. Popielewski.

"My partner."

"And at that point, did you speak with her?"

"Yes."

"What, if anything, did she say to you?"

"Objection, hearsay Judge," responded Mr. Pugh. I don't believe its sufficient foundation for an excited utterance."

"Sustained as to sufficient foundation," stated the Judge.

Ms. Popielewski continued her questioning. "Can you tell me, Officer, what was Miss Grace's demeanor at the time you saw her?"

"She was crying."

"Did you note any physical upset in Miss Grace at that time?"

"Yes, she was crying. She kept saying help, help me and I observed it, all the injuries on her face and her neck."

"And Officer, this was after you had heard a female voice screaming help, help as you arrived at the apartment, correct?"

"Yes, also from outside before we gained entry."

"Were there any other females in the apartment when you gained access?"

"No, Ma'am."

"You did speak with Julie Grace on the scene."

"Yes, Ma'am."

"What, if anything, did she describe to you at that time?"

"She had stated that the defendant and herself were involved in a verbal altercation and that he had started to punch her in the face and causing some of the bruising and scratches on her face."

"Did she describe anything further to you?"

"Yes. She also described that she was kicked in the face and the lip causing the bloody lip and that a necklace chain was ripped off of her neck and thrown off the balcony."

"Did she describe to you who committed these acts against her?"

"Yes."

"Who did she say committed these acts against her?"

"Her boyfriend."

"Did Miss Julie Grace identify the person who did this to her there on the scene?"

"Yes."

"And who did she identify? Do you see that person here in court?"

"Yes, Ma'am."

"The same person you already identified?"

"Yes, Ma'am."

"Did she describe any further incidents between she and Mr. Thompson at that time?"

"Yes, that she had tried to go to the door and at which point, that the defendant had grabbed her around the neck and pulled her away from the door, thrown her on a couch and put a pillow over her face which she said she was suffocated and she couldn't breathe."

"Did she describe to you what, if anything, the defendant, Mr. Thompson said to her as she was being stricken by him?"

"The statement was that he kept saying that I'm going to kill you."

"Did the victim state anything further in regards to what else occurred inside that apartment on that date?"

"That a bucket of water was also thrown on her by the defendant."

"Did she state whether or not she was able to contact police?"

"She did and that he kept trying to pull the phones out of the wall."

"Did she say who was pulling the phones out of the wall?"

"Yes, Ma'am, the defendant."

"Officer, did you have the opportunity to observe the interior of the apartment; the condition of the apartment?"

"Yes, Ma'am."

"What was the condition as you saw it on that date?"

"The apartment was in disarray. Furniture was turned over. I observed a bloody pillow on the couch. Clumps of hair that were also on the couch, which was similar in color and texture, I would say, to the victim's own hair."

"Okay. To your knowledge, Officer, was an evidence technician called to the scene?"

"Yes, Ma'am."

"Officer, where did you take defendant after you took him into custody?"

"The defendant was taken to the 18th District for processing."

"And once you arrived at the 18th District, did you advise the defendant of anything at that time?"

"Yes, Ma'am."

"What did you advise him of?"

"I read him his Miranda warnings from my FOP book."

"Officer, do you have an FOP book with you here today?"

"Yes, Ma'am."

"Can you take that out, please? Officer, is there a rights section in that FOP book you have in your hand?"

"Yes."

"Is it substantially the same as the rights section in the 2003 edition you had on that day?"

"Yes, Ma'am."

"Officer, if you could for us, inform the court how it was that you advised him of his Miranda warnings."

"Mr. Thompson, before we ask you any questions, it is our duty to advise you of your rights. You have the right to remain silent. Anything you say can and may be used against you in a court or other proceedings. Do you understand that you have the right to talk to a lawyer before we ask you any questions and to have him with you during questioning? If you cannot afford or otherwise obtain a lawyer and you want one, a lawyer will be appointed for you and we'll not ask you any questions until he or she has been appointed. If you decide to answer now with or without a lawyer, you still have the right to stop questioning at any time or to stop the questioning for the purpose of consulting a lawyer. You may waive the right to advice of counsel and your right to remain silent, and you may answer questions or make a statement without consulting a lawyer if you so desire. Do you understand each of these rights? The defendant stated yes. Do you wish to answer any questions at this time?"

"What, if anything, did the defendant say to that question?"

"Just nodded his head. He didn't give a response. Nothing."

"Did he continue speaking at that time?"

"Yes. We didn't ask him any questions and he just volunteered the information himself."

"What, if anything, did he say to you?"

"Stating that she, that the victim had pissed him off and that he had to kick her ass to keep her in line."

"Officer, when you took the defendant, George Thompson, into custody, did you notice any injuries on Mr. Thompson at that time?"

"Yes, Ma'am."

"What did you notice?"

"It was a scratch on the bridge of his nose, on the tip of his nose and under, I believe, under his right eye another scratch."

Ms. Popielewski approached the witness and showed him several photos of Julie and her apartment and asked, "Officer, I'm showing you some photographs. Do you recognize these items that I'm handing you?"

"Yes, Ma'am."

"Did you have the opportunity to see these photographs before testifying today?"

"Yes."

"Okay. I'm asking you in regard to People's Exhibit number 45 you have before you, can you tell us what that is?"

"It's a picture of the victim with a bloody lip and the other contusion or scratches on her look to be under her right eye, and also scratches and contusions on her neck."

"Okay. And if you could move to number 46 then, what, if anything, does that photograph depict?"

"Additional welts and scratches on her left side of her neck."

"And that photograph is a photograph of her upper torso."

"Yes."

"Number 47, can you describe, generally, what you see in the photograph and if there are any injuries depicted?"

"Another photo of the victim with injuries to her neck, to her lip, and the apartment in disarray."

"Excuse me," interrupted the judge. "Are you going to bring the evidence technician in?"

Mr. Groth replied, "Do we have the evidence technician? No, Judge."

"All right," said Judge Gaughan. "Go ahead, continue."

"Ms. Popielewski continued, "Officer, let me ask you this. Of those photographs that you just identified of Miss Grace, do they truly and accurately depict the condition of the victim as you saw her when you arrived at the apartment on that day?"

"Yes, Ma'am."

"Thank you. I'm going to show you People's Exhibit number 48. Do you recognize what is in that photograph?"

"Yes, Ma'am."

"What do you recognize that photograph to be of?"

"A picture of the apartment with the overturned ottoman and pillows on the floor."

"And next, number 49, Officer, what is that?"

"The picture of the clump of hair, which matched or which was similar to the hair of the victim."

"And where is that hair in that photograph, what is it on?"

"It's on the couch."

"And the next photograph, do you recognize what is depicted there, sir?"

"Yes, Ma'am."

"What do you recognize that to be?"

"Appears to be blood on the pillow."

"Okay, 51, what do you recognize that to be?"

"The cord of the phone ripped out of the wall and additional areas of the apartment that were in disarray."

"Now those photographs in regard to the interior of the apartment; do those photographs all truly and accurately depict the apartment as it looked when you arrived on the 7th of March?"

"Yes, Ma'am."

Ms. Popielewski showed the witness two photos (Exhibit numbers 52 & 53) of George and asked, "Do you recognize who is depicted in each one of those photos?"

"Yes, Ma'am."

"Who is that?"

"The defendant."

"George Thompson."

"Yes, Ma'am."

"Specifically on 52, can you describe what portion of the defendant's body is shown in that photograph?"

"His upper torso from his waist up."

"And in regards to 53, what portion of his body is shown in that photograph? And specifically, you noted in your earlier examination that you saw injuries to his face. Are those depicted in each one of those photographs?"

"Yes."

"Do these photographs of Mr. George Thompson, 52 and 53, truly and accurately depict the way he looked at the time you had taken him into custody?"

"Yes, Ma'am."

"I have nothing further. Thank you, Judge," said Ms. Popielewski.

Mr. Pugh began his cross-examination by asking, "Officer, what time was it you arrived at the apartment in Sandburg Village that you just testified to?"

"About 9:20 in the evening."

"Sometime after your arrival, you took George Thompson into custody, correct?"

"Yes, Sir."

"And you took him to the 18th District."

"Yes."

"When you were at the 18th District, did you have an opportunity to prepare some written reports in relation to these events?"

"Yes."

"And have you reviewed those before testifying today?"

"Yes."

"And I'm going to ask you, I'm going to mark this as Defendant's Exhibit number 4 for identification purposes. Officer, let me show you what has been marked as Defendant's Exhibit number 4, which purports to be 4 pages of a general offense case report in this case, and ask you to take a look at that and tell Judge Gaughan if that's a complete set of reports that you drafted in this case."

"Yes, Sir."

"Any other reports that you prepared, Officer, regarding this incident?"

"This is the case report. There was also an arrest report and complaints that were prepared."

"Complaints?"

"Complaints that were prepared."

"Officer, you mentioned signed complaints in this case. Did Julie Grace sign a complaint?"

"No."

"Who signed the complaints in this case?"

"We did as the police. We signed for the victim."

"Okay. And that was because she refused to sign complaints; she was uncooperative."

"Yes, that's correct."

"You documented, did you not, in these photographs, excuse me, you testified in the photographs, to injuries that you observed on Julie Grace, is that correct?"

"Yes. Yes, Sir."

"Did you offer her medical attention at that time?"

"Yes, we did."

"And she refused medical attention, did she not?"

"Yes, she refused from the paramedics."

"To your knowledge, did she go to a hospital at all that evening?"

"To my knowledge, no."

"You had testified that Miss Grace told you that she tried to call the police but that Mr. Thompson kept pulling the phone away from her or ripping the phones out."

"Yes."

"Did you document that anywhere in these reports that I just showed you?"

"I know I reviewed other reports, but I don't recall if the phone being taken away from her or pulled out of the wall is documented in the reports."

"Would you like to take a look at it?"

"Yes, please."

"Officer, look at that."

After reviewing the report, Officer Pinzine said, "No, Sir, that is not in the report."

"There is nothing in the report about Miss Grace trying to telephone the police at all, is there?"

"That's correct."

"Okay. And you agree with me that an alleged victim's efforts to call the police would be important enough to put in the report, won't you?"

"I'm sorry, could you repeat the question?"

"Sure. You would agree with me, wouldn't you, that if a victim of a crime had told you she tried to call the police and the alleged offender was preventing her from doing so, that would be something important enough for you to put in your reports, won't it be?"

"Yes, absolutely."

"Now in addition to Miss Grace, you didn't sign any type of misdemeanor complaints in this case; you had conversations with her regarding a felony complaint as well, did you not?"

"There was just about the signing the complaints."

"Did you talk to her about upgrading these charges?"

"I don't recall. I know that part of the arrest was handled via myself and my partner and that's up to the state's attorney when we call them; when we call them from the station for approval for an upgrade."

"Do you recall in the arrest report that you prepared in this case? Let me show you. I'll mark it as Defendant's 5 for defendant's purposes and have you identify it first, if I may. Officer, let me show you what has been marked as Defendant's 5 for identification purposes purported to be the arrest report in this case, ask you to take a look at it. Tell Judge Gaughan if that's the arrest report in this case."

"Yes, this is the arrest report."

"And is that your signature on it, Officer Pinzine?"

"Yes, it is."

"And the arrest report, did you prepare it or did your partner?"

"I prepared that."

"And in the arrest report, does it reflect that Miss Grace was uncooperative with an upgrade, does it not?"

"Yes, because she refused to sign the complaints."

"Okay. Well it also, the arrest report that we're talking about, said she refused to sign complaints."

"Yes."

"But an upgrade is a different thing, isn't it?"

"Right."

"What is an upgrade, please tell us?"

"If we call taking the circumstances into account, we call the state's attorney, go over the details that we have with them and they make the decision made by them on whether or not to pursue a felony charge or to go with misdemeanor charges."

"And Miss Grace was uncooperative with that procedure as well, correct?"

State's Assistant Attorney, Ms. Popielewski interrupted, "Objection, asked and answered, Judge."

Replied Judge Gaughan, "Though it's not clear. He asked what an upgrade is and we get what the state's attorney's process do in approving felony charges, which is tangential. Go ahead, overruled."

Mr. Pugh continued, "Was Miss Grace cooperative with the felony upgrade in this case?"

"She refused to sign any complaints."

"The apartment that you went to on March 7th, had you ever been in that condominium before?"

"No, I know I have not."

"And so as far as the condition of the condominium, you don't have any personal knowledge as to whether it was neat and tidy prior to your arrival, do you?"

"No, Sir."

"Or on any day prior, do you?"

"No, Sir."

"Thank you, Your Honor. Thank you, Officer."

"Officer, thank you," said the judge and he dismissed Officer Pinzine. "State, call your next witness."

The State called Officer Gina Patrick. She proceeded to the witness stand and was sworn in by the clerk.

"Officer, I want to draw your attention back to November 28th of 2002. Were you working and on duty on that particular date?"

"Yes."

"What unit were you assigned to at that time?"

"18th District beat 1821."

"At approximately 1:40 in the morning, Officer, were you working at that time?"

"Yes."

"Were you alone or with a partner?"

"I have a partner."

"Who was your partner on that date?"

"Officer Jason Walanski."

"Officer, at approximately 1:40 in the morning, were you called to the location of 1540 North LaSalle, apartment 2004?"

"Yes."

"What type of call were you going there for?"

"Domestic battery."

"Officer, when you arrived at that particular apartment, were you met by anybody?"

"Yes."

"Who were you met by?"

"I was met by the caller or the victim, Julie Grace."

"And did you have the opportunity to speak with Miss Grace on the scene?"

"Yes, I did."

"After speaking with Miss Grace, did you call any other police department personnel to the scene?"

"My sergeant was on the scene, beat 1820 and I also called for an evidence technician."

"After speaking with Miss Julie Grace at that time, was there anybody else in the apartment?"

"Yes, there was."

"Do you see that person here in court today?"

"Yes, I do."

"Can you point to that person and describe something he or she is wearing right now?"

She pointed to George and said, "The defendant in the tan shirt."

"After speaking with Miss Grace, did you have the occasion to take anyone into custody?"

"Yes."

"Who was that?"

"The defendant."

"What, if anything, did you do with the offender at that time?"

"Put handcuffs on him and then we escorted him down to our squad car and took him to the 18th District for processing."

"To your knowledge, did an evidence technician arrive at the scene?"

"Yes."

"When you spoke with Miss Julie Grace, did you have the opportunity to observe her physical condition at that time?"

"Yes, I did."

"What, if anything, did you note in regards to her physical condition at that time?"

"I noted that she had a scratch below her left eye. I noted that she had some bruising above her right eye and she had rug burns on her knees."

"Officer, when you arrived at the apartment did you note the condition of the apartment when you arrived?"

"Yes."

"What did you notice, if anything, in regards to the condition of the apartment?"

"It appeared to me to be in disarray."

"Did you have the opportunity to look around the apartment at that time?"

"Yes."

"Did you notice any damage?"

"Broken sliding glass door off the balcony."

"I want to show you a photograph I already marked as People's Exhibit 54. Do you recognize who is depicted in that photograph?"

"Julie Grace."

"Is that the woman you met at that apartment on that date and time?"

"Yes, I did."

"And what, if anything, did you notice with regard to her condition?"

"I see the scratch below her left eye and I see the bruise above her right eye."

"Does that photograph truly and accurately depict the injuries you saw on her face on that date and time?"

"Yes."

"Showing you what is marked as People's Exhibit number 55 for identification, do you recognize that?"

"Yes."

"What, if anything, do you recognize that photograph to be of?"

"Some scratch marks on her neck and red marks at the top of her chest."

"Were these visible at the time that you observed Miss Grace?"

"Yes."

"And Officer, does that photograph truly and accurately depict the scratches you saw on her neck at that time?"

"Yes."

"People's 55, do you recognize what is depicted there?"

"Yes."

"What do you recognize that to be?"

"Additional scratch marks on the right side of her neck."

"And Officer, were these visible at the time that you observed Miss Grace on that date and time?"

"Yes."

"Does that truly and accurately depict how she looked on that date?"

"Yes."

"Number 59 for identification, do you recognize what is in that photograph?"

"The rug burn on her knee."

"Does that truly and accurately depict the injury you saw on her knee on that date?"

"Yes."

"I want to show you People's Exhibit number 61 and 62 for identification. Officer, specifically in 61, what, if anything, do you recognize that photograph to be?"

"The broken sliding glass door in her apartment."

"Is that an overall view of the door?"

"That looks like a side view of the door."

"And Officer, 62, the photograph I've shown you, what, if anything, do you recognize that to be?"

"The broken window of the sliding glass door."

"A closer view?"

"Yes."

"Officer, do these two photographs, 61 and 62, accurately depict the broken window as you saw it on that date?"

"Yes."

"I have nothing further of this witness. Thank you, Judge."

"Is the E T going to testify or not?" asked Judge Gaughan.

"The E T on March 7th is not going to testify," answered Mr. Groth. "The E T on 11-28 is going to testify."

"That's why I asked," said the judge. "All right, is the E T going to testify as to what this officer just got done testifying to?"

"Actually, Judge," replied Ms. Popielewski, "there are some further photographs we're asking the E T to identify."

Mr. Pugh stated, "One quick question then. Officer"

Judge Gaughan interrupted, "Here is what I'm going to do. The E T is not going, he's not going to testify to the same photos. If you have additional evidence, fine."

"Thank you, Judge," replied Ms. Popielewski.

Mr. Pugh continued his cross-examination of the witness. "Officer, you said you contacted an E T, an evidence technician."

"Correct."

"Were those the individuals who took the photographs that you've identified?"

"Yes."

"Did you call for medical attention for Miss Grace?"

"I would have offered medical attention for her, yes."

"Did you offer medical attention?"

"Yes."

"Was it accepted?"

"No."

"And of course, had you ever been in that condominium prior to November 28th?"

"Not that I recall."

"So the condition of the condominium that you identified as being in disarray, you don't know what condition it was in the day before of course, do you?"

"No."

"Or any days afterwards."

"No."

"Nothing further, Judge," said Mr. Pugh.

Judge Gaughan instructed Officer Patrick to step down, and Ms. Popielewski called the State's next witness.

"We call Evidence Technician Wolverton."

The witness proceeded to the stand and was sworn in by the clerk of the court.

Officer Susan Wolverton stated and spelled her name, gave her star number and unit assignment, and then Ms Popielewski asked, "Officer, what are your duties as a Chicago Police Officer with that unit?"

"I'm a forensic investigator."

"I want to draw your attention back to the 28th of November, 2002. Were you also assigned to that unit working as a forensic investigator?"

"No. I was assigned to unit 377 as an evidence technician."

"Okay. Officer, I want to draw your attention to the 28th of November, 2002, approximately 2:25 AM, did you receive a call for service as an evidence technician?"

"Yes, I did."

"When you arrived at that particular location, what were your general duties at that time?"

"To photograph a domestic battery victim."

"Did you meet with a Miss Julie Grace at that time?"

"Yes, I did."

"What, if anything, did you do when you arrived at the apartment?"

"I met with Miss Grace. She allowed me into her apartment. I photographed her injuries that she indicated she had."

"When you had the opportunity to photograph her injuries, did you take several body shots of her?"

"Yes, I did."

"Investigator Wolverton, I want to show you a photograph which I already marked as People's Exhibit number 56 for identification. Do you recognize that particular photograph?"

"Yes, I do."

"Do you recognize of who that photograph is taken?"

"This is a photograph of Miss Grace's chest."

"What, if anything, do you note in that photograph and what did you see on that date?"

"It appears to be a bruising on her left breast, on her right breast and her right arm, her upper right arm."

"People's 57, do you recognize what is depicted in that photograph, Ma'am?"

"Yes, this is a photograph of Miss Grace's left wrist, looks like a small abrasion or bruise."

"Did you take that photograph of her?"

"Yes, I did."

"Number 58, do you recognize what that photograph is?"

"Number 58 is a photograph of Miss Grace's left wrist on the underside. It looks like a small scratch."

"And do these photographs truly and accurately depict Miss Grace as she appeared to you on that date?"

"Yes, they do."

"Showing you what is People's Exhibit number 60, do you recognize what that is a photograph of?"

"This is a photograph of Miss Grace's lower back area."

"And what do you see in that photograph, if anything."

"It looks like an abrasion of some sort."

"Does that also truly and accurately depict the injuries as Miss Grace showed them to you on that date?"

"Yes."

"You took that photograph."

"Yes, I did."

"Investigator Wolverton, did you take other views of the victim's body, as well?"

"Yes, I did."

"I have nothing further," announced Ms. Popielewski.

"Cross examination?" asked Judge Gaughan.

"No cross, Your Honor," answered Mr. Pugh.

The judge instructed Officer Wolverton to step down and then asked, "How long is your next witness?"

"Cross like that, not too long," answered Mr. Groth.

"Call your next one," instructed Judge Gaughan, "Thank you."

Michael Lewis is called as the next witness. He proceeded to the stand and was sworn in.

Ms. Popielewski asked, "Officer, I want to draw your attention to April 22nd, 2003. Were you working and on duty that date?"

"Yes, Ma'am."

"And what unit were you assigned to at that time?"

"I was assigned to the 18th District, car 1851."

"Officer, at approximately 5:46 in the evening did you get a call for service to the location of 1540 LaSalle in Chicago, Illinois?"

"Yes, Ma'am."

"Apartment 2004?"

"Yes, Ma'am."

"What is the nature of the call you received?"

"A domestic disturbance."

"Did you arrive at that location?"

"Yes, Ma'am."

"Were you working alone or with a partner at that time?"

"I was working with a partner."

"Who was your partner?"

"Daryl Legston."

"Once you arrived at the location what, if anything, occurred?"

"Basically, we knocked on the door, the person that had called, Julie Grace, she answered the door and let us in."

"Now can you describe for me what Miss Grace's demeanor was at the time?"

"She was visibly shaken. You could tell she was very agitated."

"Now, Officer, could you see when you arrived at the apartment, could you see anybody else in the apartment upon immediate inspection?"

"No, Ma'am."

"Once you saw Miss Grace what, if anything, did she tell you?"

"She stated she was using the phone. The offender took the phone, grabbed the phone from her hand and stated that I'll bust your head with the phone and I'll kick your ass if you don't get off the phone."

"At that time, Officer, did she identify the person who had said this to her?"

"Yes, she said he was in the bedroom."

"What, if anything, did you do when you heard that?"

"After we finished talking to Miss Grace, we went into the bedroom and approached the subject."

"Who was in the bedroom?"

"The defendant."

"Do you see the person you saw in the bedroom on that date here in court today?"

"Yes, I do."

"Can you point to him and describe something he's wearing right now?"

He pointed at George and said, "The brown uniform, DOC uniform."

"At that point what, if anything, did you do?"

"We approached him. He was laying in the bed. We asked him to stand up. We asked him what was his side of the situation."

"After that point, did you take the defendant into custody?"

"Yes, Ma'am."

"I have nothing further," stated Ms. Popielewski. "Thank you very much."

"Cross examination?" asked Judge Gaughan.

Mr. Pugh asked the witness, "Officer, you were dispatched to 1540 North LaSalle."

"Yes, Sir."

"And you had a conversation with Miss Grace when you arrived."

"Yes, Sir."

"And it was Miss Grace that had called the police, correct?"

"Yes, Sir."

"And what she told you is that Mr. Thompson had grabbed the telephone from her and threatened to bust her in the head with it. Is that correct?"

"Yes, Sir."

"But Miss Grace still managed to call the police, isn't that right?"

"Yes, Sir."

"And he went with you and he didn't resist in any fashion, did he?"

"No, Sir."

"And of course, when you got there, well, Miss Grace hadn't been struck by Mr. Thompson at that time, had she?"

"No, Sir."

Mr. Pugh ended his cross-examination by saying, "Nothing further Judge, thank you."

"Thank you," said the judge. "You can step down, Officer. How long is your next witness?"

"About 15 minutes," answered Mr. Pugh.

"Can I ask who it is?" asked Mr. Breen.

"Detective Scholtes," replied Ms. Popielewski. "We're going back to the actual date now, Judge."

The witness was called to testify and after being sworn in, he seated himself and the direct examination by Ms. Popielewski began.

"Detective, were you so assigned and on duty on the 20th of May of 2003?"

"Yes, I was."

"And what shift were you working on that particular night?"

"The first watch, which is the midnight shift."

"What were your hours of duty?"

"From 12:30 at night until 9:00 in the morning."

"I want to draw your attention to approximately 4:30 that morning. Did you receive a call to a scene located at 1540 North LaSalle Street apartment 2004?"

"Yes, I did."

"In Chicago?"

"Yes."

"Were you working alone or with a partner that night?"

"With a partner."

"Who was your partner?"

"Detective William Davis."

"And once you and he received that call, did you go to that location?"

"Yes, we did."

"Were there other officers on the scene?"

"Yes, there were."

"Approximately how many other officers?"

"I believe two or three."

"As part of the course of your investigation, Officer, did you learn anything in regards to what, if anything, had occurred at that location?"

"Yes, I did."

"And what was that, what did you notice at that time?"

"At the time it was a death investigation."

"And do you know the name of the person who was deceased?"

"Yes."

"Who was that?"

"Julie Grace."

"Do you know if she was a resident of that apartment?"

"To my knowledge, yes."

"Officer, what, if anything, did you do when you and Detective Davis arrived on the scene at that time?"

"We entered the apartment, looked through the apartment."

"What, if anything, did you note at that time?"

"I noticed it was a one bedroom apartment. We noticed there was what appeared to be blood on the floor, what appeared to be blood on the pillow on the floor, what appeared to be blood on the bed, what appeared to be blood on some blinds."

"This was in what room?"

"This was in the bedroom."

"Detective, did you have any information in regards to where the victim had been found in the apartment?"

"Yes, we learned the victim was found in the bedroom on the floor."

"What, if anything, did you do in regards to that apartment at that time?"

"We had an evidence technician come to take photographs."

"Did you remain at that apartment until the evidence technician arrived?"

"Yes, I did."

"Were you present when he or she took those photographs?"

"Yes, I was."

"After photographing the apartment that morning on the 20th, what, if anything, did you do?"

"We left the apartment and went to the hospital."

"Okay. At that point, did you know whether or not the victim was deceased?"

"That's when we learned she was deceased, yes."

"I want to draw your attention to the next day, the 21st of May, 2003. Were you also working the midnight shift on that early morning?"

"Yes, I was."

"Were you working alone or with a partner at that time?"

"With a partner again."

"Who was your partner on that particular morning?"

"That day was Detective Ed Heerdt."

"And what, if anything, was your assignment in the early morning hours of the 21st of May, 2003?"

"To return to the apartment and have another evidence technician take photos and collect evidence."

"Did you and your partner actually go to that location again?"

"Yes, we did."

"Now, previous to going to the location of 1520 North LaSalle on the early morning hours of the 21st, did you obtain any consent for entering into that apartment?"

"Yes, we did."

"And from who did you obtain that consent?"

"From George Thompson."

"And do you see Mr. George Thompson here in court today?"

"Yes, I do."

"Can you point to him and describe something he's wearing right now?"

Pointing at George, he stated, "Sitting with the brown suit there."

"Where were you when you obtained the consent from Mr. Thompson?"

"Area three Detective Division."

"And if you recall, approximately what time was it you obtained that consent?"

"I was thinking 4:00 in the morning, 4:15."

"Showing you what I've previously marked as People's Exhibit number 39 for identification, do you recognize the item that I just handed you, Sir?"

"Yes, Ma'am."

"And what do you recognize that to be?"

"This was the consent to search form."

"And was that the consent to search form signed by Mr. Thompson for that apartment?"

"Yes, it was."

"And were you a witness to that?"

"Yes, I was."

"Detective, when you arrived at the apartment with your partner what, if anything, did you and he do at that time?"

"We were met by an evidence technician and we"

"What was the purpose of the evidence technician on that second date?"

"To take additional photos and collect evidence."

"Were you present when those photographs were taken?"

"Yes, I was."

"And were you also helping to instruct the evidence technician as to what to take photographs of?"

"Yes, I was."

"Detective, you were present on both those dates, the 20th and the 21st, when the photographs were taken by the evidence technician, is that correct?"

"Yes, I was."

"When you arrived at the location on the 21st, the apartment, was it in substantially the same condition as when you had seen it on the 20th?"

"Yes, it was the same condition."

"I'm showing you a group of photographs, Detective, which have been consecutively previously marked People's Exhibits number 6 through 19. Have you had the opportunity to see these photographs before testifying today?"

"Yes, I have."

"And as a group, what are they photographs of, generally?"

"Of the apartment."

"That apartment that you viewed both on the 20th and the 21st."

"Yes, Ma'am."

"And does that group truly and accurately depict the apartment as it looked on both of those dates?"

"Yes, they do."

"If you could, very briefly describe what is depicted in People's Exhibit number 6."

"It's actually a photo of the bedroom."

Judge Gaughan interrupted, "I'm sorry, there was testimony about this already, right?"

"Yes, Your Honor, there has been," answered Ms. Popielewski.

"What is the difference? What is it going to add? As far as what is in evidence, these were the photos 6 through 19 that were taken on the 20th of May 2003, right?"

"Correct, Judge."

"What is this adding or deleting from the previous testimony?"

"Nothing Judge, I'll just merely ask the detective after having seen them. I'll say nothing more. That's all, Judge. He's identified them."

Ms. Popielewski continued to question the witness. "I'm now showing you what has been previously marked as People's Exhibit number consecutively 63 through 77. You've seen this group of photographs previous to testifying. Is that correct, Detective?"

"Yes, Ma'am."

"Generally, what are they photographs of?"

"Of the apartment, also."

"The condition of the apartment as you saw it."

"Yes, Ma'am."

"Do they truly and accurately depict that condition?"

"Yes, Ma'am."

Ms. Popielewski continued to show the witness photos of the apartment as it appeared on May 20th and 21st, asking him each time if he recognized them and if they truly and accurately depicted the condition. His responses were yes to both questions on all photos.

The State's Attorney then asked the witness, "Okay, 66, Sir?"

"It's a picture of the chair with a wrench on it."

"Is there an evidence marker on that chair?"

"Evidence marker number 4."

"Okay, 67, Sir."

"67 is a picture of the front room including the chair and the television with two evidence markers, number 4 and 5."

"And what, if anything, do those two markers show?"

"Number 4 shows a wrench and number 5 shows, appears to be another wrench."

"Okay. 68, please, what, if anything, do you see?"

"It's a picture of the front room leading to the glass sliding doors. It has sort of a tool and appears to be a tool belt, also."

"Okay, 69 please."

"A photo, close up photo of the tool belt."

"And where was that tool belt sitting?"

"On the outside on the patio."

"I have nothing further of the detective," said Ms. Popielewski. "Thank you, Judge."

"Thank you," said Judge Gaughan.

"No cross examination, Your Honor," replied Mr. Pugh.

The judge thanked Officer Scholtes and then instructed him to step down.

Judge Gaughan announced the court would take a break for lunch.

In approximately one hour, court resumed and the judge instructed the State to call their next witness.

Mr. Groth called Dr. James Footy to the stand. After Dr. Footy was sworn in, he stated and spelled his name as instructed by Mr. Groth.

Dr. Footy was a very nice elderly gentleman. He was Julie's personal physician for many years. Duard and I never questioned his judgment and were always confident he would provide the best medical care possible for Julie. We greatly admired and respected him just as much as Julie did.

Mr. Groth asked Dr. Footy, "Sir, do you have a profession?"

"I'm a physician."

"And where are you currently practicing medicine?"

"I practice at the Northwestern Medical Faculty Foundation and Northwestern Memorial Hospital."

"And what position do you hold there?"

"I'm the vice chairman of the Department of Medicine for Clinical Affairs."

"Where did you go to medical school, Sir?"

"I went to the University of Chicago."

"And did you do an internship?"

"Yes, I did."

"Where at?"

"At the University of Chicago Hospital."

"Okay. And during the course of your career have you worked in emergency rooms?"

"Yes, I have."

"Sir, were you the treating physician for a young lady by the name of Julie Grace?"

"Yes, I was."

"Sir, during the course of your treatment from January of 2001 to April 7th of 2003, what was the most prominent condition you were treating Julie Grace for?"

"I took care of essentially all of Julie's medical issues but her most prominent one was complications from alcohol."

"All right, and Julie had a number of hospitalizations between January 21st, 2001, and April 7th, 2003, is that correct?"

"Yes."

"In fact, she had a final hospitalization on May 20th, 2003, is that correct?"

"Yes."

"Now have you had an opportunity, during the course of your treating of Julie, to review her medical records from January of 2001 to April of 2003 to arrive at treatment plans and diagnoses?"

"Yes."

"And have you reviewed those before testifying today?"

"Yes."

"Would it assist you today in testifying to review the records as you're testifying?"

"Probably, yes."

"I'm going to show you these medical records, Doctor, and ask you questions regarding these. Now Sir, on January 21st, 2001, Julie was treated at Northwestern Memorial Hospital, is that correct?"

"Yes."

"And do you recall what her treatment was for at that time?"

"Yes, she came in with abdominal pain," said Dr. Footy.

"Was she treated for dehydration, vomiting and diarrhea?" asked Mr. Groth.

"Yes."

"Would those be signs of complications from alcoholism as you stated earlier?"

"Yes."

"Now on February 7th, 2001, Julie was treated at Northwestern Memorial Hospital as well, is that correct?"

"Yes."

"And what was her treatment for that day?"

"She was treated for vomiting similar to the prior emergency room admission."

"At that time, is there a notation on the medical records regarding a fatty liver?"

"Yes."

"Is that also a sign of one of the symptoms of alcoholism?"

"It's one of the signs of alcohol disease, yes."

"Sir, on the 10th of March, 2002, was Julie again treated at Northwestern Memorial Hospital?"

"Yes."

"And what was her main complaint or diagnosis at that point?"

"Her complaint was that she was having withdrawal syndrome, and her primary diagnosis was she was having adverse effects from chronic alcoholism."

"Subsequent to that treatment, did she go through a detox center at Chicago Lake Shore Hospital?"

"As far as I understand, yes."

"Now on July 10th of 2002, she was again treated at Northwestern, is that correct?"

"Yes."

"And again, what was the diagnosis at that point?"

"I can't find the exact diagnosis. She came in because she had been involved in an altercation and had a blow to the head and she was found to have some of the symptoms and signs of alcohol at that time, as well."

"Can I see the first page of your July 10th; as far as diagnosis on there, what does that indicate?"

"At the emergency room, they wrote alcohol abuse."

"But there were other problems as well that day."

"Yes."

"Okay. But on the next page, on the physician's medical records, is there additional information?"

"Yes, there is."

"And can you tell us what that is?"

"It starts out in the physician's medical record under the chief complaint, history of present illness, 40-year old and I can't read the next word, with chronic alcoholism involved in altercation two days ago when inebriated, passive blow to right orbital area."

"Doctor, I don't understand the terminology, a passive blow, how could it be passive if there was a blow?" asked Judge Gaughan.

"That means she was hit as opposed to fell down and hurt herself," answered Dr. Footy.

"Thank you," said the judge.

Mr. Groth continued, "Where is the orbital area?"

"Around the right eye," answered the witness.

"Thank you. Now on that day it also indicates that she had taken Ativan the previous day, is that correct?"

"Yes. Ativan is the brand name for Lorazepam, which is Benzodiazepine type drug which reduces anxiety symptoms."

"Now on the 3rd of September 2002, was she treated again at Northwestern Memorial Hospital?"

"Yes."

"And again, what was her primary diagnosis at that point?"

"The discharge diagnosis was alcohol abuse or dependence."

"And as far as physical signs of alcohol withdrawal, what were some of the signs that she had?"

"She was tremulous meaning that the common term would be she had the shakes, she was anxious, she had a rapid heart rate."

"Now Doctor, is there a difference between a person having seizures and a person having tremors or the shakes?"

"Yes."

"Can you explain to us what that is?"

"Well, they are totally different things. Tremors describe an oscillating repetitive movement usually of an extremity. A seizure is a complicated storm of electric chemical activity of the brain. They don't have anything to do with each other."

"Now on September 3, 2002"

"Excuse me, point of clarification. You could have a tremor without this electrical storm in the brain?" asked Judge Gaughan.

Dr. Footy replied, "Yes, the tremor has nothing to do with the electrical storm in the brain."

Mr. Groth asked the witness, "It would be a seizure that would cause a person to lose control of their body based on this electrical storm, is that correct?"

"Yes, it can," answered Dr. Footy.

"Not the tremors?"

"Correct."

"Now did Julie Grace have some secondary complaints regarding her condition on the 3rd of September, 2002?"

"She had several other diagnoses at that time. She had problems with her chemical balance, which is due to alcoholism. It's noted here as alkalosis. She had alcohol dependence, which is separate from alcohol withdrawal, and she had depression."

"Did she complain about anything else in her medical history?"

"She had not been able to eat. She described that she had been abused by her boyfriend."

"Did she give more details about what the type of abuse was?"

"There is a notation here. It says, boyfriend abuses contact with, and I can't read the next two words. And then, abuse and parenthesis, pushed out of car, end parenthesis."

"Judge, I would object. Improper foundation for this witness and relevance if it's not tied in," said Mr. Pugh.

"State?" asked Judge Gaughan.

"He's testifying as a medical expert," answered Mr. Groth. "Judge, you want to do this outside the hearing of the witness?"

"No, the doctor is a professional," replied the judge.

"Okay," said Mr. Groth. "Judge, one of the questions I was going to ask the doctor is whether or not domestic abuse is a medical diagnosis. I believe his answer will be yes. One of the things the doctor had to do when he's looking for the safety of his patient is provide her options and recommendations. Now, throwing out of a moving truck"

"Were you the treating physician on September 3, 2002, and are those your notes?" interrupted Judge Gaughan.

"No, these are not my notes," answered Dr. Footy.

"The doctor did, in fact, rely on the notes in making his diagnosis for Julie Grace. Also, the defense has been asking about Miss Grace's records through other witnesses. I think they are now in play as far as the information that is contained about her," said Mr. Groth.

"Mr. Breen?" asked the judge.

Mr. Breen replied, "I still object. I mean"

Judge Gaughan interrupted again, "You know, excuse me. There is a treating physician exception to the hearsay, okay. But Dr. Footy was not the person that was treating on September 3rd about the complaint that she was thrown out of a truck. All right. The other thing is I don't know so I can evaluate the credibility of the declarant that day. I mean, the foundation hasn't been laid other than there was alcohol abuse and there was some other things, what her condition was to evaluate her credibility. The doctor is not in a position to do that. He wasn't there."

Mr. Groth replied, "But he did rely on the medical records, that's what we're saying, Judge."

"All right," said Judge Gaughan. "Mr. Breen?"

"Judge, I object," said Mr. Breen.

"Well, give me a basis of your objection," instructed the judge.

"I object. It's hearsay, number one. Number two, it's irrelevant," said Mr. Breen.

"How is it not material and relevant?" asked Judge Gaughan.

"What does it have to do with us?" said Mr. Breen.

"State?" asked the judge.

Mr. Groth replied, "Judge, this was as far as in this case, the evidence that is shown this defendant was her boyfriend during the time period."

"Mr. Pugh commented, "She had several boyfriends, Your Honor, and she had several men in her life and I think that's what the evidence is going to show."

"And the word, boyfriend, I mean, you know again, it's not, there is not a nexus between the accused right now and the statement concerning boyfriend," said Judge Gaughan.

Mr. Groth said, "I'll move on from the 3rd of September."

"Thank you," said the judge.

Mr. Groth asked the witness, "On October 10th, did Julie Grace seek additional medical treatment, excuse me, October 10th of 2002, did she seek additional"

Once again, Judge Gaughan interrupted Mr. Groth. "Let me make the record clear. The doctor can rely certainly upon other medical records and everything and he can rely upon hearsay and make his opinion but hearsay is still hearsay no matter what. So even if the doctor reads it, he wasn't the treating physician. It's still in his formulation of his opinion but not for the truth of the matter asserted therein. Do you understand that?"

"I think I do," said Mr. Groth.

"All right," replied Judge Gaughan.

Mr. Breen followed up by saying, "We agree with the court that if he reviewed the records and based on those records he's going to render an opinion, we understand that. We don't understand what I thought, was the implication that it was being offered for the truth asserted therein."

"No, you're arriving at what you don't even have to do but you're laying a factual basis for the doctor's opinion, is that correct?" asked Judge Gaughan.

"Yes, Judge," answered Mr. Groth.

"Fine," said Judge Gaughan. "And the doctor can rely upon, just like x-rays that he didn't take, but the radiologist did and the opinion of the radiologist, and in determining those x-rays, he can rely on that which is completely hearsay to make his opinion. So, that's the basis. Those rules of evidence have been worked out for medical doctors. All right. That's my ruling, so it's clear on the record. All right. These are just matters between the doctor, his formulation of establishing basic facts to render an opinion. The truth of those facts as to the outside world, are still hearsay and they are not a matter admitted in for the truth of the matter asserted therein. He's not the treating physician."

Mr. Groth said, "Just so I'm clear so I don't think about this later on, this is not a question of admissibility."

"You're just showing me the basis for his opinion, which isn't necessary, but that's all right," replied Judge Gaughan.

"Let's jump ahead, Doctor, to October 10th of 2002," said Mr. Groth. "Did Julie come again to Northwestern Hospital?"

"Yes, she did," answered Dr. Footy.

"And what were her complaints? What was her diagnosis at that time, if you recall?"

"She had alcohol dependence and alcohol withdrawals."

"All right, and at that time again, was there a notation there regarding no entry of withdrawal seizures?"

"Could I ask for a point of clarification?" asked Dr. Footy. "I'm just unclear. Are you asking me of my memory of Julie in the hospital or for me to read the medical records? On this paper, she had no history of withdrawals or seizures."

"Again, it doesn't depend on what the records indicate, it's what the doctor based his opinion on," said Judge Gaughan. "If the doctor is doing that, that's fine, but if the doctor didn't base his opinion on the facts, they are immaterial and not relevant."

Mr. Groth replied, "This doctor was the treating doctor based on the notation of the 11th of October, the Department of Medicine Critical Care. I'll show the doctor which page numbers to make it easier."

"That's fine. Great," said the judge.

Mr. Groth continued, "Now on that sheet which is entitled for October 11th Northwestern Memorial Hospital for history of present illness, is there a notation there of no history of withdrawal seizures?"

"Yes, there is."

"Okay. Now it indicated there she was also seeking help in here or trying to quit drinking, is that correct?"

"Yes."

"Okay. She indicated that her mom was supportive of her in that type of effort, is that correct?"

"What does that have to do with his diagnosis?" asked Judge Gaughan.

Mr. Groth replied, "Well, Judge, the"

"The judge interrupted, "Where was the mother, in Chicago or Florida?"

"I believe her mother was in Florida at this time," said Mr. Groth.

The judge replied, "You're going far away and I mean here is the thing, these are ancillary. Mrs. Grace testified that she, you know, she lives in Florida. I don't know how supportive you can be in Florida and I'm not going to have you bring in experts on this, so I'll not allow that testimony."

"If I could make an offer," said Mr. Groth. "Later on in December, she indicated"

"Excuse me," interrupted Judge Gaughan once more. "We'll get to it right now. Doctor, would the geographic location of her mother have any weight on your opinion and your diagnosis?"

"No," answered Dr. Footy.

"All right, move on," instructed the judge.

Mr. Groth asked the witness, "Would the fact her mother was supportive of her and her attempt to quit alcohol have any type of relevance in your judgment?"

Before the witness answered, Mr. Pugh interrupted, "I think here lies the problem. I'm going to object to all of this testimony unless we are told what exactly he's testifying as, a treating physician, as an expert who is going to eventually render an opinion based on these records, which would mean that his observations and all that really aren't important because if he reviews the records to render an opinion. I understand how some of the stuff comes in, but what is he here for, as the treating physician or to render an opinion? That's my question."

Mr. Groth replied, "Generally would be a treating physician would be what he would be testifying about which is why I think the records are important to arrive at what his present diagnosis was the last time he saw her, as well as her physical condition on the 7th of April."

Judge Gaughan responded, "Let me ask the doctor a couple of questions then. Doctor, you have been going through these medical records from January 21st, 2001, all the way up until November 10th, 2003. Now, how much of these records, compared to how much of a treating physician, would be weighted towards your opinion, or is your opinion almost independent of these medical records?"

"I can explain that," answered Dr. Footy.

"Great," said the judge.

"It will help, I think, if I explain how we handle patients at Northwestern briefly, which is, that when a patient is admitted to the inpatient service there is an attending physician assigned who is the person whose name will be on the medical record. With my patients, I combine"

The judge interrupted again, "Doctor, point of clarification. Would the attending physician who is being assigned be the treating physician?"

"One of the treating physicians."

"Thank you. Go ahead," said Judge Gaughan.

"And I would also be a treating physician, we work collegially. In every circumstance where Miss Grace was admitted to the hospital, I went by to see her. On a few occasions, I would write notes, but most of the time I don't write notes independently. It is helpful to see the records just to refresh me in terms of the temporal sequence of things."

"All right," replied the judge. "I'm going to allow Mr. Groth to proceed with it and Mr. Breen on specific points. Certainly you will be allowed to object and I'll make rulings on those whether they are acceptable or not."

"Thank you, Your Honor," said Mr. Pugh.

"Proceed," ordered the judge.

"Now Doctor," said Mr. Groth, "we had mentioned before, is domestic abuse a medical diagnosis?"

"Yes."

"Okay. Now, on the 11th of October, 2002, in your capacity as a treating physician, did you review social work case management notes regarding Julie Grace and the domestic abuse situation?"

"Yes, I did."

"Did she express concerns to the social worker at that point?"

"Yes, she did."

"Judge, I'm going to object to the domestic abuse or diagnosis," interjected Mr. Pugh.

The judge responded by saying, "Now, if this comes within the doctor's purview as treating physician, I'm certainly going to allow it but we're getting far afield. What she told a social worker, so sustained as to that. Again, the doctor can use these hearsay things as basing his opinion but as far as an objection for the truth of the matter asserted therein, they don't, they're not truth as far as that is concerned in a court of law. Okay."

Mr. Groth continued, "Doctor, Northwestern Memorial Hospital is in the business of providing medical services for patients, is that correct?"

"Yes."

"And in the course of providing services, are these types of records created?"

"Yes."

"Now, do doctors like yourself and other professionals rely on these records for the truth of the matter asserted contained therein?"

"Yes."

"Thank you," said Mr. Groth. "Judge, at this time we seek to admit this relevant portion as an exhibit."

"I understand that," said Judge Gaughan.

"Objection," responded Mr. Breen.

The judge replied, "We're going to have to. There is a specific section in the criminal law provision about business records and I think hospital records are exempt from that. Not business records. So we'll take a short recess and get the section that covers business records in criminal law."

"Okay," said Mr. Groth. "Judge, you want me to do that?"

"Well you're not going further," answered the judge. "If you want to stand there for an hour, you can, but if you want to do that right now, go ahead."

"I understand," said Mr. Groth.

The judge instructed, "Just look at the law and then we don't have to do this method in arriving at what it means, very clear and simple if it's specifically under business records."

A short recess was taken while Mr. Groth reviewed the law.

When the court reconvened, Mr. Groth continued his questioning of the witness, "Doctor, without going into what is physically contained in the medical records, did you have concerns regarding a diagnosis of domestic abuse for Julie Grace after reviewing the October 11th through 13th medical records?"

"Objection," said Mr. Pugh.

"Basis?" asked Judge Gaughan.

Mr. Pugh replied, "It's irrelevant whether he had concerns. If he's an expert, he should be rendering an opinion."

"Sustained to the form of the question," ruled the judge.

Mr. Groth replied, "We would seek to have the doctor qualified as an expert in medicine, internal medicine and emergency medicine based on his experience."

"Just go and talk to the defense," ordered the judge.

"I have no problem with that," said Mr. Pugh.

"All right," replied Judge Gaughan. "Is that agreed upon between the parties the doctor would be qualified as an expert in internal medicine and also, as an emergency medicine doctor?"

"Yes, Your Honor," answered Mr. Pugh. "We have the doctor's CV and we agree."

Judge Gaughan ruled, "The stipulation is allowed and moved into evidence and the doctor is qualified to testify as an expert in those areas. Go ahead."

Mr. Groth asked the witness, "You have an opinion, Sir, after reviewing the records from October 10th through the 13th, 2002, whether or not Julie Grace was in danger of suffering from domestic abuse?"

"Objection," said Mr. Breen.

"Basis?" asked the judge.

"He's not qualified to render an opinion if the court were to recognize that opinion as admissible, so it's a two part objection," replied Mr. Breen.

"Mr. Groth?" asked Judge Gaughan.

Ms. Popielewski replied, "I don't understand why he's not qualified. He's an emergency room expert, internal medicine expert and an expert on medicine. He's already testified that domestic abuse is a diagnosis."

"Mr. Breen?" asked the judge.

"I object, Judge," said Mr. Breen. "I know of no recognition that the law gives to that area of expertise under Frey and the associated cases."

Mr. Groth responded, "He's not testifying as an expert in domestic abuse, he's testifying as an expert"

Judge Gaughan interrupted, "Frey sounds nice but right here, the doctor is in a field established by the scientific community. The methodology towards reaching an opinion of scientific is one thing, the opinion that would apply to Frey. You're not asking for a Frey medical opinion, are you?"

"No," answered Mr. Groth.

Mr. Breen said, "I never heard, Judge, an opinion being given that someone was subject to or in danger of domestic abuse."

"You know what I'm going to do," said Judge Gaughan, "is let the doctor render his opinion. I'm going to reserve my ruling and allow you wide latitude on cross examination to show that. All right. Proceed."

Mr. Groth continued questioning Dr. Footy. "Did you have an opinion whether or not Julie Grace was in danger of suffering domestic abuse, after reviewing the October 10th through 13th, 2002 medical records?"

"Yes," answered Dr. Footy.

"What was that opinion?"

"I believed she was suffering from domestic abuse."

"And what led you to that opinion?"

"First, my first hand observation, not the medical records. She told me."

"All right. I'm sorry," said the judge.

"Objection, Judge," exclaimed Mr. Breen.

"No," responded Judge Gaughan.

"Mr. Breen continued, "I move to strike it."

Judge Gaughan replied, "I want you to pay attention, Mr. Breen. Unless you listen and one of us talk at a time, you know, if both people talk at the same time, no one is going to learn anything."

The judge went on to say, "The doctor said, independent of the medical records, he based an opinion after consulting with Miss Grace. So you didn't use any of the medical records to arrive at your opinion, Doctor?"

"I used the medical records, but I did not need them to arrive at my opinion," answered the witness.

"Okay. All right. Proceed then. Your objection is overruled," stated the judge.

Mr. Groth asked, "Did the doctor ever answer the question? What was your opinion that day, Doctor?"

"I believed that Miss Grace was subject to domestic abuse based upon what she told me and on physical findings on a number of occasions."

"Now the 21st of October, 2002, was Julie Grace treated again at Northwestern Memorial Hospital?"

"Yes, she was."

"And what was her chief complaint?"

Judge Gaughan interrupted, "All right, I'm sorry. First of all you know, did the doctor use the medical records to base his opinion? Where are you going with this? Are you asking for another opinion or what?"

"I'm going to ask another opinion," answered Mr. Groth.

"Don't just refer to the record. Ask the doctor if he used the records. The doctor is now saying, because of an independent conversation with the patient, he formed these opinions and he didn't need the records," stated the judge.

Mr. Groth replied, "Also something I would like to clarify, brought out by Mr. Breen during his cross examination of Dr. Arangelovich, which was Mr. Breen's question that the victim in this case, Julie Grace, had cut her hand with a knife, which is not what is contained in the medical records. He was referring, specifically, to the medical records, little tough to read but I understand where the error came from. But I do want the doctor to clarify that. That's also a piece of evidence that the court, I'm sure, would consider in its ruling."

"All right," said Judge Gaughan.

"I object to that, Judge," said Mr. Breen. "The pathologist answered the question, whatever the answer was. Is he saying he's going to impeach the pathologist? Did the doctor reflect something earlier than what his witness said?"

Mr. Groth answered, "Mr. Breen approached the pathologist with the record. If Your Honor can take a look at these records. Not exactly good handwriting. Takes some deciphering to see what it says. The pathologist had an opportunity to review those records so we're not trying to impeach"

"Mr. Groth," interrupted Judge Gaughan, "get to the point. It's going to be 5:00 tomorrow afternoon before you reach a conclusion. What is the purpose of, first of all, the forensic pathologist did testify on cross examination? So what is the purpose here of Dr. Footy?"

"I'm trying to correct what may be an error in the court's facts," said Mr. Groth.

"Why didn't you do it through the doctor on redirect of the forensic pathologist?" asked the judge.

Mr. Groth answered, "There is an awful lot of medical records here, Judge, and I didn't have October 11th handy. I didn't know he would be cross examining the doctor with those October 11th records."

Mr. Breen commented, "October 21st."

"Did you give him those records?" asked Judge Gaughan.

"I did give him the records," answered Mr. Groth.

"What is your objection?" the judge asked Mr. Breen.

Mr. Pugh answered, "We need to clarify."

The judge replied, "Just inconsistencies are inconsistencies and they go to the weight of the evidence. So your objection is, I don't know what."

"I don't understand what needs to be clarified," said Mr. Breen. "I don't know."

"Then that's why you're not a prosecutor. Overruled. Go ahead," instructed Judge Gaughan.

Mr. Groth asked the witness, "On that day, did Julie Grace come in with a chief complaint?"

Again, the judge interrupted, "You're not going to read them. Ask him."

"What was her chief complaint on that day?" asked Mr. Groth.

"She came in with a laceration to her hand and multiple injuries," answered Dr. Footy.

"And where did she say the laceration from her hand came from?"

"Objection, Judge," exclaimed Mr. Pugh.

"Sustained. That's leading. Rephrase," instructed Judge Gaughan.

Mr. Groth rephrased the question by asking, "Does the record indicate where the laceration to the hand came from?"

"Yes, in the triage note, it says"

"I'm going to object," responded Mr. Pugh.

"Overruled. I'll allow you wide latitude on cross examination," said the judge.

The witness continued, "Patient presents with laceration to left hand sustained when hit; when hit with knife by boyfriend and laceration to dorsum of hand."

"I'm sorry," interjected the judge, "is that written by a doctor?"

"I'm trying to translate. It's written by a nurse," answered Dr. Footy.

"You're not qualified as a translator," replied Judge Gaughan.

"It's written by a nurse," stated the witness.

"All right. Don't interpret; just read what's there, Doctor," instructed the judge.

"He hasn't been qualified as a translator," said Mr. Groth.

"I thought I made that point but I hear an echo," replied Judge Gaughan. "All right. You know, Doctor, again, the purpose of this."

Mr. Groth asked the judge, "Could I do this, move this one particular piece of evidence into evidence so Your Honor can see why we're having trouble here?"

"Objection," responded Mr. Pugh.

"Sustained," replied the judge.

"Hard to read the handwriting isn't it, Doctor?" asked Mr. Groth.

"I'm sorry?" asked the witness.

"Is it hard to read the handwriting?"

"A little, yes."

"In fact, we were trying to decipher this in the back before you testified, is that correct?"

"Yes."

"Okay. What does it indicate as far as the mechanism of the injury that she was complaining about on the 21st of October, 2002?"

"Well the position of the injury would most likely be caused by trying to stop a blow with the left hand, stop a blow with a knife and what is written in the chart is that she"

Mr. Pugh interrupted again, "Excuse me Judge, I object."

The judge replied, "If the doctor had an independent conversation with Julie Grace, that's fine. If the doctor is saying something and giving an opinion about defensive wounds in general, sustained. You asked him a particular question, a particular question about what the medical record said. Okay, Doctor, you have to answer the question. Restrain yourself to the question. Rephrase."

Mr. Groth asked the question again, "What is your opinion of the mechanism of Julie Grace's injury on October 21st, 2002?"

"Objection," responded Mr. Pugh.

"Overruled," replied Judge Gaughan. "He's qualified as an expert in the area of emergency medicine. I'll allow you wide latitude on cross examination. Go ahead."

"Dr. Footy answered, "She sustained a laceration from a knife to the back of her left hand. I believe she did this in protecting herself against a blow."

Mr. Breen asked, "Is that his opinion or is he reading it, Judge? I object."

"Doctor, when you say the word belief, is that the same as saying this is your opinion?" asked Judge Gaughan.

"Yes," answered the doctor.

"All right. That's his opinion," commented the judge.

Mr. Groth then asked the witness, "Why do you think that?"

"Because I talked to Miss Grace after the fact," answered Dr. Footy.

"Did she indicate how the knife, how the slash got on her hand?"

"Yes."

"How?"

"Her boyfriend tried to hit her with a knife."

"Thank you."

Mr. Breen said, "Objection, there is no relevancy or to use the court's words, nexus to us."

"Let me explain something," replied Judge Gaughan. "It's the Constitution, my personal legal philosophy. Let's move on."

"Thank you," said Mr. Groth. "On November 29th, 2002, did Julie Grace again seek medical treatment at Northwestern Memorial Hospital?"

"Yes, she did," answered the witness.

"What was her chief complaint on that day?"

"Her complaint was she was assaulted."

"And again, did she indicate who assaulted her at that point?"

"Unless I'm missing it, I don't see that noted in the chart."

"On the attending physician confirmation, chief complaint, is there a notation?"

"Yes, I'm sorry. I wasn't looking at that page. She was, she presented to the emergency room after being assaulted. She reports yesterday that her boyfriend has bipolar, assaulted her for seven hours yesterday."

"Thank you. Now, on December 4th, 2002, was she treated again for alcohol detoxification at Northwestern?"

"Yes, she was."

"Okay. And again, was she treated for dehydration on December 19th, 2002?"

"Yes, she was."

"And again, for dehydration on the 21st of December, 2002?"

"Yes, she was."

"I would like to jump ahead to April 7th of 2003. Was Julie again in Northwestern Memorial Hospital?"

"Yes, she was."

"What was she being treated for at that point?"

"At that point, she was treated for pyelonephritis which is an infection of the kidneys."

"And you said infection of the kidneys."

"Yes."

"What type of infection?"

"It was a bacterial infection of her kidneys."

"How is that treated?"

"It was treated with antibiotics."

"When Julie was discharged from the hospital, was she given antibiotics to take for that condition?"

"Yes, she was."

"Doctor, if Julie Grace were to die with this infection still forcing through her, would there be evidence of it in her kidneys?"

"Yes, there would be."

"Objection," responded Mr. Breen. "Outside the field of expertise."

"Overruled," said Judge Gaughan. "Again, I'll allow you wide latitude on cross examination and subject to a motion to strike. Okay. All right. The answer will stand."

Mr. Groth continued, "Doctor, after May 20th, Julie Grace was no longer a patient of yours, is that correct?"

"That's correct."

"And I'm going to show you what has been marked as People's Exhibit number 2. See if you can identify that."

"Yes, I can."

"What is that?"

"This is a picture of Julie Grace after death."

"Now Sir, the circled area around her eye, can you tell us what that is?"

"Yes, that's an ecchymosis, periorbital ecchymosis."

"Objection, Judge, foundation," responded Mr. Breen.

"What does that mean?" asked Mr. Groth.

"I don't understand what you mean, foundation," replied Judge Gaughan.

"He's looking at a photograph," said Mr. Breen. "Is there no showing he's able to render an opinion based solely on the testimony?"

"He's certainly testifying to his opinion and that's what cross examination is for, Mr. Breen. All right. Go ahead," instructed the judge. "Overruled."

Dr. Footy answered, "It means the area is purple."

Mr. Groth asked the witness, "Okay. Have you seen that type of injury when you were working in emergency rooms?"

"Yes, I did."

"And based on your experience in the emergency room, based on your training and your education, what do you think caused that injury?"

"It was caused by a direct blow to the eye socket."

"Why do you think that?"

"This is what happens when you hit the eye socket."

"There is another injury on top of it, is that correct?"

"Yes."

"Or above it, I should say."

"Yes."

"You think those are one and the same injury?"

Judge Gaughan commented, "When you ask whether the doctor thinks, that's not asking the doctor whether he has an opinion."

Mr. Groth rephrased his question. "Do you have an opinion as to whether the bruising that is above the eye is a separate injury from this one?"

"Yes, I do."

Mr. Pugh exclaimed, "Objection, Your Honor."

"Overruled," said Judge Gaughan.

"Thank you," said Mr. Groth. "Sir, on April 7th, excuse me, April 10th, I believe. Let me back up. The course of treatment for Julie Grace that January began on April 7th at Northwestern Memorial. Did that end with her being discharged?"

"Yes, it did."

"Now prior to her discharge, did you have an opportunity to visit with her?"

"Yes, I did."

"Describe for the court, if you could, what her physical condition was, based on your observations of her."

"At which point in time?"

"When she was discharged."

"When she was discharged she was, her mental status was alert and she was oriented, which was a difference from when she had come into the hospital. Her body habitus was abnormal. She was shrunken muscle mass in her extremities, both arms and legs. She was bloated with a protuberant abdomen and a puffy face."

"Now when you say she had shrunken muscle mass, what does that mean in relation to what her physical strength would be?"

"She would not be very strong."

"She would be weak."

"She would be weak."

"Based on her condition at that point, would she be able to harm anybody?"

Judge Gaughan asked Mr. Groth, "You actually think that he's qualified to render an opinion on that? There are so many options with harming somebody."

"I'll withdraw the question," replied Mr. Groth.

"Thank you," said the judge.

"Judge, I have nothing further," stated Mr. Groth.

"Cross examination." Judge Gaughan instructed Mr. Breen.

"Thank you, Your Honor," replied Mr. Breen. He then asked the witness, "Doctor, when did you first see Julie Grace?"

"Objection, relevance," exclaimed Mr. Groth.

Mr. Breen rephrased the question by asking the witness, "When did you first begin to treat Julie Grace?"

"Objection to relevance," responded Mr. Groth.

Judge Gaughan replied, "Well, if he can't cross examine on what the doctor had stated, I'll strike the doctor's testimony."

"If we could be heard at side bar?" asked Mr. Groth.

"No," answered the judge. "Say it right now. No secrets here. Go ahead. What is the basis of your objection?"

Mr. Groth answered, "The doctor began treating Julie Grace back in 1987. There is no relevance to what her condition was from 2000. We confined our direct to 2002, 2001."

The judge replied, "I'll allow as I told Mr. Breen. I allowed you some latitude that I would give him latitude on cross examination, so go ahead."

Mr. Breen addressed the witness, "When did you begin to treat her?"

"About 1987."

"When did she begin to show the physical and emotional signs of alcoholism?"

"In about the mid to late 90's."

"So, the mid to late 1990's she was doing physical harm to herself by drinking, correct?"

"Yes."

"In fact, in 2001, when you treated her, you were diagnosing her as a chronic alcoholic, were you not?"

"That's correct."

"With major liver damage, were you not?"

"That's correct."

"And in 2001, did you know that George Thompson hadn't even been in her life prior to that?"

"I'm unfamiliar until I came in today with the name George Thompson."

"Let's talk about your familiarity, Sir. In 2001, she was a full fledged chronic alcoholic, correct?"

"Yes."

"Did you ever at any time during the course of her alcoholism ever seek to commit her?"

"By committing her, are you asking me to have her hospitalized against her will?"

"Yes."

"No, I did not."

"She was killing herself by drinking, was she not?"

"Yes, she was."

"And one of the criteria for a commitment is, as you are well aware, is to commit someone because they are a danger to themselves, correct?"

"Yes."

"She was a full fledge danger to herself, was she not?"

"Yes."

"And you and Northwestern Hospital never sought a commitment proceeding?"

"No, it's not correct."

"Did you attempt to commit her; did you seek a commitment proceeding?"

"During one hospitalization, we initiated committing her involuntarily and then she agreed to be hospitalized."

"Is that anywhere in any notes or reports that you have received?"

"I think so."

"All right. When was that?"

"I would have to go through the notes and look it up."

"Do you have any summary in front of you or anything?"

"It's in one of these."

"Please take a look at it."

After a short pause, Mr. Breen continued, "There is a suggestion of the date you can look at, Doctor. Did you find it on your own?"

"Yes," answered Dr. Footy.

"Okay, and is the date March 10th, 2002, or is it earlier in 2001 that she went to Lake Shore?"

"It was at one of the hospitalizations."

"Well, she went twice, correct?"

"I remember one."

"And what year and what month was that? In fact, I believe the date that was suggested was in error. I believe it was in March of 2001 that she first went to Lake Shore. Is that what your notes reflect?"

"I don't have that. I do have a note from March of 2002."

"I ask these be marked. I'm going to show you Defendant's Exhibit number 6 for identification. Sir, does this reflect an admission to Lake Shore Hospital in March of 2001, of your patient Julie Grace?"

"Yes, it does."

"And is that when you recommended to her that she go to Lake Shore Hospital or be committed?"

"I don't remember this date. I remember the other date."

"Well, did you? What was the other date?"

"It was in her admission of March 10th, 2002."

"All right. Did she go to Lake Shore Hospital, do you know?"

"I believe so, yes."

"Did she come out?"

"Yes."

"Did she continue to drink?"

"Yes."

"Did she continue to show the symptoms and diagnosis of chronic alcoholism?"

"Yes."

"Did you at any time during that period of time following Lake Shore Hospital in March of 2002, did you ever attempt to involuntarily commit her?"

"Not after 2002, no."

"Yet she continued to show the same problems, dehydration, ethanol abuse, correct?"

"Yes."

"Sir, you have rendered various opinions today. Are those based in part on the medical records and in part on your personal observations?"

"Yes."

"Have you ever written a report that summarizes the testimony that you were going to give today relative to your opinion?"

"No."

"When was the first time you were asked your opinion that you shared with the court today?"

"I don't remember the exact date. I met with or spoke with Mr. Groth in, I believe, it would have been the autumn probably of the year Julie died."

"The year she died."

"I think so."

"Was he taking notes?"

"You know, I don't remember."

"When did you next opine as you have today?"

"I remember speaking to Mr. Groth by telephone on two occasions. The most recent one was to arrange this court date so they would have been in the last six months."

"Did you give your opinion on that telephone call?"

"At some point, yes."

"Now these two occasions that you gave an opinion similar to the one you've given now, you've indicated that you never wrote up any kind of a report regarding those opinions, correct?"

"Correct, I don't remember writing any reports."

"Now your opinion is based on your personal observations, your reviewing records and your personal observations. If I'm doubling up, I'm sorry. Is that right?"

"That's correct."

"Did you ever talk to George Thompson?"

"I don't remember."

"Did you ever send a social worker out to Julie Grace's home to talk to her and her boyfriend or boyfriends?"

"I never did it directly. I don't send social workers, but perhaps my nurse did. I don't remember."

"Well your notes don't refer to any kind of a recommendation that someone go speak to this couple, this boyfriend/girlfriend."

"I don't believe so."

"Your records that you reviewed today indicate that Julie Grace's behavior was violent and aggressive, isn't that right?"

"Objection to foundation," responded Mr. Groth. "Which one of the dates?"

"Sustained. Rephrase," directed Judge Gaughan.

Mr. Breen continued, "Do you have the July 10th records in front of you?"

"That would be July 10th, 2002?"

"Yes, Sir."

"Yes, I do."

"Do those records reflect she was violent and aggressive?"

"I don't see it as I'm looking through, but if you point me to it, I will be happy to turn to the page."

"Are you familiar with an incident where she struck a doctor on July 10th, 2002?"

"Mr. Breen, the doctor asked if you'd point that out to him," commented Judge Gaughan.

"I'm just asking him, generally, right now," said Mr. Breen. "I'm not trying to play games with him."

"I know that," said the judge. "But I'm certainly going to keep it on the record. You are a gentleman and outstanding lawyer. Go ahead."

The witness spoke up and said, "I do see where she was put in restraints."

"What does it say about that?" asked Mr. Breen.

"On the page I'm reading, it just said she's put in four point restraints."

"Why would somebody be put in four point restraints?"

"Generally because the person would be violent."

"Point of clarification, Doctor, what are four point restraints?" asked the judge.

"All four extremities would be restrained so you would tie down both hands and both feet," answered Dr. Footy.

"Thank you," replied Judge Gaughan. "Either side is allowed to ask questions concerning the point of clarification. Go ahead."

"I found it, Judge, the specific part I was referring to. I'll mark this as Defendant's Exhibit number 7," said Mr. Breen. He continued by saying, "Let me show you this, Sir, and see if this is in your July 20th, 02 packet. I'm showing you what I marked as Defendant's Exhibit number 7 for identification. Can you identify that piece of paper? It was in the back of my packet, Doctor; maybe in the back of your packet."

"Yes, I can."

"Now would you please relate to the court what, if anything, those records reflect regarding her aggressive conduct in the emergency room? Sir, does it reflect her behavior in the emergency room as it relates to being violent or aggressive?"

"Yes, it states that patient hit MD and the reason for restraints is checked off violent or aggressive behavior."

"Now, was she being the victim of domestic abuse there in the emergency room?"

"No."

"You did know her to be aggressive and violent."

"No."

"Had you ever been with her when she was intoxicated, drunk, inebriated?"

"Only in the emergency room or in the hospital, yes."

"In the emergency room, at least on one occasion when she was inebriated she was aggressive, correct?"

"Correct."

"All right. Now, Sir, if I understand you correctly, your opinion regarding domestic abuse is based on hearing Julie Grace's version of events, correct?"

"That's correct."

"You never did any kind of independent investigation to find out what Julie Grace, what actually occurred, correct?"

"Correct."

"You never found out, you never did any testing to determine whether or not she was aggressive or violent when she was drinking, correct?"

"Correct."

"Now you did see in these records did you not, the phrase mutually abusive? Did you see that?"

"I can't remember but if you point to it, I'll look it up," said Dr. Footy.

"Are you familiar with the term, mutually abusive relationship?"

"Yes."

"What is that?"

"That would mean, I used it myself, that would mean that two people in a relationship were both abusive to each other."

"And possibly violent to each other."

"Yes."

"Did you do anything, Sir, to investigate whether or not this is one of those mutually abusive relationships? During your treating of Julie Grace, did you do anything beyond listening to her version of the events that may have caused her injuries?"

"No, I did not."

"Did you, Sir, in rendering or as a treating physician review her Lake Shore reports regarding her admission to Lake Shore or her, you know, the treatment that she received at Lake Shore?"

"I don't remember, no."

"Well you indicated to us that you had told her, I believe, that you were going to involuntarily commit her and she came back with, I'll go in voluntarily, correct?"

"That's correct."

"Okay. Did you do anything to incorporate the Lake Shore records into the Northwestern records so you could review them as her treating physician?"

"No."

"Would you agree, Sir, that the records and treatment that she received at Lake Shore Hospital would be beneficial to someone who wanted to render an opinion whether or not there was a domestic abusive relationship?"

"Objection to foundation, Judge," responded Mr. Groth.

Judge Gaughan asked the witness, "Doctor, do you understand the question?"

"I think so," answered Dr. Footy.

"Also, going to object to relevance, Judge," said Mr. Groth. "The Lake Shore records he's talking about predate the relationship with this defendant. This is where they met, the second intake or second treatment trip to Lake Shore. So as far as the abusive relationship goes, it's irrelevant."

"When was the first admission into Lake Shore? Was that 2001?" asked Judge Gaughan.

"Right," answered Mr. Groth.

"I have October 11, 2001, Your Honor," interjected Mr. Breen.

"Overruled," stated the judge. "The doctor testified that he's been treating Julie before that time. All right, go ahead. You can ask the question."

Addressing the witness, the judge continued, "Doctor, you don't have to think whether you understand the question or not. If you have any doubt, make the lawyers explain it to you."

"Thank you," replied Dr. Footy.

Mr. Breen asked the witness, "Do you remember the question?"

"No, I don't."

"I'll try it again. You rendered an opinion regarding Julie Grace, correct?"

"Yes."

"Okay. As a purported expert in that field, do you think that it would be beneficial for you to have reviewed the 2001 treatment she received at Lake Shore and/or the 2002 treatment she received at Lake Shore?"

"If I could have reviewed the record, yes, I think that would be useful."

"All right. As you indicated before, that you told her that she was going to be committed if she didn't go into treatment or she voluntarily went into treatment. Did you ask her for those records at any point in time to see how seriously she had taken her treatment?"

"I don't believe so."

"Now Sir, you made a distinction for the benefit of us, the difference between tremors and seizures, correct?"

"Yes."

"Without going through the differences again, where did you learn the difference between tremors and seizures, the University of Chicago Med School?"

"I don't think I can pin down the specific place I learned one thing."

"It would have been during your medical education, correct?"

"My education doesn't stop, so somewhere along there, yes."

"Doctor, a little bit of your undergraduate, it would have been in medical school?" asked Judge Gaughan.

"Well I take continuing education courses and have an interest in neurological disorders," replied Dr. Footy. "I may have learned more subsequent to my training. Not trying to be cute."

Mr. Pugh followed up by saying, "You're not and I'm not trying to be cute when I say something, not something they teach in iron worker's school, correct?"

"Correct," answered the witness.

Mr. Breen continued his questioning. "To tap into your continuing medical education, what are the D.T's as we, as I've used the expression, if you know what I mean?"

"DT's is short for delirium tremens which is a syndrome that's caused by alcohol withdrawal and it consists of tremors, neurological autonomic nervous system instability and hallucinations."

"If we were to see someone going through DT's, what would we see that person do?"

"Objection," interrupted Mr. Groth.

"Basis?" asked Judge Gaughan.

"Withdraw, Judge," said Mr. Groth.

Mr. Breen rephrased the questions and asked the witness, "Physically, what might we see symptomatically?"

"It depends on the level of consciousness of the person. The person would be tremulous, the blood"

"What does that mean?"

"Would be shaky."

"Okay."

"The blood pressure and pulse would be up and down irregularly, the person would be sweating, the person would be disoriented to some degree to where he or she was, and may be actively hallucinating, usually with visual hallucinations, meaning seeing things that aren't there."

"Might a person be vomiting?"

"Yes."

"Might a person be heaving?"

"Yes."

"Doctor, just a point of clarification," commented the judge. "Would the DT's, as stated by Mr. Breen, be caused by the toxicity of alcohol or the withdrawal from alcohol?"

"It's the withdrawals," answered the witness.

"So, it won't be a toxin. Cells in the body would be dependent on alcohol," stated Judge Gaughan.

"That's correct. You would be correct."

Mr. Breen asked Dr. Footy, "Doctor, is your opinion based in part on your review of March 10th, 2003, Northwestern records?"

"Yes."

"I would like to call your attention to the last, the second half of those reports, to a psychological social case formulation, page 13, could you find that for me, please? Did you find that?"

"Yes, I have it."

"Okay, Sir, I'm referring to the records, Judge, Defendant's Exhibit number 3 for identification which would show up on cross examination of the State's witness yesterday, the forensic pathologist. Doctor, the opinion that you had given us today regarding domestic abuse, is the following statement contrary to the opinion you had given today; that being that Julie Grace was in a mutually abusive relationship with a boyfriend?"

"No, that would not be contradictory."

"Does the fact that Julie Grace broke into her boyfriend's apartment and was arrested, would that be contrary to your opinion today?"

"No."

"What is the difference between a mutually abusive relationship and a domestic abuse relationship or that she suffered from domestic abuse? What is the difference between those two things?"

"Domestic abuse refers to a situation which there is violence that is centered in the home or in the family or in close relationships. A mutually aggressive relationship would not necessarily be confined to a domestic relationship."

"I see. So a domestic abuse relationship is not necessarily the impetus to that, is not necessarily one person. It could be two people, correct?"

"Correct."

"The note that you referred to in rendering your opinion indicates that the type of relationship she was in was one where both parties were aggressive and violent, isn't that right?"

Mr. Groth interrupted, "Object to the form of the question, Judge."

"Doctor, do you understand the question?" asked Judge Gaughan.

"Yes, but I don't see the part here," answered the witness.

"Mine was highlighted," said Mr. Breen. It's easy for me. Let me show it to you."

"Thank you for helping me," said Dr. Footy. "Now I forgot your question."

"I may ask it to be read back," replied Mr. Breen.

"Rephrase or repeat," instructed the judge.

Mr. Breen rephrased the question. "The phrase, mutually abusive relationship, suggests that it may be a two party problem. In other words, both people are being aggressive or violent."

"Yes."

"Okay. I have nothing further," said Mr. Breen. "Thank you, Doctor."

"Redirect?" the judge asked Mr. Groth.

"Based on Julie Grace's records for January of 01 and February of 01, there is no complaint there about domestic abuse, is that correct?" Mr. Groth asked the witness.

"That's correct," answered Dr. Footy.

"And it isn't until after she's treated and sent to Lake Shore Hospital in

March of 02 that the words, domestic abuse, begin appearing on her medical records, is that correct?"

"That is correct."

"Just so we're clear on the whole tremors versus seizure issue, tremors are often referred to as the shakes, right?"

"Yes."

"Now a person's hands are shaking or if their extremities are shaking, that's not going to thrust them out of a chair or anything, is that correct?"

"That is correct."

"And a seizure would be something different. A seizure would be the storm you were talking about in the brain which would cause a person to have a seizure, right?"

"Correct. I don't have any other way to describe it better than that."

"What are the ways a person acts when they're having a seizure? What are the actions they have?"

"It's very broad. It, being a one extreme, the person can sit catatonic and simply not be interactive with the environment. At the other extreme, there can be jerking activity of all the muscles in the body with loss of consciousness and loss of control of normal functions."

"Now based on your review of Julie Grace's records, from January to April, excuse me, January 21, 01 to April 7, 03, she had never exhibited seizure activity as far as her medical records are concerned, is that correct?"

"That's correct."

"In fact, when you spoke to the police about this case, you told them she had no history of seizures, is that correct?"

"That is correct."

"Up until her medical records of April 7th, 03, when you last saw her alive, she had no history of seizures, is that correct?"

"That is correct."

"Thank you, thank you for letting me clarify that."

Mr. Groth had no more questions for the witness. The judge asked the defense if they wanted to recross-exam the witness.

"Doctor," you don't have an opinion of what may have ailed her between April 7th, 03 and May 20th, 03, correct?" asked Mr. Breen.

"To be more precise, between the day she was discharged and the day she died," answered the witness.

"What day was she discharged? He just asked you about that. I thought it was April 7th."

"That was when she was admitted."

"When was she discharged?"

"I think April 12th."

"So you did not see her between April 12th and May 17, 2003, correct?"

"That is correct."

"I have nothing further, thank you," concluded Mr. Breen.

"Doctor, thank you very much," said Judge Gaughan. We appreciate your time."

Dr. Footy stepped down, and the judge called a short recess and instructed the attorneys to meet with him in his chambers.

While we sat waiting for the judge and the attorneys to return to the courtroom, I could only hope that the judge had thoroughly analyzed Dr. Footy's testimony and had not been swayed by Mr. Breen's twisting of the facts. Dr. Footy made it very clear that Julie was an alcoholic, but she did not have any seizures and she did not die of alcoholism; but based on Mr. Breen's cross-examination of Dr. Footy, I wasn't convinced Judge Gaughan would look at it that way.

After the recess, court reconvened, and Mr. Groth called his next witness, Edward Heerdt. Mr. Heerdt was sworn in and seated himself in the witness stand. He stated and spelled his name and gave his star number.

Mr. Groth began the direct examination of the witness.

"How long have you been a Chicago Police Detective?"

"I have been a detective for four years."

"And how long have you been a member of the Chicago Police Department?"

"Approximately ten years."

"Sir, I would like to draw your attention, if I could, to May 20th, 2003 approximately 4:00, excuse me, 4:15 in the morning. Were you working the midnight shift at that time?"

"Yes, I was."

"Did you have a partner?"

"Yes, I did."

"Who was that?"

"Detective Neal Francis."

"Now, as part of your duties, were you assigned to assist in the investigation of the homicide of Julie Grace?"

"Yes, I was."

"As part of that investigation, did you have contact with anyone that you now see in this courtroom?"

"Yes, I did."

"Identify that person, please?"

"Yes, it's the gentleman to the right of Counsel with the tan DOC uniform, George Thompson."

"Sir, can you describe for the court how it was, what your first contact with the defendant was about?"

"My first contact that day?" questioned the witness.

"At 6:17 in the morning."

"He was in custody at the Area Three Violent Crimes Office and my partner and me went in and introduced ourselves to him."

"Did you advise him of anything?"

"Yes, I did. I advised him of his Miranda warnings per my Fraternal Order of Police Organizer book."

"Did the defendant indicate he understood those warnings?"

"Yes, he did."

"Did he agree to speak with you?"

"Yes, he did."

"Describe for the court, please, what it was he told you at 6:17 in the morning at Area 3 police headquarters on May 20th, 2003."

"Mr. Thompson had described to us that he had been, he was the boyfriend of Miss Julie Grace and that he had been living with her at her condominium for approximately one year. He also stated that during his courtship with her there were domestic instances in the past, and that he had been, he had knowledge of an order of protection that was against him naming him as the respondent and Julie Grace as the Petitioner. He added that during the weekend of the incident, he stated that Miss Grace had been drinking a lot and as he referred to it, had gone on a drunken bender."

"Did he indicate to you what Miss Grace going on a drunken bender as he called it, required him to do?"

"It required him, specifically, to help lift her up off the ground at times when she fell, and he went so far as to describe that that was the cause of the bruises that were under her arms."

"Did he indicate anything else about what he did that weekend with Julie Grace?"

"Well, he stated that during these drinking incidents that Miss Grace was jumping around wildly during the weekend and that she had fallen down on different occasions, once off a lazy boy chair and hitting a table, once falling off the toilet after using the restroom facility and hitting her head, possibly on the shower adjacent to the toilet."

"Did he indicate if, at any time during the weekend, he tried to reach out to anybody else?"

"Yes, he did."

"What did he tell you?"

"He stated that he tried to call Miss Julie Starsiak to get assistance in getting Julie Grace to go to the hospital to receive treatment. Miss Starsiak, as Mr. Thompson related, indicated that she would not come out to assist him in that and had suggested to him that he dial 911 and leave the premises if he were concerned about issues of the order of protection or the appearance that a domestic violence incident had occurred."

"And did he indicate to you whether or not he had any fears about that?"

"Yes, he did."

"What did he tell you?"

"He said that he was concerned exactly about that, giving the appearance that a domestic had occurred and again reiterating his knowledge that there was an order of protection against him as the respondent and Julie Grace as the Petitioner."

"Did he indicate to you what had happened shortly before he called 911 that day?"

"Yes. He stated that Miss Grace had a vomiting spell and that he had attempted to perform CPR on her."

"And did he indicate what he was doing about Miss Grace's physical care or keeping her clean?"

"He had indicated that he spent a lot of time cleaning up the vomit and other bodily fluids involved in Miss Grace's ailments throughout the weekend and that he had helped to change her clothes numerous times and that was the explanation for the discovery of the nude Julie Grace body upon arrival of CFD and CFD personnel."

"Did he indicate any other types of things that had occurred between himself and Julie Grace that weekend, specifically, what he had done for her prior to the arrival of the fire personnel?"

"He stated that he attempted to perform CPR, that her lips were turning blue and she was in a very sickly condition and did his best to perform CPR."

"Did he indicate to you why it was that the police or fire department wasn't called sooner in this case?"

"He stated that Miss Grace in the past, has been in this condition before and he had hoped that she would, and she had pulled out of it and go back to sobriety and normalcy. He was hoping it would be the same instance this time."

"Did he mention anything about the order of protection at this time?"

"That he was afraid that if the police were to arrive, he's on the scene, his knowledge of an order of protection, he could be arrested for that violation."

"And you talked about how the defendant related to you that Miss Grace was in a lazy boy on either Saturday or Sunday. Did he indicate any type of unusual activity she had at that point?"

"He stated that she may have what he believed, to be a possible seizure and that she was in the lazy boy chair and had fallen down on a table nearby causing a loud noise which he assisted in helping to pick her up, and he was not certain what the injuries were if any, but she had sustained that type of a fall."

"Did you ask him about the black eye that Julie Grace had?"

"Yes, I did."

"What did he tell you about that?"

"That's when Mr. Thompson related that Miss Grace had fallen off the toilet after using the toilet and struck her head causing that injury, and he believed it, as noted in my general progress report note, that he believed that it may have been the shower portion of the bathroom area that she struck her eye on causing that injury."

"After that statement from the defendant regarding the eye injury, did you have any further contact with him at that time?"

"At that time, no."

"Okay. Now 9:00 in the morning on the 20th, did you again interview him after advising him of his Miranda warnings?"

"Yes, I did."

"Did you confront him with anything at that point?"

"I confronted him with information I had received from Ruth Grace, Julie Grace's mother, who I had spoken to on the telephone. And unfortunately, I was unable to notify her in person and I had to notify her of the circumstances over the telephone which I'm sorry I had to do that way, but I did receive information from her of a phone call that she had attempted to make during this span of incident which had occurred where she attempted to call her daughter."

"Okay. And did you confront Mr. Thompson with what Ruth Grace had told you about the phone calls she had made about trying to contact her daughter?"

"Yes."

"What did Mr. Thompson say?"

"He acknowledged that phone calls had been made by Ruth Grace and he stated that it was actually Ruth Grace who had hung up on him and not him hanging up on her and using cursive language as Ms. Ruth Grace had indicated to me."

"Thank you," said Mr. Groth. "I tender the witness."

"Sir, what time of the day on May 20th did you first see George Thompson?" asked Mr. Breen.

"I first saw him when I entered the interview room at 0617 hours and introduced myself to him."

"On what day?"

"On I believe, that was May 20th."

"Okay. May 20th. And that's military hours you just gave me. What time in a lay person's time?"

"That would be 6:17 in the AM."

"Okay. And where was he at that time?"

"He was in one of the interview rooms in the Area Three Violent Crimes office."

"And what day of the week, Sir, was Thursday; what was that date?"

"You can go either way. Which week are we talking about?" asked Judge Gaughan.

"The week before that, prior to May 20th," answered Mr. Breen.

"I would have to consult a calendar to know that," replied Detective Heerdt.

"What day of the week was May 20th?"

"I believe it was the Tuesday that he was in custody."

"And then May 17th, what day was that?"

"That mathematically, that would be the Thursday prior to."

"At the time you were talking to him, did you know that the relevant period of time that he was talking about"

Mr. Groth interrupted, "I'm going to object, Judge."

"I'm sorry, no, the thing is what?" asked Judge Gaughan.

"May 20th," answered Mr. Groth.

"Right, the deduction wasn't correct," said the judge. "If May 20th is Tuesday, May 17th is certainly not Thursday."

"It's not my question," said Mr. Breen. "You did know the dates of the week between May 17th and May 20th when you were talking to him."

"Specifically, how do you mean, did I know?"

"Was there not some confusion during your interview of him as to the day and the time that Julie Grace got injured?"

"First of all, we spoke in terms of days of the week, we didn't use, we didn't speak of dates, we spoke of days, refer to Friday, Saturday or Sunday, not putting a numeric date on it."

"What do you say happened Friday night?"

"He did not say in specific terms, except one time he used a general, either Saturday or Sunday night, in speaking of one of the instances that I already testified."

"What he did say happened Saturday and Saturday night."

"Saturday night, either Saturday or Sunday night was the night when he spoke of her having, what he believed was a seizure, and her being in the Lazy Boy chair and falling down and hitting the table causing some type of injury."

"What day did he tell you that occurred?"

"As my report indicates, he called it either Saturday or Sunday. He did not specifically know which one."

"Okay. And what happened on Monday?"

"Monday, there is no specific mention of any Monday activity in my report."

"Did you ask him about Monday?"

"Monday, no, that I recall specifically, no."

"So, you didn't even ask him about a whole day between May 17th and 20th?"

"I left my interview very open ended to Mr. Thompson and allowed him to tell me the information."

"And what time did that interview conclude?"

"I didn't specifically document the exact time that it ended. And I couldn't even give you an approximate amount of time that that interview took."

"When did you talk to Mrs. Grace in Florida?"

"If I could refer to my detective sup I do have the time specifically documented that I spoke to her."

"Was it 7:40 in the morning?"

"That sounds correct."

"Okay. And you told Miss Grace at that time that there was a death investigation, correct?"

"Yes."

"You didn't tell her it was a murder investigation, did you?"

"No, I did not."

"As a matter of fact, it continued to be a death investigation until the State's Attorney's Office directed your area to charge him with first degree murder, isn't that right?"

"I was not present at that point in time when the state's attorney approved the charges, but that's the protocol."

"Were you ever present for any other interviews of George Thompson after the interview you had with him on May 20th, in the morning hours?"

"The two separate interviews I had were the only contact I had during any investigation with Mr. Thompson until the point I'm sitting here right now."

"Okay. He did tell you, Sir, that Julie Grace had been taken to the hospital on numerous occasions before that."

"I don't recall that, no."

"Did he tell you that Julie Grace had been violent on earlier occasions?"

"I don't specifically recall violence being mentioned, no."

"But there was, he did tell you, did he not, about fights that they were having?"

"He stated that there were several times of drunkenness and he alluded to domestic disputes."

"And he told you about an order of protection, or you asked him about it, which was it?"

"I don't recall whether I asked or he volunteered it, but it was mentioned by him."

"So you knew that there was a domestic case somewhere in the system, correct?"

"My assumption, yes."

"Did you ask him at all about his relationship with Julie?"

"In specifically what?"

"Where they met?"

"Yes, that they had met in rehabilitation program they were going to."

"Did you ask him about Julie's behavior after they met in the treatment facility?"

"No, I did not."

"But your conversation was kind of brief, correct?"

"It's fair to say, yes."

"What was the purpose of your conversation?"

"The purpose of my conversation was to ascertain Mr. Thompson's account of what had occurred and how these injuries had occurred to Miss Julie Grace."

"Did you show him any pictures, Detective?"

"I do not believe I did."

"Did he tell you, Sir, Julie had gone into convulsions minutes prior to calling 911?"

"Yes, he did."

"And he had told you that she had similar episodes in the past but that she had always come out of it, isn't that right?"

"That's correct."

"And that that's why he didn't call 911 earlier, correct?"

"That's correct."

"I have nothing further; thank you, Sir," concluded Mr. Breen.

"Redirect?" the judge asked Mr. Groth.

Mr. Groth asked, "That wasn't the only reason he gave for not wanting to call the police or the fire department, correct?"

"Correct," answered Detective Heerdt.

"What were the other reasons?"

"His concern of the order of protection and his presence in Miss Grace's condo."

"Thank you," replied Mr. Groth. "Judge, I have nothing further."

"Any recourse?" the judge asked the defense.

Mr. Breen addressed the witness and asked, "Did you discuss the amendments to the protection order that being that he was allowed to live there?"

"No, I didn't know any existed," answered Detective Heerdt.

"You didn't know what?"

"I did not know there were any amendments that existed. I only know the information that Mr. Thompson told me."

"Did you ask him why are you living there if there is a protection order?"

"I don't specifically recall asking that question, no."

"I have nothing further. Thanks Detective."

"Thank you, Detective. You may step down," instructed the judge.

Mr. Groth was asked to call his next witness, Nick D'Angelo. The witness came forward and was sworn in.

"Sir, do you have a profession?" asked Mr. Groth.

"Yes, I'm a prosecutor."

"Are you licensed to practice law in the State of Illinois?"

"I am."

"How long have you been so licensed?"

"Approximately 14 years."

"What is your current assignment?"

"I'm in the Felony Trial Division assigned to the 6th District which is Markham."

"Back in May of 2003, did you have a different assignment?"

"Yes, I did."

"And what was that assignment?"

"I was assigned to the Felony Review Unit working here out of the building at 26th and California."

"Sir, I would like to draw your attention to the late evening hours of May 20th going into the early evening hours of May 21st, 2003. Were you working felony review at that time?"

"Yes, I was."

"And day shift or night shift?"

"I was working the night shift, would have been the 5 PM to 5 AM shift."

"And did you get an assignment regarding the investigation of a homicide of Julie Grace?"

"Yes, I did."

"Did you go anywhere when you got that assignment?"

"Yes, I went to Area Three Violent Crimes located at Belmont and Western."

"About what time did you get there? Do you know?"

"I got there shortly before midnight."

"Did you talk to anybody?"

"Yes, I did. I talked to the detectives that were assigned to the case: Detective Villardita, Detective Redmond and Detective Thesan."

"Did you get an update about this case?"

"Yes, I did. I spoke to them about the case and reviewed some documents."

"And did you speak to anybody else about this case?"

"Eventually I spoke to the suspect, yes."

"Do you see him in court?"

"Yes, I do. He's sitting right here in front of me in the brown DOC."

"When you spoke to him, how did you introduce yourself?"

"Detective Thesan introduced me as the assistant state's attorney and I introduced myself as a prosecutor."

"Did he indicate he understood?"

"I asked him if he knew what a prosecutor was and he told me that he did."

"Did you advise him of anything else?"

"I told him that I was a lawyer but not his lawyer and I asked him if he wanted to talk to me and before I could talk with him, I gave him what are commonly referred to as Miranda rights."

"And how did you do that?"

"I did that by memory."

"What did you advise him of?"

"I told him that he probably had heard this thousands of times on TV, but I was going to tell him again. And I asked him if he understood everything I was saying to let me know. I told him that he had a right to remain silent and that if he didn't remain silent anything he told me could be used against him. He had a right to have an attorney present and if he couldn't afford an attorney one could be appointed for him."

"And did he agree to speak to you?"

"I asked him if he understood those rights and he said that he did. I asked him if he wanted to talk with me and he said he did."

"Did you talk to him about the events of May 17th, 2003, up to the events of May 20th, 2003?"

"Yes, I did."

"And did you talk to him about memorializing that statement?"

"Yes. I talked to him for about an hour and after our conversation I gave him some options. I asked him if he wanted his statement videotaped and he told me that he did. I told him there was some paperwork I needed to prepare and I would call the videographer."

"Let me back up a minute. I apologize. At some point, did you speak to Mr. Thompson alone, outside the presence of any detectives?"

"Yes, I did."

"What did you ask him about then?"

"During that time when we were alone I asked him how he had been treated since he had been at the area."

"Did he have any complaints?"

"No, he didn't."

"Now the statement that he gave you, was it memorialized in some way?"

"Yes, it was. After he told me that he wanted, he agreed to have his statement videotaped, I told him there was some paperwork I needed to prepare and forms for him to sign and I called for a videographer from our office to come to the area."

"Okay."

"Then once the videographer arrived, he set up the equipment and we had the defendant, his statement videotaped."

"You mentioned a consent form for videotaping, is that correct?"

"Yes."

"Did anybody sign that?"

"Yes."

"Who did?"

"The defendant signed it. I signed it."

"Okay. Did the detective sign it?"

"Yes, he did."

"And I'm going to show you, did you use any other documents in the taking of the statement?"

"There was basically, some introductory remarks where, when you view the videotape, know who the defendant is, the person making the statement, where we're at, what it's about and I told him I filled in some blanks on a form with material on it and there was some photographs that I used with the defendant and had him mark in our conversation previous and then I used those as exhibits during the statement itself."

"I'm going to show you what has been marked as group Exhibit number 93 and ask you to take a look at these items and see if you recognize them."

"Yes. This is the videotaped consent form that I filled out and had the defendant sign. I signed. The detective signed on May 21ˢᵗ, 2003. The next, there is an opening remark for the videotaped statement that I referred to and then the closing remarks and also some Miranda rights that go along with the statement process that I referred to and read from in the statement itself.

"Then the other parts of the group exhibits are two Polaroid photographs that I had shown Mr. Thompson, and during our conversation which he made some markings on, and that he signed on the front, and I put identification numbers, what they related to on the back. Then there are photos that I used, as well, during our conversation and interview which the defendant marked. One of them in an area, circling the area and the other one, just describing the area, and I had Mr. Thompson place his signature on the back of those and I used those in the videotape. And there are some notations how to track them. Then once they were all prepared and the statement was over I put them all in an envelope and took the envelope with me."

"These group Exhibit 93, is it in the same or substantially the same condition as it was on May 21ˢᵗ when you were done with the statement?"

"Yes, they are."

"Now I'm going to show you Exhibit number 91, see if you recognize what that is."

"Exhibit number 91 is a copy of the defendant's videotape statement."

"Have you had an opportunity to review Exhibit number 91 prior to testifying today?"

"Yes, I have."

"Does it truly and accurately depict the statement the defendant and you, the conversation the defendant had with you on May 21ˢᵗ, 2003?"

"Yes, it does."

"I'm going to show you, you did say you had reviewed People's Exhibit number 91, and it truly and accurately depicts the statement the defendant gave?"

"I have reviewed Exhibit number 91 on a previous occasion, and it does truly and accurately depict the statement that Mr. Thompson gave me on May 21ˢᵗ of 2003."

"I'm going to show you Exhibit number 92. What do you recognize that to be?"

"Exhibit number 92 is a transcript of the statement of the video on People's number 91."

"Does that truly and accurately transcribe what is contained on 91?"

"Yes, I have had an opportunity to read the transcript as well as watch the tape, and it does truly and accurately depict the statement that Mr. Thompson made to me on May 21st, 2003."

"With the court's permission, I seek to move into evidence People's Exhibits number 91 through 93, a copy of the transcript for Your Honor and one for the court reporter."

"Any objection?" asked Judge Gaughan.

"No, Your Honor," answered Mr. Breen.

"Okay," said the judge. "The identification marks on those exhibits will be stricken and they will be moved into evidence."

"Thank you," replied Mr. Groth. "With the court's permission, I'm going to publish the statement."

"Sure. Subject to cross examination," replied the judge.

Mr. Groth then played the tape. When I heard George's voice, it was obvious to me, just as it was in his 911 tape, that George was not remorseful for killing Julie. There was no emotion in his voice, and he sounded like someone without a conscience. Listening to his statements, I sat mortified and amazed and wondered why Julie ever allowed someone as evil and devious as George Thompson into her life.

After the tape ended, Mr. Groth asked Mr. D'Angelo, "Is that the statement the defendant gave to you on May 21st, 2003?"

"Yes, it is."

"Thank you."

"Cross examination?" asked Judge Gaughan.

"Thank you, Your Honor," answered Mr. Breen.

"Counselor, as of May 20th, 2003, how long had you been an attorney?" Mr. Breen asked the witness.

"Since a little over ten years."

"And that ten-year period, Sir, what did it consist of? What did you do as an attorney?"

"I was in private practice for a short period of time and handled general cases as well as criminal defense."

"And you tried cases in private practice, did you not?"

"Yes, I did."

"And when did you join the State's Attorney's Office, what year?"

"I believe I joined the State's Attorney's Office in 94."

"All right. So, from 94 to 2003, during that period of time you were an assistant state's attorney, correct?"

"Yes, Sir."

"You were assigned prior to being on felony review to a trial courtroom, were you not?"

"Yes, Sir."

"And you had tried multiple cases as a prosecutor, had you not?"

"Yes, Sir."

"On May 21st, 2003, at 3:24 in the morning, were you in a hurry to get through this statement?"

"No, Sir."

"Well, did somebody put some kind of a time limit on your statement you were going to take from George Thompson?"

"No, Sir."

"Why did the statement end in 14 and a half or 15 minutes?"

"The statement was over because that's the statement he had made to me."

Mr. Breen countered, "The statement was over when you decided it was over, isn't that right?"

"No, Sir."

"Wait a minute. You were asking the questions, correct?"

"Yes, I was."

"George Thompson wasn't asking the questions, correct?"

"No, he wasn't."

"The questioner, the interrogator was the one that determined to stop asking questions, isn't that right?"

"I stopped asking questions when we were done with the statement that he had already given me, yes."

"When you say you were done with the statement, you decided you were done with the statement."

"No Sir, the video is a memorialization of the statement that he had already given me. We were done covering that material. I stopped asking questions because there were no more questions to cover."

"There were no more questions, in your opinion, to ask."

"Based on the statement that he had already given me, no."

"So in a 15-minute period you covered what George Thompson, everything you wanted to cover, correct?"

"I covered everything that we went over in the previous statement that he had given me, yes, Sir."

"You could have asked him any question you wanted to, couldn't you have?"

"I was asking him questions on the video based on interviews that I had already conducted with him."

"You could have asked him any questions you wanted to during the interview of him or during the video, couldn't you have?"

"As it relates, I guess in the interview, of him I could have asked him anything germane to the crime that was being investigated. And on the video

I could have asked him any questions as it related to the interview that he had already given me, yes, Sir."

"So the answer to my question, Counselor, is yes, you could have asked him any question you wanted to relative to the death investigation, correct?"

"Yes, that's fair to say."

"Your own statement is entitled, let's see, what is it entitled, a fight investigation, excuse me, referred as regarding an investigation, parenthesis, fight with Julie Grace, correct?"

"Yes, that's correct."

"And you could have asked him any question in the pre-video or during the video regarding his relationship with Julie Grace and what occurred in the days before he called 911, isn't that correct?"

"Yes."

"And as a prosecutor and as a trial lawyer you know what a leading question is, don't you?"

"I do."

"And the first 4 pages of your statement, your video statement from George Thompson, are all leading questions, aren't they?"

"In the first 4 pages, I'm not sure, Counselor."

"Well why don't you take a look at the transcript? Have you identified it?"

"I have."

"Is it in front of you?"

"It's not."

"Have you reviewed it?"

"I have."

"Was this the first statement you ever took from a suspect?"

"No, it is not."

"Why don't you take a look at this, Sir, and look at the manner in which you asked the questions of George Thompson in the first 4 pages. On page 1 of this transcript you are identifying yourself, is that not correct?"

"Yes, Sir."

"And you asked him whether or not you have explained to him that you're a state's attorney. His answer is yes, isn't that correct?"

"Yes."

"Page 2 has the following answers of George Thompson. Yes. Correct. Yes. Correct. Correct. Yes. Correct. Yes. Sir, those are his answers, are they not?"

"Yes, Sir."

"On page 3, George's answers are, that is correct. Right. Most of it, yeah. Correct. Right. Yes. Correct. Those are his answers, isn't that right?"

"Yes, those are his answers."

"And you were asking him all leading questions attempting to summarize what you say, was your interview before the videotape was turned on, isn't that correct?"

"Yes, that's what that portion was for."

"Do you anywhere during this statement, ask him about what Julie Grace was like in the last year of his relationship with her?"

"No, I did not."

"Did you at any time ask George Thompson if she was violent and aggressive?"

"In this portion?"

"In this video statement."

"In the video statement, I did not."

"Did you at any time, ask George Thompson whether or not he ever filed a complaint against Julie Grace and got a protection order?"

"On the video, no I did not."

"Did you in the pre-interview?"

"In the pre-interview, he never indicated to me that he had an order of protection issued against her."

"Did you ask him?"

"I asked him about his relationship with her and he indicated to me, on several times, he had beaten her up before and she had an order of protection against him."

"So he only apparently mentioned his conduct towards her, is that it?"

"Yes."

"Did you ever ask him about her conduct towards him?"

"Well she was dead, Counsel."

"Did you hear my question?"

"I did."

"Would you answer my question?"

"He did not tell me that she ever had, that he had ever had any order of protection against her."

"Does George Thompson ever use, during the course of this video statement, the words jealousy or jealous?"

"He says that things were with her and other guys and stuff like that. And to clarify"

Mr. Breen interrupted the witness, "Excuse me. You did hear my question."

"Objection, the witness is answering the question," responded Mr. Groth.

"No, he's not," said Mr. Breen.

"It's not responsive. Mr. D'Angelo, answer the question," instructed the judge.

"He never uses the word jealous," replied the witness.

"Did you, Sir, take any notes of your pre-video interview?"

"No."

"You did not."

"I did not."

"During the course of the video, he indicated to you that she struck her head on the dresser, is that correct?"

"Yes."

"Let me show you what has been marked as group 93 and let me show you that photograph. Is there a photograph of a dresser in that photograph as well as the other photograph?"

"There appears to be a photograph of what may be a dresser next to the credenza that the television and VCR is on."

"That may be a dresser as opposed to a Hyundai."

"Objection," responded Mr. Groth.

"That is a dresser, is it not?" asked Mr. Breen.

"I wasn't in the bedroom, but it could be a dresser. I don't know what it is."

"How old are you?"

"44."

"In the 44 years you've been on God's green earth, have you seen dressers?"

"I have."

"Do you know what a dresser looks like?"

"I do."

"Does that photograph look like it's a photograph of a dresser?"

"Well, Sir, it's only a quarter of whatever the piece of furniture is."

"Okay. Let me ask you this. Assistant State's Attorney, did you ask him to circle in the photograph where Julie Grace struck her head after he pushed her?"

"I did not."

"You had these photographs with you, did you not?"

"I did."

"You had a purpose, did you not, Sir, when you were interviewing him, and that was to charge him with the murder case before you even heard his answers, isn't that true?"

"That's not true, Sir."

"Are you telling me you sat down with him during the pre-video interview, and during the video interview with an open mind looking at both sides of this fight?"

"Yes, Sir. I never approved charges, Sir."

"Are you telling us that you told the investigators, based on your investigation and your statement of George Thompson, that you would not approve first degree murder charges?"

"I left things for them to do, but in my opinion, Mr. Thompson should be charged with murder, based on what he told me, yes."

"So you did recommend first degree murder charges?"

"No, I gave the detectives a list of things to do, but if you're asking my opinion, my opinion is based on what he had told me. He should have been charged with first degree murder, yes, Sir."

"Actually, I didn't ask you what your opinion was. I asked you what you did. Did you direct and approve first degree murder charges against George Thompson?"

"No, Sir."

"Yes or no?"

"No, Sir."

"Who approved those charges?"

"Another assistant state's attorney did."

"Did you ever see him in the interview room with George Thompson?"

"No, Sir, I was there. Like I told you, I gave the detectives a list of things to accomplish."

"The photographs of Julie, these Polaroids, you had George circle certain bruises that appear on her body, correct?"

"Yes, I did."

"And on page 7 of the statement, line 10 through maybe 15, you're talking about those Polaroid photographs, I'm sorry, 7 through 15 you're talking about those Polaroid photographs, aren't you?"

"Yes, Sir."

"And you asked if there are some bruises that have been circled by you, is that right? Answer. Yes. And you signed the bottom of that. Answer. He indicated something. Question. The bruises that are on Julie's body, some of them came from the fight that happened Saturday night? Yeah, all of them, probably."

Mr. Breen continued, "Is he referring to the circled bruises or don't you know or, strike that. Do you know what he's referring to there?"

"I believe he's referring to all the bruises on her body."

"But you were talking to him about the circled bruises, were you not?"

"I talked to him about the circled bruises and then I asked him, generally, the question was the bruises that are on Julie's body. Some of them came from the fight that happened Saturday night. Answer. Yeah, all of them, probably."

"He's looking at the circled bruises on the photograph, is he not?"

"He was looking at the photograph."

"Sir, what did he tell you what happened on May 17th, 2003? What did he tell you happened on that day during his pre-interview or his videotape?"

"He told me that on May 17th, he was upset because she had called him and she was with another man and in his apartment and later came home with another man and that he had shooed him out of the apartment and sometime later he and Julie began to drink vodka and once they were drinking they had a fight about her having been involved with these other men and the fight became physical. It started in the bedroom where he slapped her somewhere between 10 and 20 times and he punched her five times; that he pushed her from behind into the dresser next to the bed and that she struck her head and fell to the ground and that's when the fight ended."

"How many times did Julie strike him during the incident on May 17th, Saturday?"

"He never told me that she struck him at all."

"Did you ever ask him?"

"I asked him what happened during the fight. He never told me that she hit him."

"Did you not notice injuries on Mr. Thompson?"

"I did not notice any serious injuries, no."

"I didn't ask you about serious. Did you notice any injuries on Mr. Thompson, yes or no? You may answer that."

"I noticed that he had two small scabs on one of his cheeks."

"Did you notice anything on his left arm?"

"No."

"Did you ask him about any injuries that you observed, the ones on his cheeks?"

"No, I did not."

"You didn't ask him how he got those."

"No. They weren't very significant. No, I did not."

"Let me show you what has been marked as People's Exhibit number 40 and 41 for identification. Sir, is 41 a photograph of George Thompson?"

"Yes, it is."

"And do you see on his face, Sir, marks on his right lower cheek area?"

"Yes."

"Do you also see a mark on his left part of his nose and the nostril area?"

"I do."

"Do you see a photograph of People's Exhibit 41? Do you see that this is a bare chested bare armed George Thompson?"

"Yes, it is."

"Do you see marks on the left arm, forearm area?"

"There is some discoloration it appears, yes."

"And at any point in time, Sir, did you ask him about those discolorations or injuries or insignificant or significant?"

"No, I did not."

"What did he tell you happened on Sunday, May 18th, 2003?"

"I don't believe he told me anything happened on Sunday."

"It's your testimony, Sir, that he did not tell you that on Sunday she was fine, that they had fun, that she ordered more vodka, food and cigarettes from the grocery store across the street. He didn't tell you that."

"No, he did not."

"Did you ask him about Sunday?"

"I asked him about what had happened. He did not tell me anything until Monday when she started to have seizures and convulsions."

"Sir, you were a lawyer with over ten years experience. He is a person being interrogated by you. You didn't think it was important to ask him everything that occurred after May 17th, 2003?"

"I didn't ask him everything that took place between the fight and when Miss Grace was found dead."

"But you could have, you would agree with that, wouldn't you?"

"Oh sure, I guess I could have."

"You could have asked him all about Sunday, right?"

"Yes, I could have."

"You could have asked him all about Monday, right?"

"I could have, yes."

"He did tell you that Monday night, she began to vomit, isn't that right?"

"I think he told me Monday she started to have seizures and convulsions."

"He did talk to you about her vomiting."

"Later, she started to vomit blood."

"He did tell you she again got better and she showered and she returned to normal."

"No, he never told me she had ever returned to normal after the beating."

"Well, you didn't even ask him about Sunday when she ordered booze, food"

"Rephrase, rephrase," ordered the judge.

Mr. Breen complied by asking the witness, "You didn't ask him anything about Sunday when she ordered food."

"Objection," responded Mr. Groth.

Mr. Breen continued, "And alcohol, strike that. She's right. She's absolutely right. Withdraw the question. You didn't ask anything about Sunday, right?"

"He didn't mention to me anything about Sunday," answered the witness.

"You're an interrogator. You didn't ask him."

"I didn't ask him."

"Objection to the question," interrupted Mr. Groth.

"He didn't put a question mark on it. More like a statement. You want to rephrase it, Mr. Breen, that's fine," said Judge Gaughan.

Deciding not to press the issue, Mr. Breen asked the witness, "Sir, will you go to page 8 of the transcript of the video?"

"Yes, Sir."

"Page 8, you say in a question. Okay now, George, can you tell us how the fight started, correct?"

"Yes."

"All right. And he talks about Saturday, a fight occurring on Saturday, is that right?"

"Yes, Sir."

"He never tells you, nor is there any inquiry made regarding her showing any ill symptoms until Monday, later on Monday when she has seizures, isn't that right?"

"No, Sir."

"Then correct me."

"Well, he says that after the fight"

"Counsel," interrupted the judge, "what page are you talking about?"

"Well," replied the witness.

"Just give me the page number. Not a trick question. What is at the bottom you're looking at?" asked Judge Gaughan.

"Page 8 is the one I'm on," responded Mr. Breen.

"I'm talking to the witness," replied the judge.

Mr. D'Angelo said, "I'm looking at page 9 where he's talking about the bruises and the black eye are from the punching and the bruise to the chin; that all occurred during the fight. And then, I believe, it's on the bottom of the page he described how he pushed her from behind, and she hit the dresser and he talks about. First, I need to find it."

"Counsel, could you tell me what line this is?" asked the judge.

The witness replied, "On page 10, on the bottom of page 9, he says"

"Let's start with page 9," interrupted Mr. Breen.

The witness responded, "21 through 25 is the answer that talks about the punching and then it ends with when I pushed her and then she struck the dresser with her head. And then the first question on page 10 is, and the black eye that you already identified; the black eye resulted from pushing Julie into the dresser, and he said that's right. And then he goes on to talk about the other injuries from hitting the dresser and starts, the answer starts on line 9 and goes on to say, I mean that she had, she had a goose egg to begin with and then, and then it finally went down."

Mr. D'Angelo continued, "And then Sunday evening is when she started to have the black eye. So it wasn't Monday, Counselor, that the black eye started. It was Sunday, and we did apparently talk about what happened on Sunday, for your previous question. And that's when he says that there is already injuries, bruises that happened immediately after the goose egg. The goose egg happened after she hit the dresser, but the black eye didn't occur until the next day."

"Fair to say, as a result of the dresser, there was a goose egg shown almost immediately, correct?" asked Mr. Breen.

"That's what he told me."

"Is that correct?"

"Yes."

"And is it correct to say that the black eye began to show itself Sunday, correct?"

"That's what he said."

"And it was not until Monday that she began to have what he described as convulsions or seizures, isn't that correct?"

"That's what he told me."

"And you still didn't ask him anything about what he did on Sunday, did you?"

"I asked him as it related to him calling for help or getting her help, and the answer was, he never did anything until he found that she wasn't breathing."

"And that was on Monday or was that on Tuesday morning?"

"I believe that was on Tuesday morning."

"So my question is, you still didn't ask him what he and Julie did all day Sunday, did you?"

"I asked him what he did as it related to calling for her during the period of time after the fight."

"But you didn't, you didn't ask him what he and Julie did during the course of Sunday."

"No, I did not."

"All right. You again asked him the questions you wanted to ask him, isn't that right?"

"Yes."

"You, at no time, turned to him and said George, would you like to just talk and tell us everything you remember that occurred from Friday to Tuesday morning. You never said that, did you?"

"Well when we did the earlier interview, when we were just talking, I asked him the questions that are on the transcript based on what our previous interview was."

"Then I'll ask the question again. At any time during the course of the pre-interview or during the video, did you ask him, George, why don't you just tell us what happened from the 17th to the 22nd of May, you never asked him that, did you?"

"Certainly, the first thing I asked him was if he wanted to tell me what happened as it resulted in the fight. That was the first question that I asked him. He could have told me anything and then I made certain follow up questions after that."

"And none of those follow up questions asked the following: What did you do on Friday? What did you do all day Saturday? What did you do all day Sunday? What did you do all day Monday? You didn't ask those questions. You would agree with that, wouldn't you?"

"Well, Counselor, the fight didn't take place until Saturday night. So I don't know if I would have even cared about what happened on Friday."

"So their prior relationship to you would have nothing to do with your investigation, is that what you're telling us?"

"No, I asked him about their previous fights, yes."

"Where does he discuss the fact that he pushed her from behind in the transcript?"

"I believe it starts on page 9 and goes to page 10. He says that he pushes her. I went to get out of the bedroom and that's when I pushed her and she struck the dresser with her head, and the black eye that you already identified, is the one that's in the photograph. The black eye resulted from me pushing Julie into the dresser. That's right. Then he goes on to say, I asked, can you describe, besides the black eye, were there any other injuries from hitting the dresser? Then he talks about the goose egg, to begin with, and then when it finally went down, and then Sunday evening."

"Counsel, listen," interjected the judge, "I went through this before and you didn't answer my question. Where did he say he pushed her from behind, not that he pushed her, all right? Where does it say from behind?"

The witness answered, "Judge, I don't believe it actually says from behind, but when he pushed her and the injury was to her face and her eye, I assumed since that's what struck first he propelled her into the dresser. So, I guess that was my assumption."

"Thank you. Thank you," replied Judge Gaughan.

Mr. Breen asked the witness, "You're not assuming things that aren't in the transcript, correct?"

"Well, Counselor"

"Sir, are you assuming things that aren't in the transcript, yes or no?"

"I guess that was an assumption on my part how she would have been propelled into the dresser, yes."

"You said, he said she was coming at him, correct? She kept coming at me, isn't that what he said? Counsel, the bottom of page 9."

"That's when he threw her on the bed and she kept coming at me and that's when I punched her in the chest one time. And then she was coming at me more and I just wanted to, you know, get out of the bedroom and that's when I pushed her."

"And you're assuming that he pushed her from behind, but he could very well have done exactly what he said, pushed her from the front, and she could have turned around and fallen, isn't that right?"

"Objection," responded Mr. Groth.

"I have no further questions. Withdraw the question," replied Mr. Breen.

Mr. Groth was asked if he wanted to redirect. He addressed the witness and stated, "Counsel asked you questions and I just ask you to direct your attention to page 8. Counsel asked you about the fight starting, or asked you questions about the fight starting, and on page 8, your question and statement is, okay. Now George, can you tell us how the fight started. Answer. It was over Saturday morning, she had taken off. I thought she was going to the bank she said. And then, and then she called me later on. She said she's at this guy, Bill's, house down the street, and I asked her to come home. She said she was going to go to the bank and go get something to drink and I said okay. I was still sleeping. And this is about 10:00 or so. And then, and then when she came home later, she brought another guy with her to the house. I finally ran him out of there, you know. I told him to leave and then later on that night we started getting into this, you know. That was the question you asked and the answer he gave. Is that correct?"

"Yes."

"Okay. And then he continues on. And you asked, okay, and he continues with his answer and says she went and got a bottle of liquor and started drinking and then later that night, Saturday night, that's when we started fighting. Is that correct?"

"Yes."

"Okay. So, according to this defendant's answers, actually his narrative about what happened that night, the person who was in the apartment was long gone when they started fighting, is that the way you understand that?"

"Yes."

"And you actually followed up and said you were jealous, excuse me, okay. And you were jealous that Julie had been with these other guys. Answer. Correct. Yeah. And that's when you were asking the defendant what caused him to have this fight with Julie Grace, isn't that correct?"

"Yes."

"That was the answer that he gave."

"Yes."

"And then you asked him again at the bottom of page 9, okay. And then during the fight, how did the fight end, George? Answer. I had finally, we were standing around and then I think I pushed her on the bed once, and she kept coming at me and that's when I punched her in the chest one time, and she was coming at me more and I just wanted to, you know, get out of the bedroom and that's when I pushed her and she struck the dresser with her head. That was the full question and answer regarding the injury to her eye, the defendant's version, is that correct?"

"Yes."

"On pages 7 and 8 you were shown a photo of the bedroom that you drew a circle around and you asked him, can you tell me what the circle represents and the defendant in his answer said that's where we started fighting, you know. I mean she was in the bedroom, she had come out, she came out into the living room and then came back in the bedroom and then I came in there, and then we started. And then you said okay, George, go on. Or actually okay, George, can, and he continued saying fighting or something in that area. Okay. And you signed the back of that photo before I showed it to you. Correct, I did was his answer. Those were some of the questions and answers he gave, is that correct?"

"Yes."

"Judge, I've got nothing further," said Mr. Groth.

"Recross?" Judge Gaughan asked Mr. Breen.

"No questions, Your Honor," answered Mr. Breen.

The judge instructed the witness to step down. He then said, "All right. Approximately 5:00. So State, you have additional witnesses for Monday."

Mr. Groth replied, "I do, Judge."

"All right, trial commenced and continued to Monday morning," stated Judge Gaughan.

Glenn and I left the courtroom and proceeded to the airport to catch our flight back home to Florida. It had been a tough and grueling two days, and we were ready for a break. However, once we got home we found it was very hard for either one of us to relax. The courtroom testimonies kept playing over and over in our heads, and there was no way to turn them off. We both desperately wanted the trial to end soon even though we were not comfortable with the way things were going. In spite of everything, we tried to remain optimistic that the judge would see that George was a hard, cold murderer, and he would convict George and lock him up for life.

CHAPTER 12
DAY THREE OF GEORGE'S TRIAL

S oon after everyone assembled in the courtroom on May 15th, 2006, Judge Gaughan opened by asking Mr. Groth, "How much more testimony?"

"Our case is very short, a stipulation, a couple certified copies of things and the detective to testify to his height and weight," answered Mr. Groth.

"I have a brief witness," added Mr. Breen.

"Let's complete the State's case, recess on yours, go on to the other case," replied the judge. "All right. Mr. Thompson, have a seat with your attorneys over at counsel table. State, will you proceed?"

"Judge, we will call Detective Redman," said Mr. Groth.

The witness came forward and was sworn in.

"Sir, how are you employed?" asked Mr. Groth.

"By the Chicago Police Department."

"In what capacity?"

"As a detective."

"How long have you been a detective, Sir?"

"26 years."

"Sir, I would like to draw your attention, if I could, to May 20th, 2003, approximately 9:00 in the evening at Area 3 police headquarters. Were you working on that date, time and location?"

"Yes, Sir."

"And were you assigned to assist in the investigation of the homicide of Julie Grace?"

"Yes, Sir."

"As part of that investigation do you see anyone in court who was taken into custody at that time?"

"Yes."

"Identify that person, please."

"The young man seated to my left with the khaki Cook County jail outfit."

"As part of the booking procedures, were certain identifiers taken of this defendant?"

"Yes, Sir."

"And part of those booking procedures, did he list a height of five feet nine inches and weight of 160 pounds?"

"Yes, Sir."

"Sir, I am going to show you what's been marked as People's Exhibits 40 through 44. Do you recognize those photographs?"

"Yes."

"Have you had an opportunity to review them before testifying today?"

"Yes, Sir."

"Do they truly and accurately depict the defendant as he appeared on May 20th, 2003 at Area 3 headquarters?"

"Yes, Sir."

"Thank you. Judge, I have nothing further for Detective Redman," said Mr. Groth.

"Thank you," replied Judge Gaughan. "Cross examination?"

"No questions, Your Honor," answered Mr. Breen.

The judge excused the witness and then asked, "State?"

"Judge, if we could proceed by way of stipulation at this time," requested Mr. Groth.

"I know it's been two days but do you have a copy of the stipulation?" asked Judge Gaughan.

"Judge, that lesson did stick. I put it up on your bench before you got up there. It may have gotten hidden in the interim," replied Mr. Groth.

"I'm sorry, here it is," said the judge. "Thank you. I appreciate that. Proceed will you please, Mr. Groth?"

"Sure, Judge. It is stipulated by and between the parties that if called to testify, Marirose McManus would testify that she is a lawyer licensed to practice law in the State of Illinois. She was assigned to the domestic violence section of the Cook County State's Attorney's Office on March 28th, 2003, and was the prosecutor for People versus George Thompson, Case No. 03-216154. That this case arose out of the events of March 7th, 2003, at 1540 North LaSalle, Apartment 2004.

"On that date, the Honorable Daniel Panarese found this defendant guilty of domestic battery. That Exhibit 94 is a certified copy of conviction for that case and that also on that date, the Honorable Donald Panarese entered a plenary order of protection with Julie Grace as the Petitioner and George Thompson as the Respondent.

"Exhibit 95 is a certified copy of the plenary order of protection entered under case 03-216154. So stipulated."

"So stipulated," responded Mr. Breen.

"That stipulation is allowed and moved into evidence," replied Judge Gaughan.

Mr. Groth continued, "We have one final piece of evidence which goes to the violation of the order of protection count and that is a certified copy of conviction for this defendant under 02-272629. We would ask that that go into evidence."

"Certified copy of conviction of what?" asked the judge.

"Domestic battery," answered Mr. Groth.

"Dated, the date of the conviction?" asked Mr. Breen.

"12-10-02, this goes to the November 27th, 28th," answered Mr. Groth.

"All right. Is that stipulated, too?" asked Judge Gaughan.

"Yes, Your Honor," answered Mr. Pugh.

"Thank you," said the judge. "That stipulation is allowed and also moved into evidence."

"Judge, at this time we would rest our case in chief," stated Mr. Groth.

"Okay. Defense?" asked Judge Gaughan.

Mr. Breen called his first witness, Jeffrey Iwamuro. "If you will stand up here and face the court, they are going to swear you in," he said.

The witness stated and spelled his last name and then Mr. Breen asked, "Mr. Iwamuro, what is your occupation?"

"I'm a grocery store manager."

"And what store do you manage?"

"Pottash Brother's Supermarket."

"Where is that located?"

"1525 North Clark Street in Chicago."

"What is the phone number for the grocery store?"

"312-337-7537."

"Sir, in May of 2003, as of that month, did you know a woman by the name of Julie Grace?"

"Yes, I did."

"Approximately how long had you known Julie Grace?"

"Probably five to six years."

"Did you see Julie Grace on any kind of a regular basis?"

"Probably weekly, shopping."

"Had you seen Julie Grace intoxicated or under the influence of alcohol?"

"Yes."

"Had you also seen her when she was sober and not under the influence?"

"Yes."

"Sir, I would like to call your attention, specifically, to Sunday, May 18th, and ask you whether or not you were working at the grocery store in the evening hours?"

"Yes, I was."

"What would your normal, back in May of 03, what would your normal hours be?"

"My working hours?"

"Yes, Sir."

"It would be 1:00 to 10:00."

"10:00?"

"Yes."

"On May 18th, Sunday, did you receive a phone call from Julie Grace?"

"Yes, I did."

"Do you know approximately what time that phone call would have come in?"

"Sometime after 7:00."

"Do you recognize Julie's voice?"

"Yes."

"Can you tell us, based on your experience in dealing with Julie, whether or not she sounded intoxicated or sober at that time?"

"She sounded intoxicated."

"What was the nature of the call that you had with her, what was it about?"

"She wanted some groceries delivered."

"And do you recall, as you sit there now, what it was that she wanted delivered?"

"Not exactly."

"Do you know, generally speaking, what it was that she wanted?"

"It was food items."

"Anything else?"

"There was some alcohol."

"Would you tell us the internal mechanisms at the grocery store there, in other words when she would call, specifically, when she would call, who took her order?"

"On this particular instance?"

"Yes."

"I took that order."

"How was that order processed?"

"She would tell me over the telephone what she would like. I, in turn, noted it. And either I remembered myself, I shopped that order."

"By shopping that order, what does that mean?"

"Picking out the items."

"And after you shopped the order, what is done?"

"We run it through the register, check out system."

"And after that, what occurs?"

"Depending upon the method of payment, either credit card, this particular one was COD, cash on delivery, and we have someone walk it over to her house."

"Your Honor," said Mr. Breen. "I would ask to be allowed to show Defendant's 8 to the witness please."

"Sure. Go ahead," replied the judge.

"Sir, sometime in, I believe, it was October of 03, myself and an investigator, John Ireman, visited you at the store, correct?"

"I recollect that, yes."

"And we asked you about this May 18th, this Sunday night order, did we not?"

"Most likely, yes."

"Did you go through your records at that time and deliver to us by way of fax, a receipt that reflects Julie's order?"

"Yes."

"I am going to show you, Sir, Defendant's Exhibit No. 8 for identification. Are you able to identify that receipt?"

"Yes."

"Is this a copy of, Xerox copy of the receipt that reflects Julie's order?"

"Yes."

"Does that receipt reflect the date of Julie Grace's order? What is that date?"

"5-18-03."

"Does it also reflect the time that it hit the cash register?"

"Yes."

"What time is that?"

"7:46 PM."

"Does it reflect the items that you shopped for her and had delivered to her?"

"Yes, it does."

"Would you please, if you have no independent recollection of exactly what she ordered, I believe you will be able to use that document, could you tell us what it was she ordered on May 18th?"

"Item for item?"

"Yes, Sir."

"Any objection, State?" interrupted Judge Gaughan.

"Judge, I would object," answered Mr. Groth. "The exhibit would speak for itself. He can say this is a true, accurate copy of the receipt. I think that's good enough."

"Well if it's going into evidence, then he can read it. If that's your objection, overruled, then he can read it. It's going in anyway so all right," replied the judge.

"Go ahead, Sir," Mr. Breen instructed the witness.

Mr. Iwamuro said, "I have three cans of Chef Boy R D Ravioli, one package of cigarettes. It looks like a pound or half pound of our own turkey breast, a 1.7 liter of Absolute Vodka, Fritos Cheese Puffs, five single bagels, a little over a pound of Holland tomatoes, six-pack of Diet Coke, dozen large eggs, Cinnamon Toast Crunch Cereal, package of chicken gizzards, half gallon of whole milk, two 32-ounce Gatorades lemon-lime. It looks like a pound of fresh Chuck, Cracker Barrel Kraft sharp cheddar cheese, one Vidalia onion, three cans of Campbell's Chicken Soup with Stars, Newman's Lemonade and a Minute Maid Orange Juice, twenty-nine items."

"When she was giving you this order, Sir, do you recall whether or not she appeared to be reading from a list, a shopping list?"

"Objection," responded Mr. Groth. "Calls for speculation."

"I will withdraw the question," replied Mr. Breen.

"Sustained," said the judge.

Mr. Breen continued. "Had she asked for deliveries in the past?"

"I don't recollect, but I would imagine so."

"Do you know how it was Julie Grace would normally pay for her grocery items, if you know, Sir?"

"Yes. I would think it could be check. It could be cash."

"Okay. Do you recall whether or not the delivery was, in fact, made?"

"Yes, it was."

"And did your delivery boy return after making the delivery?"

"Yes."

"Where was her apartment, Sir, in relationship to the grocery store?"

"Directly west of us about a block."

"Thank you very much, Sir. I appreciate it," said Mr. Breen.

"Are you through?" Judge Gaughan asked Mr. Breen.

"Yes, Your Honor," answered Mr. Breen.

"Cross examination, Mr. Groth?" asked the judge.

"Sir, would it be safe to say that Julie Grace usually paid for her groceries by check?" asked Mr. Groth.

"I couldn't remember. I couldn't tell you because I am not on the register at the time she is purchasing."

"As part of your duties as the manager of the grocery store, you would be aware of how many checks are coming in?"

"Yes."

"Would it be safe to say that Julie Grace's name appeared on an awful lot of checks?"

"Yes."

"In fact, almost on a daily basis she was writing checks, is that correct?"

"I don't know if it was daily. Weekly, weekly I could say."

"And sometimes she would, or actually except for this occasion, she would come in, buy some groceries, is that correct?"

"Correct."

"And you said that you had known Julie for approximately five years. Is that correct?"

"Yes."

"Now you also said that when she was on the phone you thought that she was under the influence of alcohol. Is that correct?"

"Yes."

"And you had actually seen her in person in the store under the influence of alcohol. Is that correct?"

"Yes."

"When you spoke to her on the phone, her speech sounded slurred."

"Yes."

"She sounded"

"Her speech sounded a little disoriented."

"Yes."

"Sounded a little confused."

"I don't know, confused. She was able to rattle off her list from memory or most people don't have a list. They just know what they want."

"But this was the first time that Julie Grace had called in an order for delivery that you had recalled, is that correct?"

"Yes."

"Now the young man who went to go deliver the groceries, did he have any paperwork generated on this?"

"No."

"So, he just went up and delivered it?"

"Yes, he has a receipt."

"Where is that receipt today?"

"I believe that was a copy of it we were looking at."

"So, no one signed for the order."

"No, he was paid one way or another."

"And again, you don't know how he was paid whether it was cash or check, is that correct?"

"Right, I do not."

"Now, Counsel said that he had come out and talked to you with an investigator, is that correct?"

"Yes."

"That was back in October of 2003?"

"Sometime in 2003."

"Do you recall the investigator if he had like a policeman's or investigator's notebook in front of him when he was talking to you?"

"I don't recollect that."

"Did you ever talk to me in the hallway and you said maybe they did?"

"Okay."

"So maybe they did."

"Maybe they did, yes."

"Okay. How many times was George Thompson in the Pottash Store?"

"I maybe saw him five to ten times with her."

"With her?"

"Yeah."

"Thank you, Judge. Nothing further, Your Honor."

"Redirect?" the judge asked Mr. Breen.

"Yes, just a couple," he answered.

"Sir, until Mr. Ireman and I came out and spoke to you, had any Chicago policeman or any state's attorneys come out and spoke to you about this order?"

"No."

"Nothing further, thank you."

"Anything else, Mr. Groth?" asked the judge.

"Not based on that, Judge," answered Mr. Groth.

"Thank you. You can step down," Judge Gaughan said to the witness. He instructed Mr. Breen to call his next witness.

"Judge, we will call George Thompson."

George approached the witness stand and was sworn in. I was surprised his attorney called him to testify but when I heard him speak, I understood why. Just as he was when he made his recorded confession, he showed no emotion in his voice. Furthermore, he remained very calm and composed while he blatantly lied about the circumstances that ultimately led to Julie's death.

169

"Would you tell us your first, your middle and your last name?"

"Yes. George Kenneth Thompson, Jr."

"How old are you today?"

"I am thirty-six."

"And where were you born?"

"I was born in Charleston, South Carolina."

"Who were you born to?"

"Maxine and George Thompson."

"Did there come a time when you left the Charleston area?"

"Yes, I left one time in 78 to 80. And then another time I left and came up here in 85, I believe it was."

"What is the extent of your formal education?"

"I dropped out of school my freshman year and got my GED."

"All right. When you came to the Chicago area originally, what year was that about?"

"That was 19, the first time was in 78. The second time I moved back up here was in 85."

"Okay. In 85, where did you stay when you came back here?"

"I stayed in South Holland."

"With whom did you stay in South Holland?"

"Maxine and my stepfather, Glen."

"And are they the folks that are here?"

"Yes, Sir."

"Where did, they lived in South Holland did you say?"

"South Holland, Illinois."

"How old were you about when you stayed with them in South Holland?"

"I was fifteen."

"Where did you go to high school before you dropped out?"

"Thornwood."

"Is there a point to this?" asked Judge Gaughan.

"Just going through his background, Your Honor, because I thought the court would want to know something about his educational background," answered Mr. Breen.

"Okay. Go ahead," replied the judge.

"Now that was in 85. Did you work after dropping out of school?" Mr. Breen asked.

"I worked during school. I was a stock boy at Jewel Food Store."

"I am going to move us along, Mr. Thompson, into, let's say 1990 or 1991. Where did you live in that year?"

"That year I was living in South Holland. I moved back up from South Carolina."

"What type of work did you do?"

"Local 1 Iron Worker."

"I want to call your attention to March of 2002. Were you at the Lake Shore Rehab Center on Sheridan Road here in Chicago?"

"Yes, I was."

"What is it, Sir, that landed you at Lake Shore Hospital in 2002?"

"I am an alcoholic and I was having problems with alcoholism again and decided to check myself into rehab."

"How long did you stay in rehab?"

"For two weeks."

"During your rehab there, did you meet a woman by the name of Julie Grace?"

"Yes, I did."

"And how is it that you came to meet her at the Lake Shore Rehab Center?"

"It was females and males and we had meetings daily and programs there and we met that way."

"Do you remember, and if you don't remember that's fine, but do you remember the date that you were discharged from Lake Shore Hospital?"

"I believe it was early April, first week in April."

"Do you know if Julie was discharged before or after you?"

"She was discharged approximately a week, five days before I was."

"Did you talk to Julie Grace while you were at Lake Shore and she had been discharged?"

"When she had already been discharged?"

"Yes."

"Yes, I talked with her on the phone."

"When you got out of Lake Shore Hospital, where did you go or who did you call?"

"When I was to be released, I was supposed to go to a three-quarter house in Lisle and that was the following day, but I spent the night with her, that night before I went there."

"Were you drinking that night?"

"No, I wasn't."

"Was she drinking that night?"

"Yes, she was."

"When you say you were scheduled to go to a three-quarter house in Lisle, what is a three-quarter house?"

"That's, it's a program you live with other men in an apartment and you can go to work and then you come home and you do, you have programs and meetings that you have to attend."

"Did you in fact, reside at the three-quarter house?"

"Yes, I did."

"And about how long did you do that?"

"That was approximately from April until I would say June, three months or so."

"Between April and June while you were residing at the three-quarter house, did you see Julie Grace on a regular basis?"

"Yes, I did."

"What were the circumstances under which you saw her during that time period?"

"We were girlfriend and boyfriend pretty much. And I would come down to her. I was working downtown at the time so I would stay sometimes with her. It was okay with the guys at the three-quarter house as long as I wasn't drinking. Then they would, there was no problem and I made my meetings out there, also."

"Was she drinking during that course of time?"

"A few times she did."

"Did you and Julie at any time travel outside of Chicago?"

"We flew to Orlando to meet her mother and father and brother."

"Do you know the month that you did that?"

"That was June, I believe, of 2002."

"And were both of you sober during that trip?"

"Yes, we were."

"Where did you meet her mother and father?"

"At their house in Eustis, Florida, I believe."

"And after visiting with her parents there, where, if anywhere, did you and Julie go?"

"We also went to Jacksonville to meet my sister. She was living there. And I took her up to Charleston to meet my real dad and my stepmother."

"After that trip, did you come back to the Chicago area?"

"Yes, we did."

"Where did you live when you came back to the Chicago area?"

"I was still at the three-quarter house, but about a month later I quit and I was living with Julie."

"Were you drinking by that time?"

"I think I had relapsed in July, I believe."

"Did you have any other apartment other than"

"Excuse me, Mr. Breen," interrupted Judge Gaughan.

The judge then called a brief recess. After a few minutes, the judge instructed Mr. Breen to proceed.

"I believe, and I may be wrong on this, George, I believe we were talking about whether or not you maintained an apartment after the three-quarter house."

"Yes, I did. I had an apartment in the same Four Lakes subdivision out there and I got an apartment out there."

"And that is in what town again?"

"That's in Lisle."

"Now you would stay with Julie Grace while you had the apartment out there."

"Yes, I would. I was working downtown and sometimes it was easier for me just to stay at her place instead of driving out to the suburbs."

"Let's talk about after, say July of 2002. Were you drinking on a regular basis?"

"Not all the time but I was relapsing. I was trying to do my meetings out there but when we would get together we would start drinking."

"Was she maintaining any kind of sobriety after July of 2002?"

"No, I wouldn't say so."

"What was your relationship with her; was it boyfriend, girlfriend?"

"I really wouldn't call it that. It was, we were intimate. We would have sex with each other but I wouldn't exactly call it girlfriend, boyfriend."

"I want to call your attention to November 28th, 2002, or thereabouts. Were you arrested by the Chicago Police Department for a domestic battery?"

"Yes, I was."

"Would you tell the judge what it was that occurred on November 28th, 2002, between you and Julie Grace?"

"She had come out to my apartment and was wanting to make amends, makeup. She had a lady bring her out there. She wanted to actually go out to dinner that night and I said sure, I would be downtown later on. And later when I came down there, she was already out with some other people that went to dinner."

"What did you do?"

"I contacted her. When I got to the apartment she wasn't there. So I called her cell phone and then she came home about a half an hour later."

"In November of 2002, did you have a key to her place?"

"Yes, I did."

"How long had you had a key to her place?"

"Since like May I would say, of 2002."

"What happened when she came home?"

"She came home and I asked her where she was, what happened to us going out, you are out with these other people. And she, we got into an argument. She said she would go out with whoever the F she wanted to. And we started getting into an argument and then it turned physical. She started slapping me and the police were called after we got to fighting."

"On November 28th, who struck who first?"

"Julie struck me."

"Had Julie struck you before November 28th, 02?"

"Several times, yes."

"Tell us what the circumstances are that would cause her to do that."

"The circumstances were being drunk, her being drunk and we would just get to arguing and she would throw things. I would throw things and it would get physical. She would turn physical."

"Did you ever strike her first?"

"No, I haven't."

"Did you throw things first?"

"No."

"Did she throw things?"

"Yes."

"You got arrested on November 28th, and after that, where did she go and where did you go?"

"After November 28th, I went back out to my place and she had stayed at her apartment.

"Are you saying that night or just generally after? Just generally speaking after that, the next two or three days, how did you guys relationship go? Did you split up for awhile?"

"I believe I was in jail for the two weeks. And then after that I had got evicted from my apartment. So she asked me to move in with her."

"Did you move in with her?"

"Yes, I did."

"You got evicted from your apartment, I believe, late November of 2002."

"Yes."

"I want to call your attention to a date mentioned in this trial, March 7th, 2003. Do you remember a Mr. Goldstein testifying here?"

"Yes, I remember him."

"Where did he live, to your knowledge?"

"He lived across the street some floors up on the northwest side of the building. I believe this is the same gentleman because we were having sex one night and all of a sudden a red laser pointer comes into the bedroom and it came from up that way. So I figured that this is the same gentleman who had called the police when we had this fight."

"On March 7th, 2003, would you please tell Judge Gaughan what it is that occurred earlier in the day before the police arrived and arrested you?"

"We were having, we were drinking in March. We had gotten into a verbal altercation. She was drunk. I was drunk. She had slapped and hit me. I hit her back. I left. Then I came back later. And she was just getting really, Julie is a very belligerent drunk and a very mean drunk, the things that she would say to you.

"My sister had actually miscarried a child and she was saying something to the affect of your sister is a fucking snob and blah, blah, blah and her husband is a piece of shit, things to that affect to get me fired up. She would, that was what she would like to do. She would get me fired up and loved to fight and start throwing things at me. It's just how she was. She was very, very belligerent when she would get to drinking."

"Tell us about any physical altercation that you had with her on March 7th, 2003."

"She clawed me up pretty good that day if I remember correctly. And we got into, we got to fighting on the sofa in the bedroom, or I mean in the living room and that's how Mr. Goldstein had seen us."

"All right. How far would you approximate Mr. Goldstein's apartment is from the apartment that you and Julie lived in?"

"It's 100 foot across the street and about 80 foot up. We are on the 20th floor. He said that he was on the 28th."

"What is it exactly that occurred when you said something about the sofa in the living room? What happened in the living room area?"

"We were in the living room. Julie was striking me, scratching me in my face. I pushed her down on the sofa. I am trying to hold her down and she gets very crazy. And I have that pillow that I put over her face, you know, just to get her to calm the hell down. And she just continually is clawing at me."

"Were you arrested on March 7th?"

"Yes, I was."

"And when was it that you were released from custody?"

"On my birthday, March 10th, she bonded me out, I believe."

"Where did you go that night?"

"Back to the apartment."

"Now on March 7th when you were arrested, police officers came to that apartment, correct?"

"Yes, they did."

"And you heard a policeman testify here to a statement that you made where you said that you needed to keep her in line or something like that, correct?"

"Right, right. These officers have been called to the apartment before.

They know of our domestic issues and we were generally joking around. They said something to the effect of Julie is getting fucking crazy or wild again. And I said something to the effects of yeah, I had to tune her up or keep her in line."

"Were you saying that seriously?"

"No, this was going downstairs in the elevator. We were just bullshitting. This wasn't said serious."

"By the way, Sir, had there been, as of March 7th, 2003, had there been an incident that you saw, where Julie was playing with knives?"

"Yeah, I had come over one night and don't know what she was raged up about, but I came in the door and she starts wheeling knives all over the place at me. And she was running. She went into the elevator and went downstairs somewhere and came back up still acting crazy so I left the building."

"Do you know if she went to the hospital as a result of that?"

"No, I don't know what she did that night."

"By the way, Sir, did you know from June of 2002 to let's go to May of 2003, did you know of Julie having to go to the emergency room from time to time?"

"Yes, she went several times, numerous."

"And what was that for?"

"For dehydration of her drinking. She gets the shakes. She starts puking, you know, crapping her pants, things of that nature."

"And she had actually done that prior to, before May of 2003, is that right?"

"Yes, several times."

"Who would clean up after her?"

"That would be me. I would be the babysitter."

"I want to call your attention now to a specific weekend and I want to talk about, let's start with Saturday morning May 17th, 2003. Do you have that day in your head right now?"

"Yes, Sir."

"I want to talk about that Saturday. What happened in the morning of May 17th?"

"On the morning of May 17th, earlier in the morning, probably about 5:00 AM, this fellow Bill calls. He is a friend of Julie's and he was wanting to come to the house and party, but we didn't want any of that. So, then later on Julie wakes up, probably around 9:00, I guess."

"Let me stop you for just a moment. Do you know Bill's last name?"

"Bambridge or Bangbridge or something."

"Who was your understanding as to who Bill was?"

"Objection to hearsay," interrupted Mr. Groth.

"It goes to his state of mind," said Mr. Breen.

"Overruled," ordered the judge.

"Okay," said Mr. Breen.

George continued, "He was a fellow that lives a couple blocks over. He is a bisexual older gentleman and they had had a relationship at one time. He was one of several partners that Julie had."

"Well when Bill called at 5:00 in the morning and said he wanted to party, what did you understand that to mean, come over to drink?"

"To drink, do some coke."

"And who answered the phone at 5:00 in the morning?"

"Julie had answered it."

"What happened after that phone call?"

"We went back to sleep that morning."

"What happens next?"

"She wakes up, says she is going to the bank and she was going to go over to Pottash to get something to drink. And it ends up she called me approximately an hour later that she was at Bill's house with some other guy, and that they were just hanging out, drinking and partying."

"What time of morning do you think that was?"

"That was about 10:00 or 10:30."

"What did you say to her at that time, anything?"

"I told her I really didn't care for her being over there with these guys and, you know, with the drugs around. I didn't know of Julie to do any drugs, but when Julie gets drunk she is very susceptible to other people. I didn't want her there to be taken advantage of or a gang bang could be in process or I had no idea what's going on."

"Well when she got so drunk, would she pass out?"

"Julie drinks. Julie cannot drink more than three drinks. Then she will have to pass out for an hour at the most. Then she gets up again and has more drinks. This is a continuous cycle that she has."

"Did she drink in the morning after getting out of bed?"

"She drank around the clock pretty much."

"Now we are still talking about May 17th. What happens next after you have this phone call with her?"

"I call back several times to this Bill. I am like, send Julie home. I don't want her over there with you. I wasn't going to go over there. I didn't want to cause a scene or whatever. But nonetheless, she doesn't come home until probably about 4:00, 3:30."

"When she comes home, who is she with?"

"She was with Bill's bisexual partner, I guess."

"Do you know his name?"

"I do not know his name."

"Where were you when Julie and this other man came into the apartment?"

"I was in the bedroom just watching TV."

"All right. Did you get out of bed right away when they came in?"

"I heard them come in and she wanted to introduce me to this fellow and, you know."

"What happened?"

"I shook hands with him, you know, told him my name and then I went back in the bedroom and they were in the front room talking for about an hour or so."

"Were they drinking, also?"

"I think there was a little bit to drink around the house. I think they might have had a couple cocktails. I really didn't go out there because, I am not prejudiced against gays or anything, but I don't know the guy from a can of paint, so I am not interested in meeting him."

"What happens next?"

"Eventually she and this fella come into the bedroom and say that they are going to go over to Burton Place bar, and they are going to have some cocktails and get something to eat. And I told him, you are not going anywhere with Julie. I said it's time for you to just leave."

"And did he leave?"

"Yes, he did."

"Now, tell us what happened."

"After that, Julie went over to Pottash, got another bottle of liquor, and she came, she brought a lady friend of hers, Ellen was her name, up to the house to introduce to me. She was, she is an AA member."

"When Ellen came to the house, did you talk to Ellen?"

"Yeah. We talked for about an hour and a half or so."

"What did you guys talk about?"

"Objection to relevance, Judge. Its hearsay," interrupted Mr. Groth.

Mr. Breen rephrased his question, "What did she talk about?"

"We were talking."

Judge Gaughan interrupted, "Excuse me. Wait a minute, Mr. Thompson. How is this material and how is this relevant?"

"I'm just trying to lay out the whole scenario, the totality of the circumstances. That's all," answered Mr. Breen.

"Well let's just move on. Sustained," said the judge.

"I will move on," replied Mr. Breen. He then asked the witness, "Did Ellen eventually leave?"

"Yes, she did leave. After Julie was drinking, she has to go to the bedroom to pass out. So Ellen and I talked for another half-hour and then she left."

"Now what happens on Saturday, May 17th?"

"Now I'm drinking, I started. I have me a few cocktails and I have the radio going. Julie finally comes out of her thing and wants to have more drinks. And she has a couple and then goes and lays back down and comes back yelling at me to turn the stereo down, and after that I, she goes back into the bedroom. Then I come back in there and we start getting into a verbal altercation."

"When you say verbal altercation, I want you to get more specific."

"She"

"Tell us who is saying what."

"I was asking her what was with the deal bringing that guy here. I wasn't really too concerned about that. The thing that made me madder or mad, I was concerned about, was when Ellen was there, Julie, when she drinks she likes to tell everybody our business and my business, specifically. She was talking about my sister to her, you know, in a negative way. She talks about my mom, you know, my parents, that type of thing. She just, and I told her, I said if I would like Ellen to know about my personal business, I will tell Ellen. I just met this woman and she is already telling her my personal life."

"Tell us about how this thing progressed, this verbal argument."

"She like, she will tell whoever the fuck she wants to talk to who about what. And she will bring whoever the fuck she wants to bring to the house. She is going to do it. It's her place and that type of thing. And then she slaps me. Then I push her away. She is coming at me some more. I punch her to get her off of me. And I mean we are doing like this to each other, too."

"Let the record reflect that his hands are open and flailing."

"And finally she scratches me again in the face and then I push her hard to get her away from me and this is when she strikes her head on this dresser."

"Now I want to back up for just a second here. Prior to this, had you ever had Julie arrested?"

"Yeah, I have had her arrested before."

"Prior to this, had you ever sustained injuries from Julie attacking you?"

"Oh, yeah."

"How many times?"

"Several times. She broke my nose one time with the cordless phone. She scratched me, bit me, kicked me several times. These weren't times that the police were ever called. These are times that were just let go. These happened both in Lisle and at her place."

"When we talked about on earlier occasions when she had to go to the hospital, correct?"

"Right."

"Have you ever nursed her or taken care of her during any of her DT's or seizures or whatever?"

"Several times. It was a fulltime job babysitting Julie."

"Did you ever take her anywhere other than your apartment for that?"

"I have taken her to my parent's house a couple of times."

"For what purpose?"

"Because I didn't want her to, I had meetings that I had to make, you know. This was going back a little bit, but I had meetings that I had to do and I was still sober. So, I took her there instead of taking her to the hospital. We actually called her mother and, you know, it was okay for her to go out there."

"By the way, did you ever see her mother in the Chicago area?"

"No, I didn't."

"You only met her in Florida, correct?"

"Yeah, just the one time."

"Now getting back where we left off on May 17th, you indicate that you had pushed her, correct?"

"Yes, I did."

"What happened to her as a result of you pushing her?"

"She pretty much, her feet came from up under her and she fell into the dresser."

"What happened after that?"

"I immediately went and assisted her to pick her up, and probably a half an hour later she had a pretty good goose egg on her temple."

"After you picked her up, where did you put her or where did she go?"

"She stood up, probably used the bathroom, I believe. We mixed a couple more drinks, being the sick alcoholics that we are, and called it a night after that."

"About what time do you think you went to bed that night?"

"Probably around 10:00, I would say."

"Were you both intoxicated?"

"Yes, very much so."

"You mentioned that she had a goose egg on her head."

"Yes."

"At any time did she ask you to go to the hospital that night?"

"No, she didn't."

"At any time, I mean, did you ever deny her the use of the phone?"

"No."

"I want to talk to you about the next day which is Sunday, May 18th. I want you to walk us through as best as you can, Sunday, May 18th. Tell us what time you got up and what you guys did."

"Sunday, probably got up around 10:00, 11:00. Julie had got up earlier than I because she gets up early and she has to have a drink right away. So that's the first thing she does. She goes back to bed. She didn't go to sleep, but she was just laying in the bed with me. We were watching TV. Finally, I get up. I go take a shower. I take the dog out. She didn't take the dog out because she had this black eye, you know, it was developing."

"Let's stop here for just a minute. In the apartment was you and Julie and the dog, correct?"

"Yes."

"How many times would you take the dog out during the day?"

"I would take Bronte out a couple times and Julie, we would share."

"But on that Sunday, you took the dog out both times, correct?"

"Probably about four times that day."

"What else did you guys do that day?"

"We just hung around the apartment mostly. We didn't go out or any of that because of this black eye that was developing, just sat around, watched TV."

"At any time during Sunday did she say she wanted to go to the hospital?"

"No, not at all."

"At any time Sunday had she begun to vomit or anything?"

"No."

"Okay. What else did you do on Sunday?"

"Later in the evening, we ordered some groceries from Pottash."

"Now when you say, we, who, in fact, made the phone call?"

"Julie made the phone call."

"Do you know how it was that she had these items in mind? Did you see her reading from notes or did she just tell them? Were you there when she made the call?"

"Yes, I was."

"And what do you remember her ordering?"

"Some of the items that were earlier read off, the food items and vodka and cigarettes."

"Had you run out of cigarettes?"

"Yes."

"She did not smoke, correct?"

"No, she didn't."

"Had you run out of vodka?"

"Yes, we did."

"By the way, where do you keep your vodka at the house?"

"In the freezer."

"What happened after she ordered this food from Pottash?"

"Probably about a half an hour later or so, the delivery boy comes to the door and we receive the groceries."

"Where were you when those groceries arrived?"

"I was in the kitchen."

"And did Julie go to the door?"

"She was in the kitchen, also."

"Now you had a key to the apartment, but how is it people would be able to go through the vestibule and go to the apartment in Sandburg Village?"

"Byron, the door man, would let them in."

"Do you remember whether or not you had got a buzz that the deliveryman was there?"

"I think Byron may have called upstairs. I am not positive, though."

"So the alcohol and the cigarettes and food items arrive, right?"

"Correct."

"Now Gatorade, Lemon-Lime, do you know who drank that?"

"That's, Julie orders that. She usually mixes it with vodka."

"And the orange juice, would you use that?"

"Both of us would use it."

"What happened after the delivery was made?"

"We started drinking a few drinks and ate a little bit and went to bed."

"Now I want to talk about Monday, May 19th. Do you remember the morning hours of May 19th?"

"Yes, I do."

"What happened in the morning?"

"In the morning it was pretty much a repeat of Sunday. She's up having cocktails early in the morning. I get up approximately the same time. I take out the dog. I get, I make us something to eat. She eats and then later on probably, about 12:00 or so, was when Julie had called, Julie Starsiak and"

"I am going to object to foundation, 12:00 noon or 12:00 midnight," interrupted Mr. Groth.

"Sustained. Lay the foundation," said Judge Gaughan.

Mr. Breen asked George, "Was it 12:00 noon?"

"Yes."

"You are just approximating, right?"

"Yes."

"Did you talk to Julie Starsiak?"

"Yes, I did."

"What was that conversation all about?"

"Julie had called to see what we were up to and I said that we weren't doing much. I told her about, Julie had got a black eye. I said we were fighting over the weekend. Julie ended up, she got a black eye. And I said she is in the bedroom. Because Julie Starsiak is very familiar with Julie Grace's having a few drinks, going, passing out for awhile."

Julie Starsiak was a few years older than Julie, but the two of them had been very good friends for several years. They met during the time when Julie worked for the late Senator Paul Simon and Julie Starziak worked as a lobbyist.

"What else was discussed?" Mr. Breen asked George.

"We had a discussion about her getting to the hospital because of dehydration. She wasn't doing good. I was pretty much, I was tired of babysitting Julie. I have to babysit Julie constantly and it's a pretty big effort on my part to have her not drink. And without all being in the house, it's just not going to happen, to get her rehydrated where she is functional."

"So there was some discussions about her going to the hospital for hydration problems, correct?"

"Right."

"What happens after that phone conversation with Julie Starsiak? How does the afternoon progress?"

"Later on we have a drink. I start drinking later on, probably I started drinking around 3:00, I would say. Julie was up drinking with me. I go into the bedroom to watch TV. There was a TV in the living room but I never watched TV in there. I always just watched it in the bedroom and she is out in the front room. She sits in this Lazy Boy that has a window right there. That's where she likes to sit to look over at the park and the lake."

"So you are in the bedroom."

"Correct."

"To your knowledge, she is in the living room in the Lazy Boy. What happens?"

"I hear some commotion in there. There is a table that always is falling down. Sometimes the Lazy Boy will hit it. It's real unstable. So I go out there and I see Julie is on the ground and she is, apparently, I am catching what the end of looks like a seizure or convulsion of some type of nature."

"Now had you, and there has been talk here as to what a seizure is. You never went to medical school, right?"

"Iron worker school, not medical school."

"What did you see her doing physically? Describe what she's doing."

"She was laying on her side and her hand was shaking, not her legs, just her hands were shaking."

"Have you seen her in that condition before?"

"Not quite as shaky, but I have seen her like that before. Yes, I have, falling down. She is constantly falling down all over the place."

"Okay. What happens then?"

"She gets up and that, it was right there, I had had enough of her. I told her that was it for the drinking and I wanted to push water. So, I told her to get into the shower, go lay down, you know, babysitting is coming into full effect now because I am scared shitless."

"Why are you scared?"

"Well I am scared because she is not feeling good and I have really, would really, I don't want to babysit her and I would rather somebody else do it. I have to do this. I have done this for a year straight, this babysitting routine. And I would rather have somebody else do this."

"What happens next?"

"So, she goes in and lays down. I try to give her something more to eat but she says she is not hungry. So, I am out in the front room. I hear her. She is laying down. I hear her up in the bathroom puking. I go in there. She has puked on herself, missed the toilet, made a mess of the bathroom. This is why I don't like this babysitting job. But I clean her up, get her back in bed, have her start drinking some of the Gatorade, or I was pushing water for her, something like that."

"Now when you say that you cleaned the bathroom, first of all, you know, I need to get a little specific here. When you would say she was puking up, what was she puking up?"

"She is puking brownish looking, it's just brown looking. I really don't know what it was. She pukes all the time, same stuff she always puked up."

"When you say you clean up the bathroom, did you literally go in and clean up whatever it was she was heaving?"

"Yes, it was all over the place."

"What happens then?"

"She goes back into the bedroom and that episode happens another time, probably around midnight, I would say."

"Did she seem relieved after she had vomited?"

"Yeah, she always seems like she feels a little better."

"Did you talk to her after the bathroom incident?"

"Yeah."

"What did you say to her?"

"The typical thing I would say to her, ask her if she is feeling any better, do you want something to eat or want something to drink? She is wanting to drink booze because that booze is the only thing that makes her body feel better. That's part of being a chronic alcoholic."

"Now let's take it to midnight that night. Where are the two of you around midnight?"

"She's in bed, but she gets up one more time and she goes and pukes again. So I am going through this episode again of getting her up, cleaning up the bathroom and put her back, helping her back to the bedroom."

"What happens next?"

"I go to bed, probably maybe twenty minutes later after I am done cleaning up, I go to bed and we went to sleep."

"What happens next?"

"Now later on, this was 3:30 or so, 3:45. This is when I am woke up with her puking very seriously bad. It looks like blood, she looks like she is puking up. It's hurled. It was on the blinds, I believe, in some of the photos that I saw."

"So for the record, you just put your hands from your mouth indicating that the puke was actually parallel to the ground."

"Exactly, yes."

"What happens next?"

"She has made a mess of herself and of the bed, the pillow, the wall, because she lurches. This vomit comes out so the stuff is everywhere. Now what I do, I take her clothes off of her. I get the sheets because these are pretty much ruined. And there is a garbage chute out in the hallway. I take these and throw them down the chute. I come back and I am looking for new linens to put on the bed. Then I come into the bedroom and she is on the ground. Now she is having a convulsion and she is blue in the face."

"This is after you returned from putting the laundry down the chute?"

"Right, and I had also ran a pillow out to the balcony."

"What happens now?"

"Now I'm on the phone right away. I have called 911, and I am waiting for these paramedics to arrive, and I am trying to assist her, give her CPR. I am trying to clear her throat and I am talking to her. Well, we have heard the 911 tape."

"We did hear the 911 tape. There is a point in there and it's a little muffled but where you are supposedly saying, break the fucking window, or something to that effect. What was that all about?"

"That was the paramedics where, because I have the phone on with 911, I am not thinking about having to buzz them into the building and the doorman leaves at midnight. And these guys seem like they are taking forever. And, you know, I don't know if the lady knew this. I mean Julie is sitting here, I think dying in front of me. And I just want these guys to break these fucking windows and get in the building already. I mean, if I would have had my head on straight, I probably should have went and put her in the elevator and took her downstairs. But I mean, this is all, you know."

"Did they come to the apartment?"

"They finally got up there, yes."

"And what happened next?"

"I was, I told them to go in here. I told them to come into the bedroom and then the police took me out into the living room."

"Did the police take you over to Area 3 at Belmont and Western?"

"Yes, they did."

"When Julie had been hospitalized in the past, before May 20th, did you take her to the hospital?"

"Yeah, I have taken her to the hospital several times."

"And then, getting to May 17th when you pushed her and she struck her head, did the fight end at that point in time?"

"Oh, yeah."

"I am going to show you some photographs, People's Exhibit 6 for identification. What is that a photograph of?"

"That's from the hallway looking into the bedroom."

"And People's Exhibit 7, what is that?"

"That's the little, walking a little more into the bedroom."

"People's Exhibit 8 for identification."

"That's a picture of the bed."

"Now did, go ahead"

"And the dresser is right there, also."

"The bed does not have sheets or a blanket on it, correct?"

"Correct."

"Do you know what happened to those?"

"Those are the ones that, the one that she puked on the most, it was a sheet not the bedspread, I guess you would say."

"People's Exhibit 9, that's a photograph of the bed."

"Uh-huh."

"People's Exhibit 10, what is that piece of furniture seen in that photograph?"

"That's the dresser that she struck her head on."

"People's Exhibit 11, do you know what caused those spots on the carpet?"

"No, I don't know what caused that. It looks like maybe when the paramedics were there or something, that's something from them."

"People's Exhibit number 12 for identification, which seems to be a photograph of the blinds. Do you see spottage on those blinds?"

"Yes."

"What is that?"

"I believe that was where she had lurched this vomit."

"People's Exhibit 13 and 14 appear to be photographs of a pillow. What is that pillow?"

"That's the pillow that was on the bed."

"People's Exhibit 65, I see kind of a wicker chair in that photograph."

"Yes."

"That isn't the Lazy Boy you were speaking of or is it?"

"No, that's not it."

"By the way, Sir, there were some tools in the apartment, were there not?"

"Yes, tools from my tool box."

"What are those? What kind of tools are those?"

"A spud wrench and crescent wrench."

"I want to show you People's Exhibit 72 and 73 for identification and, as it relates to March 7th, 2003, the Goldstein matter. Is that the couch where you struggled with Julie?"

"Yes, it's in a little different position then it was then."

"Where was it then?"

"Then it was more of a 45-degree angle to the corner of the wall there. More of it was to the window there."

"By the way, on March 7th, Sir, did you ever kick her?"

"No, not on March 7th."

"When was it, Sir, that you ever kicked her?"

"I kicked Julie one time, the time when she broke my nose with the phone. When I was laying in bed she wanted to go out west somewhere shopping, and I wasn't moving fast enough, I guess, so"

"People's Exhibit 71 for identification, can you identify the piece of furniture in that photograph?"

"This is the Lazy Boy that she likes to sit in and look out of the window."

"People's Exhibit 74 for identification, are you able or not able to tell us what is located against the wall in People's Exhibit 74, by way of furniture?"

"There is a desk. We use it as a desk. There is a laptop there. There used to be. Then there is this little round table that falls over. You can see it fell over that Monday afternoon. I didn't really put it back together."

"Thank you."

"I have no further questions, Your Honor," said Mr. Breen.

"Cross examination, Mr. Groth." said Judge Gaughan.

"Sir, you indicated that you worked as an iron worker, is that correct?" Mr. Groth asked George.

"Yes, I have been an iron worker, Local 1 for 13 years before I got locked up."

"What kind of work is that?"

"I am a connector on structural steel."

"And the tool belt that you talked about, those tools, those are part of your stock and trade; is that correct?"

"Yes, it is."

"That looks pretty heavy, is it?"

"The heaviest thing I carry is an eight-pound beater."

"It might be heavy for a guy like me but for you, it's part of your everyday life; is that correct?"

"Yes."

"As an iron worker, you have to be pretty strong to work all those I beams and connectors and rivets and fasteners, all that stuff."

"That's not necessarily true. If you know how to work with a crane, you don't have to fight it; you can finesse it."

"Well you have to carry that eight-pound beater you said, right?"

"That's, most of that weight is carried on my shoulders. It's a big full body harness."

"What do you use to drive the rivets into the iron?"

"There is no rivets, just bolts."

"You have to get them nice and tight so they don't fall apart."

"That's usually up to the detail gang."

"Okay. You have done that for how long would you say?"

"13 years before I got locked up."

"Okay. And before you got locked up, did you have plans to return to it?"

"I never quit it."

"Well when was the last time that you worked as an iron worker?"

"Probably about two weeks before this incident."

"That was when you got laid off in March."

"Not in March, no."

"How did you stop working that iron working job?"

"The job had ended. It was over here on the blue line, the Douglas branch."

"Since you have been locked up, have you talked to anybody specifically, from the press about this case?"

"Yeah, I talked to a reporter."

"You talked to a Jennifer Tanaka from Chicago Magazine, is that right?"

"Yes, I don't remember her name."

"When you talked to her, you told her that you got kicked off the job site for fighting, is that right?"

"Yeah, that was in May of 2002."

"And then when you went to rehab was in 2002 as well, is that correct?"

"In March, correct."

"And how long were you in the rehab did you say?"

"For two weeks until my insurance ran out."

"There is a little confusion in my mind. Were you in there as an inpatient or outpatient?"

"It was inpatient."

"Tell us about what happens when you go into inpatient rehab."

"You get a roommate, probably about ten dorms for women on one wing and ten for men on the other. And you have meetings daily."

"What are the meetings like?"

"Excuse me?"

"What do you learn in the meetings?"

"You learn to work the twelve steps of Alcoholics Anonymous."

"And other than that, do they try to motivate you in other ways to stay off alcohol?"

"How would you mean motivate?"

"Do they tell you alcohol is a great thing but your body has a bad reaction to it so you must stop, or do they tell you about what your body's reaction to alcohol means?"

"Most people know it's a bad reaction."

"Most people would include you, right?"

"Yeah."

"So you know that continued exposure to alcohol is going to progressively weaken a person over time, is that correct?"

"Most probably, I would say."

"In fact, that's what happened with Julie; is that correct?"

"That's a good assumption, yes."

"And those trips to the hospital that she made, sometimes you took her, is that correct?"

"I have taken her several times to the hospital."

"You took her in your truck."

"Yes."

"The truck that was parked at the bottom of 1540 North LaSalle, correct?"

"Right."

"Now on the 17th of May, 2003 you indicated that you had an altercation with her, is that correct?"

"Yes."

"And that altercation was several hours after, whatever the subjects were you were arguing about, is that correct?"

"Yes, it was. Well, we were arguing and then the fight happened all in the bedroom at the same time. We were never fighting beforehand."

"Right. It was several hours after she had come home with this bisexual gentleman, is that correct?"

"Yes."

"And in the interim, she had gone to the liquor store a couple times."

"One time."

"Her friend, Ellen Corley, came over."

"She did."

"Her friend, Ellen Corley, and you chatted for awhile."

"Yeah."

"Then you started arguing again, is that correct?"

"Yes."

"Now, when you were arguing, at one point she goes into the bedroom."

"There is no arguing again. We weren't arguing to begin with. There was one argument that led up to the fight."

"Okay. So at some point in this argument she goes into the bedroom while you are in the living room, is that correct?"

"Yes, she does."

"You follow her in there."

"Right, when she came out and told me to turn down the music."

"And then you followed her back into the bedroom at that point, is that correct?"

"I went in there a few minutes later."

"She came out in the living room and talked to you about the radio, went back into the bedroom and that's when you followed her in there."

"Right."

"That's when the argument started, is that correct?"

"Yes."

"You started fighting."

"Yes."

"That's what you told us earlier."

"Yes, Sir."

"Now how many times did you actually punch her during that fight?"

"One time I punched her in the chest."

"How many times did you slap her?"

"We were flailing at each other. It was multiple times I would say, back and forth."

"How many times did you slap her, Sir?"

"I wasn't counting. I don't think anybody counts that."

"All right. How many times did you grab her by the arm and throw her around?"

"I didn't throw her around at all."

"Now you have seen this photograph, right? These three photographs, People's Exhibit 22, 21 and 24. I am going to show you 21, all those bruises on her chest area. That came from the one punch you threw."

"This one did."

"And the others, you don't know where they came from, is that right?"

"No, I do not. That, I might have grabbed her to keep her from, you know, she was trying to go at me like that."

"On the inside of her arm is where you were able to grab her."

"I grabbed her like this, that way."

"How would you grab her, Sir?"

"From the front."

"Your Honor," said Mr. Groth, "may the record reflect the witness has his hands spread out, all fingers about half an inch away from each other."

"When you would grab her from the front, she would be facing her front towards you, is that right?"

"Yes."

"So your thumbs would be right here on the biceps."

"Yes."

"These are the same bruises on the other side that's from the same grab, is that correct?"

"Yes, that would be the same arm."

"Now these bruises on her chin, how did she get those?"

"I have no idea how she got those bruises. It could have been when the arms were flying I might have struck her on the chin."

"Well, you remember telling Assistant State's Attorney D'Angelo, in your video, most of those bruises that were on her in the photos came from the fight. Is that correct?"

"The ones that were circled, yes."

"So, these ones under her chin, you don't know where those came from, is that right?"

"Well I just stated that that could have happened when we were flailing at each other."

"Okay. How about the one under her breast; do you have any idea where that came from?"

"It may have been from the fight. I couldn't tell you."

"How would you leave that kind of mark under her breast during the fight, Sir, do you know?"

"I may have when I pushed her away."

"So you got under her breast and pushed her away and left a bruise. Is that right?"

"That's correct."

"Now back on November 27th of 2002, you had another one of these altercations with Julie, is that correct?"

"Yes, Sir."

"What was the basis for that?"

"That was when I had came from out from Lisle and her and I, we had plans to go out to dinner and she was out with some other people."

"So she stood you up basically, and you got mad, is that right?"

"I was upset. I was looking forward to going out with some other people and when I got there, I didn't know if we had our times crossed or whatever, but I called her and she came home."

"Now you had another fight with her on that day. How is it that her hair came out of her head that day, Sir?"

"Objection," interrupted Mr. Breen. "Assumes a fact not in evidence."

"Sustained. Rephrase," said the judge.

"I am going to show you People's Exhibit 49. Do you see that on the couch there?"

"Uh-huh."

"What is that?"

"That's either her hair or mine."

"Okay. What color is that hair?"

"I would say its blondish-brown."

"That hair there is blondish-brown?"

"To me, it looks like its blondish-brown."

"Can you describe the texture of the hair? Long, short, wavy, straight."

"It's a little long."

"A little wavy, too."

"From this picture, it looks to be wavy."

"Sure. How about People's Exhibit 54. Does it look like it came from the person in that photograph?"

"It looks like it may have."

"But it's too long to have come from your hair."

"I don't remember what the length of my hair was at that time. I do wear my hair pretty long, if you see in the police photo."

"Right. That's, so you think this could actually be your hair."

"It could be either one of us."

"Did you pull her hair out of her head that day?"

"Not that I recall. No, I didn't."

"This is a photo of People's Exhibit 53 where you are talking about on March 7th, where your hair is very long, is that right?"

"No, it's not real long there. My hair has been a lot longer. It's actually pretty short."

"Okay. And these marks on your face in People's Exhibit number 53, that's when Julie was able to fight back against you, right?"

"That's when Julie attacked me."

"That's when she attacked you."

"Yes."

"You are the one that pled guilty on March 28th to domestic battery on her, right?"

"On March 28th, yes."

"That was based on the March 7th incident where she allegedly attacked you?"

"Objection, Your Honor," interrupted Mr. Breen.

"What's the basis?" asked Judge Gaughan.

"It's an improper question," answered Mr. Breen.

"What's your response?" the judge asked Mr. Groth.

"It's not an improper question. He has set forth the idea he basically, made inconsistent statements. He said she attacked him therefore, he has self-defense on the March 7th incident and on March 28th. Three weeks later he is pleading guilty."

"Overruled. You can answer," replied Judge Gaughan.

"Mr. Groth said to George, "You did plead guilty to that charge."

"Yes, I did."

"Thank you. Now Mr. Breen asked you about the neighbor who testified, his name is actually Goldsmith, not Goldstein."

"Goldstein, I believe."

"It's not Goldsmith."

"It's Gold something."

"And he is the neighbor, right?"

"Correct, across the street."

"He called the police on you on the 7th of March, is that correct?"

"Yes."

"Now aside from the fact that you think that one night when you were having relations with Julie, he is the person who shined a red laser light into the two of you, you have never seen him or had anything against the man."

"Prior to that night?"

"Well let me ask you this."

"Rephrase it, Mr. Groth," interrupted the judge. "There is a compound question here."

Mr. Groth continued, "You believe that at some time Mr. Goldsmith shined a red laser light in the room when you were having relations with Julie, is that correct?"

"I believe it was Mr. Goldstein."

"Okay. And other than that, you have never had any kind of bad blood with him before, correct?"

"Never met the man in my life."

"Never met him before. That building at Sandburg Court, that's not the only apartment that faces you and Julie's apartment, is that correct?"

"No, there is several."

"Now you said that you had taken Julie to the ER on several occasions, is that correct?"

"Yes."

"How many times?"

"Three, four times maybe."

"So you knew where Northwestern Hospital was, right?"

"Oh, yes."

"And then later on in your testimony Julie always came out of it you said, is that also right?"

"In my statement?"

"Yes."

"When she was feeling badly and going through her things with the dehydration, puking, she usually would come out of it. That's when she went to the hospital and also when I would babysit her."

"So she would need medical attention to help her come out of it, is that correct?"

"Objection," exclaimed Mr. Breen.

"No, that's not correct."

"The answer will stand," ordered the judge.

Mr. Groth asked George, "Now at the time when you were, as you put it, her babysitter, you had to take care of her, is that correct?"

"On several occasions."

"What did that involve?"

"It involves helping her up, picking her up when she is falling down drunk, cleaning up after her puking, cleaning up the house, taking the dog out. It entails a lot of stuff taking care of a person who's drunk and can't take care of themselves. I don't know if you have ever been around a bad alcoholic but it's not a very pretty sight."

"Frustrating, right?"

"Not frustrating, but it did get old after awhile."

"So how is it not frustrating then?"

"Objection, Judge," interjected Mr. Breen.

"Sustained. Argumentative," ruled Judge Gaughan.

"It got tiresome." said Mr. Groth.

"After awhile, yes," replied George.

"Get on your nerves because she would be making incessant demands how to do things for her, correct?"

"I would help Julie out of the kindness of my heart. She wouldn't make any demands of anything. When you see a person in the condition that she is, you help her. We had a relationship so I would take care of Julie."

"But you weren't boyfriend and girlfriend as you stated earlier, right?"

"At that time we weren't. That's when I lived in Lisle. When I moved in after November of 2002, we were girlfriend and boyfriend."

"So you were boyfriend and girlfriend with her back in November when Mr. Goldsmith, or excuse me, when you had the fight with her back in November, is that correct, November of 2002?"

"So so."

"And you were her boyfriend."

"I was living out in Lisle so she had actually came out to my place and wanted me to come and take her out."

"Hadn't you been evicted from Lisle at that point?"

"No, I didn't get evicted until December, December 1st or something."

"You didn't get arrested in Lisle at that time, by the 23rd of November, for damaging the apartment."

"Right. I had got arrested."

"And the landlord let you stay there after you had been arrested."

"Yes, I had to get all my stuff out of it. He let me stay for approximately another ten days, I believe."

"Now on the day of May 17th when you had that fight with Julie, you went to bed shortly after, is that correct?"

"About 10:00 that evening, yeah."

"Then she woke up the next morning and she had drinks, is that right?"

"Yes."

"She had the drink in the afternoon."

"She had drinks all day long."

"Okay. That pattern continued on Monday, is that right?"

"Sunday and Monday."

"So, she had drinks pretty much all day, Monday as well?"

"Not all day. I would say she probably stopped drinking around, maybe 5:00. Whenever she had that type of seizure when she fell off the chair, that's when I cut her off of the booze."

"So at 5:00, she has a seizure that causes her to fall off the chair. That's 5:00 in the afternoon, and it's not until 11 hours later that you called 911."

Mr. Breen spoke up, "I object to the statement that she had a seizure which caused her to fall out of a chair. He wasn't there so that is not his testimony."

"Sustained. Rephrase," ordered the judge.

Mr. Groth rephrased the question. He asked George, "Around 5:00, you had left Julie shortly before that sitting in a Lazy Boy, is that correct?"

"Well I wouldn't say I left her. I was in the bedroom. She likes to sit out in the front room and look out the window. I was watching TV."

"She was in the Lazy Boy in the front room."

"Yes."

"That was around 5:00."

"Right."

"A short time later you heard the crash."

"I hear some commotion. I hear the table fall over."

"Where is Julie laying when you find her?"

"In front of the chair."

"And she is having difficulty at that point, is that correct?"

"She looks what appears to be some shakes, maybe a seizure. I caught the very end of it."

"And at that point, you didn't call the hospital for her, is that correct?"

"No, I didn't."

"But you were already worried from Sunday when Julie Starsiak had contacted you, is that correct?"

"No, that's not correct. Julie Starsiak called on Monday about noon, between noon and 1:00."

"Well you were worried when you talked to Julie Starsiak, is that correct?"

"I wasn't worried. I told Julie Starsiak about, they are very good friends, they are best friends, I believe. And I said Julie is on her same, you know, with the drinking, and I had mentioned that she had hit her head and had a black eye."

"Well you had mentioned to Julie Starsiak that you wanted her help in getting Julie to the hospital, is that correct?"

"I asked her if she wanted to come over and take Julie. I asked if she wanted to take her. She doesn't want to get involved. I don't know if Julie has ever taken her but when she gets like that, they don't talk anyway, so."

"And you were reluctant to take Julie Grace to the hospital because of all the injuries, is that correct?"

"I wouldn't say I was reluctant but I was, with the black eye it wouldn't look very good."

"It wouldn't look very good because of the past history between you two, right?"

"Yes, Sir, that's correct."

"So at 1:00, you are able to recognize Julie Grace needs to go to the hospital, but you don't want to take her because of the injuries, am I correct on that?"

"I recognize Julie had to go to the hospital. She could have went to the hospital any time from Sunday until Monday. She lives in a perpetual state of needing to be hospitalized."

"I am going to ask it again. It's a yes or no question, Sir. At 1:00 on Monday you realized that Julie Grace needs to go to the hospital but you didn't want to take her because of the injuries, yes or no?"

"That's correct, yes, Sir."

"Now you said that she had gotten a black eye, is that correct?"

"That's correct."

"And during your testimony, I believe you said she got it during the initial fight on Saturday when you pushed her, is that correct?"

"That's right."

"And she was coming towards you when you pushed her, is that correct?"

"Yes."

"And then you said her feet come out from under her and that's when she hit her head on the dresser, is that right?"

"Right."

"Now you also told Detective Heerdt that she fell off the toilet and hit her head and that's what caused the black eye, is that correct?"

"Right, well during Monday"

"Is that correct, Sir?"

"Yeah, that's what I told him."

"Now when you first talked to Detective Heerdt, Sir, you didn't mention this fight that you had with her at all did you?"

"I believe I did."

"When you talked to him you indicated that she had been drinking, she was a bad drunk and you had to spend most of your weekend picking her up and taking care of her. That's Detective Heerdt, the detective that testified in court."

"I know who he is. I know him privately."

"How did you know him privately?"

"He knew Julie in some capacity and when we would fight he would sometimes intercede and we would talk on the phone."

"He always wanted you to come in and talk to him to work these cases out, is that right?"

"Come in."

"Come into the Area to talk about the other cases, is that correct?"

"No, that's not correct at all."

"In fact, you told Detective Heerdt that Julie fell off the toilet on Saturday and hit her head and may have hit the shower."

"I may have."

"You didn't tell him that she hit her head on the dresser when you two were arguing and fighting, is that correct?"

"You're right."

"You didn't want to tell him that because again, she has got all these injuries on her, right?"

"I didn't want to tell him what happened because I was scared at the time."

"Now you also told him that you told Assistant State's Attorney D'Angelo that you were scared because of the order of the protection, is that right?"

"Yes, I did."

"But the order of protection was amended to allow you to live there, is that right?"

"Yes, it is."

"So there was nothing to be afraid of at that point because she was the one who attacked you all those time, right?"

"Well if they see a black eye and it was amended that we not fight with each other was the amendment on the violation."

"So again, Sir, you are not doing anything unlawful when you are defending yourself against her. There is nothing to be afraid of as far as that order of protection goes."

"Well if she gets a black eye and the police come, I am going to jail."

"Again, Sir, you haven't done anything wrong, right? That's your testimony today."

"She attacked me, yes."

"So you really"

"That doesn't work like that. When the police come, I am going to jail regardless."

"Right, because all these injuries she got was just an accident, is that right?"

"Except for the ones that I pointed out that I did."

"So the other bruises on her body, under her breast, on her chin, on her shoulders, on her legs, on her elbows, on her back, all of those you didn't cause?"

"The one on the back I did cause and the one under the breast I may have caused also, but other ones, Julie is a fall down drunk constantly."

"Right. How does she fall down and hurt her arms, on the interior of her arms?"

"I have no idea. I said I took claim for that one."

"Nothing further, Judge," said Mr. Groth.

"Redirect?" Judge Gaughan asked Mr. Breen.

"I have no questions," answered Mr. Breen.

"You can step down Mr. Thompson," instructed the judge.

Mr. Breen stated that he had no more witnesses.

After a brief discussion between the judge, Mr. Breen and Mr. Groth, the judge announced, "Now defense rests. Any rebuttal?" he asked.

Mr. Groth said, "We have a stipulation to his felony conviction out in DuPage County. Do you want us to do it now or do you want us to write it up?"

Co-defense attorney, Mr. Pugh, replied, "Criminal damage to property."

Judge Gaughan asked, "Are you all clear so that we can have an oral stipulation? Go ahead then."

Mr. Groth continued, "It would be stipulated by and between the parties that the defendant was convicted of criminal damage to property in DuPage County, and I will get the date."

Mr. Breen spoke up, "I understand that the State is moving for the admission of this as it may or may not affect his credibility in People versus Montgomery."

The judge replied, "And if it's the criteria, then I did the balancing test, so it's not overly prejudicial. So it will come in. State."

Mr. Groth went on to say, "Criminal damage to property, defendant was found guilty on October 13th, 2004 by George Bakalis."

"That was a felony." stated Judge Gaughan.

"Felony," replied Mr. Groth.

"So stipulated, Your Honor," responded Mr. Breen.

"That stipulation will be allowed and moved into evidence. Anything else in rebuttal?" asked the judge.

"No, Judge," answered Mr. Groth.

"You rest?" asked Judge Gaughan.

"Yes, Judge," answered Mr. Groth.

"Anything in surrebuttal?" asked the judge.

"No, Your Honor," answered Mr. Breen.

"Fine," said Judge Gaughan. "What I would like to do is have closing arguments tomorrow." He went on to say that each side would have 25 minutes. "This trial is commenced and continued to tomorrow for closing arguments."

CHAPTER 13

DAY FOUR OF GEORGE'S TRIAL
AND CLOSING ARGUMENTS

The trial was over. All the witnesses had given their testimony. Tomorrow, Glenn and I would hear George's long-awaited verdict. Both of us spent a very restless night in our hotel. It seemed like tomorrow would never come. When it finally arrived, Glenn, Julie's friends, members of the media, and I made our way into the courtroom, and anxiously waited for the last day of the trial to begin. I wasn't feeling good about the way the trial had gone, and my only hope was that Mr. Groth's closing argument would be compelling enough to convince the judge to convict George of first-degree murder.

At 11:00 AM on May 16, 2006, court reconvened. The judge opened by asking both Mr. Groth and Mr. Breen if they were prepared to proceed with closing arguments. Both stated they were. The judge instructed Mr. Groth to make his closing statements for the State.

Instead of Mr. Groth, Ms. Popielewski stood up and stated the following: "Your Honor, in this case of People versus George Thompson, we are asking that you make a finding, a finding that comports with the evidence, and that finding would be a finding of guilty of first degree murder.

"Your Honor, what is the evidence that proves the defendant guilty of first degree murder beyond a reasonable doubt? We believe that evidence shows that the defendant performed the acts which caused the death of Miss Julie Grace, caused the death of Julie Grace, his acts.

"He admits to you in a video-taped confession, as well as here on the stand, that he punched Julie Grace on the 17th of May, that he slapped her, that he pushed her. It is these acts which caused the blows to her body, the subdural hematoma.

"As you well know, Judge, the law of causation in a first degree murder case does not require that the defendant's acts are the sole and immediate cause of death. They require that they are a contributing factor and you heard from the medical examiner in this case.

"The medical examiner told you that Julie Grace died as a result of blunt force trauma and the complications thereof. It is beyond a reasonable doubt proven that it is this man's acts that caused the death of Julie Grace.

"What else has the evidence shown for you? We also must prove that when he caused these acts, when he gave her that brutal beating, he intended to kill and do great bodily harm to Miss Grace, or that when he beat her, he knew that his acts caused a strong probability of great bodily harm to Miss Grace.

"Your Honor, I am asking you to look at three specific factors to determine this man's intent when he beat his girlfriend. First, I want you to look at the severity of the injuries to Miss Grace's body, two subdural hematoma, black eye, fresh bruises to her lower face in the chin area, large pattern of fresh bruises to her chest, her arms, her back, her hip, her legs. These show the severity of this beating. All you have to do is look at that severity to know what the intent was there and that was certainly to do great bodily harm.

"However, Judge, the other factor I'm asking you to look at is the escalating pattern of violence between Mr. Thompson as he engaged in it against Julie Grace. And specifically, look at the progression of the injuries from November to March of 2003, to finally May 20th, when she expires. Look at what the defendant has to say, coupled with the severity of the injuries on the 17th, the broken lip, bruises on the body.

"Julie Grace, thru that police officer, was able to tell us that this defendant said, I'm going to kill you on that day. He also speaks to the police on that day and says to them, I had to kick her ass to keep her in line. Well, Your Honor, that pattern of violence was finished for Mr. Thompson when he actually carried out that threat, I'm going to kill you. He did that when he beat her on the 17th of May.

"The third thing I want you to look at, Judge, in regard to the defendant's intent when he committed this horrible act, is to look at the defendant's actions after this brutal beating. He does nothing to get Julie Grace any medical attention even though he admits to you on the stand, he knew she needed it. Once he realized that his goal has been reached, he killed her.

"What does he then do? He lies to the police about what he's done and once he is confronted with the fact that the injuries to her body do not comport with his version of events, he minimizes, he minimizes in that videotape and he minimized on the stand yesterday to you. He's doing anything he can to get away from his responsibility.

"Your Honor, a picture speaks a thousand words. This photograph of Julie Grace in death speaks louder than any words that George Thompson could put on video or could say from that stand. The severity of this beating proves to you what his intent was at that time. His intent was to commit first degree murder and we are asking you for a finding of guilty."

"Thank you," said Judge Gaughan. "Mr. Breen."

Mr. Breen's closing argument was as follows: "I said in the beginning of this case that their murder theory, their first degree murder theory, was a stretch, a real stretch. As the court well knows, they must prove beyond a reasonable doubt each of the elements of their first degree murder indictment that they brought against George Thompson.

"The court said something very interesting, and it may have been an aside but I took a note of it, and that was there are no secrets in a courtroom. And that is so true, Your Honor. There are no secrets anymore about Julie Grace and her lifestyle and her abuse with alcohol. The evidence has shown and we have attempted to spotlight that evidence, of her problems with chronic alcoholism, not to demean her name, not to demean her, but to do what I don't believe anybody did prior to George Thompson being charged with this offense, which is, to investigate completely, independently and openly as to what may have occurred on May 17th, 2003.

"We didn't go into the fact that in January of 2001, and in February of 2001, she was dehydrated, that she was puking, dry heaving, that she was showing signs of alcohol abuse, you know, so much alcohol to your system that it has a toxic reaction.

"We didn't go into her two treatments at Lake Shore Hospital for the purposes of defiling her or mocking her. We didn't go into the March of 02 ethanol abuse or the July 10th ethanol abuse at Northwestern Hospital or why she was admitted to the emergency room.

"We didn't go into the fact that she had aggressive, violent behavior while intoxicated, that she struck a doctor, that she had to be restrained, we don't do that, Your Honor, to demean her. And we didn't do all the other medicals showing constant need to be dehydrated, constant toxic results of alcohol use. We didn't go into the fact that she suffered so severely from her drinking that her liver had almost been destroyed.

"We didn't do that to demean Julie Grace. It is a fact, and it is a fact of life, and you have to decide the facts on May 17th, 2003.

"Why did we go into it? It has at least two extremely relevant; it goes to two very relevant things in this case. One, Your Honor, it does go to cause of death and it goes to the condition of the body as seen in these photographs.

"What do I mean by that? The court heard from the pathologist, or heard from a pathologist, not the pathologist who performed the autopsy. You heard from a pathologist who rendered an opinion who did not have a complete set of her records regarding her prior medical history. When she testified, she did not have a full set of Julie Grace's medicals. But put that aside. The cause of death that Counsel wants to say is so plain and simple, took months for the Cook County medical examiner to determine. It is a complicated cause of death where she indicates that a major contributing factor to her death was her chronic alcoholism and her fatty liver.

"That, Your Honor, is very important because it explains why bruises on her would seem so exaggerated in these photographs. And the doctor testified that a bump in the dark would cause major bruising in a chronic alcoholic because the liver is not able to react properly, clot the blood properly to prevent the bruise. So these photographs that Counsel says are worth a thousand words are not worth a thousand words until you look at the facts behind these photographs.

"What are the other facts behind the photographs? The mutually abusive and physical relationship that George had with her. Her chronic alcoholism, Judge, didn't just result in a bad liver from easy bruising. It didn't just result in all of that, it resulted in a few other things, violent behavior.

"And George told you about their relationship and he also told you, and the evidence happens to be absolutely uncontradicted on that point, that Julie would become violent and attack him. It would start verbally, then it would turn physical and she would attack him and he would respond.

"The prosecution wants to tell you that somehow, between November and March, his conduct toward her escalated. That is not true. Her conduct toward him escalated, that's what occurred. He, too, had been injured in some of these domestic disputes and he, too, well knows that the guy goes to jail on a domestic abuse case. And whatever he said in the moment of anger, I'm going to kill you or whatever was not in fact his intent.

"When he says to the policemen on the elevator going down and he's talking to policemen who he knows, and the policemen knows that situation because they're familiar with Julie Grace, and he is making a smart ass comment that he shouldn't have made that sounds like he's cold, I had to keep her in line. Judge, there is no evidence whatsoever that that's what he ever tried to do. The evidence is uncontradicted that he attempted to defend himself from time to time.

"Now, let's talk about May 17th, 2003. On May 17th, 2003 the evidence is that Julie became violent and aggressive. Who cares what the topic was that caused her and George to have a mouth fight that she went after him, that she scratched his face, and whether the scratches are small or whatever, it doesn't make any difference that she scratched his face and that he hit her in the chest to get her away, and that she kept coming at him and then he pushed her and she fell, and she fell and he saw her hit her head onto the dresser, and that was the end of the fight. That he went over and picked her up and put her on the bed.

"And the court heard the testimony yesterday, so I won't go into the details of it, but what is so important, Your Honor, is the fight had ended, that was it, it is over. George Thompson and Julie Grace spend an evening together and the next day.

"And it is so obvious, I probably shouldn't even bother the court with it, you know, he is an iron worker; he's not a medical doctor. What he sees the next day, later in the day, is a black eye developing. Earlier, he had seen a welt.

"She never complained, she never asked to go to the hospital. She had access to the phone. She could have called anyone. She could have called 911. She could have called a cab. She could have called her mother. She was not being held incommunicado, which I believe was their original theory.

"What does she do? At 7:15 or so in the evening, she calls the neighborhood grocery store for a delivery. She gets a 1.75 liter of vodka, cigarettes and food. That is what she does and she makes that phone call. And you'll see phone activity, by the way, Judge, on their own phone records. She's not being held incommunicado.

"She speaks to Jeff, who spoke to her in the past, and gets an order. Why is that important? It is important for a whole bunch of reasons, but it is most important because it absolutely positively corroborates what George Thompson has been saying, that after that fight on May 17th, she was fine, we went about our business. It corroborates him, it is independent, completely independent of him, and it is documented. She is fine on that day of May 18th. It is only later on May 19th, that she begins to fall again, gets sick again.

"Now what is interesting is how we all care so much after the fact of Julie Grace's death. We're all concerned we've lost someone and I'm concerned, too, and I feel for her and her family, but who is in charge of her on May 17th, 18th, 19th and 20th? Her friends don't want anything to do with her, nothing. There's nobody there to rescue her from her chronic alcoholism, from her vomiting, her dehydration problems.

"George is there and George told her, and again is corroborated by the medical records, that the symptoms she showed on the 19th and 20th were symptoms he had seen before. Does he know the difference between a tremor and seizure like Dr. Footy does? No. Has he seen her go thru dehydration and DT's and shake and tremble? Yes. Has he seen her projectile vomit, defecate in her pants? Yes. He has personally seen that in the past, and he sees her going thru that still again.

"And everybody wants to criticize him for why didn't you call 911. Why didn't you get her to a hospital? Well, Judge, it was kind of a usual thing in the life of George Thompson and Julie Grace; that is why he didn't. And when the time came, and after cleaning up after her at 4:00 in the morning, he returned to that room and saw her on the ground, and for the first time knew that this was different from all other occasions, he called 911.

"Their story, Judge, isn't a story of a sitcom family. Their story isn't a Norman Rockwell portrait. Their story is a sad, sad, depressing story that too frequently occurs from two chronic alcoholics joining each other in their alcoholism. Neither is good for the other. Tragedy will always lurk right around the corner.

"George Thompson is terribly sorry that Julie Grace died. You can see that in the videotape. The fact of the matter is, Your Honor, she did not die as a result of George Thompson intentionally or knowingly, without lawful justification, doing harm to her, that is not how she died. To give the State the complete benefit of the doubt, she died as a result of hitting her head on a dresser, falling on that dresser because George pushed her away from him. And to look at these photographs, maybe a lay person would prior to the pathologist report, say, oh, my God, she must have been pummeled. Well, Judge, when we get behind the photographs and get to the scientific evidence, we know she wasn't pummeled.

"They want to say how strong George is. Well, Judge, if he attempted to attack her or pummel her in some way, she would have had more significant injuries than this. She never has a fracture. She never has a broken bone. She has bruises as any chronic alcoholic who is falling and bumping in the dark would have.

"The case law, Your Honor, that is applicable to this case is right on point. The State has given us some cases, and I won't get into a big legal argument at this point in time, I don't know if the court wants it. But their cases that they have cited to date, don't even come close to the facts of the situation that we have.

"We look, Judge, in this case at the following: The mutual abusive relationship, the evidence that she was violent and aggressive, the uncontradicted fact that even came out in the videotape, much to the chagrin of the assistant state's attorney, taking it no doubt, that she attacked him and he pushed her away, which resulted in her falling on the dresser.

"I would ask the court look at a case called People versus Divincenzo, 183 IL 2d, 239, a 1998 decision. I would ask that the court take a look at People versus Tainter, 304 IL Ap 3rd, 847, a 1999 case, and there are others here, Your

Honor,People versus Burnette, 35 IL Ap 3rd, 792; People versus Holmes, 246 IL Ap 3rd, 179; People versus Hancock, 113 IL Ap 3rd, 4564. And at best, Your Honor, at best what the law says under these facts, is that his conduct under the totality of the circumstances may have been reckless. And if reckless is the proper mental state, then first degree murder must be dismissed, aggravated battery must be dismissed, and the tryer of fact and the court, according to the law, may consider involuntary manslaughter only.

"Your Honor, it is just a tragedy and if anything, it should be a learning experience for all of us. But a tragedy Judge, occurred, not induced or intended by George Thompson. And let's not double the tragedy by stretching the law to some degree or the facts and find him guilty of first degree murder, because neither the law nor the facts, Your Honor, would support that. Thank you."

"Thank you," said Judge Gaughan. "Mr. Groth."

"Judge," said Mr. Groth, "the law and the facts, common sense, human experience and the laws of physics completely support a first degree murder conviction.

"Let's talk about the injury that was caused to Julie Grace, the series of injuries to her face that was caused by, as the defendant put it, her coming at him, him pushing her so violently that she left her feet, and somehow in that trip off the ground, she did a 90 degree turn, moved over about 2 or 3 feet and made contact with the dresser.

"Now, unfortunately for the defense, the doctor's testimony, Dr. Arangelovich, completely destroys that theory. The questions I asked her about the abrasions on the temple wound completely destroy that. The fact that there are no straight line injuries to her head completely destroys that. This defendant, if you look at the other pictures here, Judge, if you look at the pictures from the bruises to Julie Grace's arms, under Julie Grace's breasts and in between her breasts, are completely consistent with somebody who lost a fight. The bruises on her arm are consistent with someone kneeling on her arm and pasting her a couple right in the face. That is why there is two distinct injuries on her temple and on her eye socket.

"The defendant came up with this incredibly improbable story because he doesn't want to admit what he did, and that is just the way this defendant is, Judge. You saw that in the evidence of proof of other crimes. You saw that on March 7th. If Peter Goldsmith doesn't call the police, we are here in March of 02 trying this case because it happened on that day. You heard how he was taking running kicks at her. You saw the physical evidence of the victim's and nobody else's hair on the sofa. You saw what she looked like when Julie could actually put up a fight.

"This defendant took an oath and stood up in that stand and said that the hair on the sofa is his. These two pictures were taken the same day. By no stretch of the imagination could the hair on the sofa be this defendant's. It is completely consistent with Julie Grace, but again, this defendant is trying to lie and do whatever he can to escape responsibility.

"You heard from Dr. Footy. The victim came into the hospital and told him she had gotten her hand cut by her boyfriend. Dr. Footy told us that it was consistent with that and this defendant gets in here, takes an oath and says, oh, no, she was playing mumble depeg in the kitchen.

"November 28th, you have rug burns, scratching, bruises above her right eye. April 22nd, 2003 when Julie Grace tries to use the phone in her apartment, and what does this defendant say, I will bust your head open. Also, on March 7th, because you see again the defendant's methods of operations, he pulls the phone cords out of the wall. You have got pictures of those.

"You have the defendant's explanation for the injuries and these are critical. This is People's Exhibit 29 and People's Exhibit 31 showing the hemorrhages on both sides of the skull. That does not come from a fall. None of this stuff came from a fall. That is just the story he came up with.

"Here's the man acting in self defense or recklessly. He's got two shaving cuts on him and that is 3 or 4 days after the original fight. And you heard from Dr. Arangelovich, he's got fresh blood on his fingers. Julie Grace wasn't bleeding openly. This defendant was wise to the system and he knew what was going to happen. He opened those wounds up."

Mr. Breen interrupted, "Objection. This is truly speculative."

"Sustained. Move on, State," replied Judge Gaughan.

Mr. Groth continued. "You have the evidence of Mrs. Grace making desperate phone calls. You will have her records showing she is making call to call to Julie on that day, this defendant hanging up, which he initially did. He lies, but subsequently admits. You have the 911 tape showing, once again, this defendant is not a good actor. You heard his tone. It was one of annoyance. She's puking on me all night. Listen to me, I'm giving her mouth to mouth, huff, huff.

"You heard from Paramedic Greer who is by no means a layman, someone who has the experience of working as a paramedic on the streets of Chicago, he takes one look at her. He knows what happened. She got beat up. Everybody knows what happened. You have Dr. Arangelovich's testimony which is crucial, several irregular areas of bruising on the chest. That didn't come from one punch. The ten by ten centimeters under the breasts, which defendant cannot account for. Bruising under the breast sounds like someone who doesn't like women attacking them in the area that most represents their womanhood."

"Judge, object," interjected Mr. Breen.

"Sustained," replied Judge Gaughan. "State, stick to the evidence, all right, and don't try and inflame me."

Mr. Groth continued, "She's got one small defensive wound on her hand and that goes to show her helplessness, the same way Dr. Footy's testimony described her helplessness. Look at her injuries in the protocol. They are all isometrical on the sides of her body. The bruising to her hips, each one has a mate on the other side. It is all very consistent with someone kneeling on her or squeezing her or doing something to inflict injury.

"The law in the State of Illinois is clear. We cited all those cases to you so I'm not going to cite them. You've got them all, and they all said the same thing. If the defendant's acts are a contributing factor, he's guilty of murder, but we haven't got that. We have got her prior existing condition being a contributing factor. She died as a result of the bronchopneumonia caused by him beating her on the head on two sides.

"There was no sign of infection in her kidneys. Dr. Arangelovich testified her kidneys were fine. Dr. Arangelovich talked about the sheer force required to do these types of things. Force required to move things forward and backwards and that is important because if you fall, you are only going to hit one time, the one thing. She talked about how Julie was an alcoholic and the alcoholic needs to drink to the detriment of everything else. She had higher tolerance. She could handle more. And yet, when this defendant is done with her, Judge, she's got no alcohol in her system.

"They have gone to great lengths to show what a horrible alcoholic she was. Well, this defendant beat her into sobriety. She never got the chance to hit rock bottom.

"You heard Detective Heerdt talking about trying to explain the bruises to her body as part of his care taking function, and it is crucial he never told Detective Heerdt to say, hey, it was an accident. I may have pushed her too hard. He denies everything. He denies any type of wrongdoing. He comes up with, she fell off the Lazy Boy. She fell off the toilet. She was flopping around. She was whirling like a dervish.

"He said he was afraid to call the police because of the order of protection. Later on, he said he knew this order of protection was amended, so it is just him lying. He talked about she had random seizures. Well, we know from Dr. Arangelovich that the seizures were a symptom of the blunt force trauma. He didn't know at that point. Counsel pointed out he went to iron workers school but he didn't go to medical school.

"You heard, to the defendant's additional version, the one he gave to Nick D'Angelo, probably all the bruises were caused in the fight, he says. Then on the stand he says, no, it was just the circular one, the rest are a mystery especially the ones under her arm as he could not account for those bruises.

"He told them before, Julie only had insignificant bruises when they fought. This defendant told Nick D'Angelo what he wanted to tell him. You have his version, the DT's caused withdrawal, she is still drinking when she seizes up.

"Counsel talks about how his testimony is uncontradicted. It is also uncorroborated. Where is the evidence that this defendant got a broken nose? Where is the evidence that this defendant suffered any harm whatsoever at the hands of Julie Grace?

"They talk about a mutually abusive relationship and I know Your Honor listened to the testimony that took place before she met this defendant, and that was something involving her getting arrested for no violence."

"Judge, objection," said Mr. Breen. "That was March of 03. The doctor said absolutely abusive."

Judge Gaughan interrupted, "So it was. That pertained to the July, 2002. All right. Go ahead."

Mr. Groth replied, "My mistake, Judge. It was in the records in a different date. There is no evidence of her starting any fights.

"This defendant said that Julie started all the fights with him and yet he goes into court and pleads guilty every time. He goes into court and admits that he is the guy who did it. He's not the one who was acting in self defense. All those are admissions showing that he was the aggressor in the past, and he's trying to blame everything. In the video, he actually tries to blame his father for showing him the way to beat women. This defendant is throwing everything he can against the wall. All the bruises come from the fight. Yesterday when he testified, it was only the ones I circled and I can't explain the others.

"Victim Julie Grace had set this defendant off on that day, May 17th. She went to go see her friend, Bill. She brought her bi-sexual friend home. She told family secrets he didn't care to hear. This set him off and he got angry. There is provocation because their defendant admitted it took place too far away from when the original provocation occurred and it is not provocation. The law is clear. You can't have strong words lead to murder.

"Defendant talked about how he didn't give any care to Julie Grace's injuries. He was acting out of the kindness of his heart. He babysat for her. He didn't want to take care of her. He wanted someone else to do it. Well, Northwestern Hospital is a short truck trip away. 911 is a phone call away. What is the reason for him not getting her some type of medical attention except for the consciousness of his guilt regarding her injuries and he as much said so in the video.

"He tries to come up with the story about how she leaves her feet and somehow makes contact with the dresser. That is nonsense.

"This defendant is the same person who wants you to believe all these lies he's told about Julie cutting herself with a knife, about his hair being on the sofa, about that back slip into the dresser. All these things.

"Julie Starsiak was telling him to call 911 and leave and he didn't want to do that because he knew that is something he can't control. Defendant admitted on the video that he had just gotten out of jail and he wasn't in a hurry to go back.

"They talk about the delivery. The only person they called regarding the delivery was somebody who talked to Julie over the phone, and Your Honor is going to see from the bank records that this was a big deviation from what Julie normally did. She normally went in there and paid for things with checks. She had never had things delivered to her before. She's so disoriented. She's so confused she can't do anything like she normally would, go down there, meet and greet people, be the social person she was. She's got to have the delivery guy come up here. And where is the delivery guy? There is nothing to show that. All the defendant's statement, 911 tape, video, testimony, they show several things. He inflicted the beating, didn't want to get caught, delayed calling because of consciousness of guilt. He lied because defendant did have consciousness of guilt and he is so desperate that he is willing to smear Julie Grace.

"I do want to point out, Judge, that the cases Counsel cited all go toward instructions, whether or not the jury gets an instruction on an issue except for People versus Holmes, which Counsel cited and I checked before I came to court. They provided me with these cases earlier today and that's been overruled by People versus Ripley which has got a great sentiment as far as this case goes. It is an agg bat to a child case and the defendant, not surprisingly in Ripley, said hey, I didn't mean to do it, just like this defendant and the court stated, 'However we conclude that Holmes was wrongfully decided. We find that circumstantial evidence, including medical testimony regarding severity of the injuries, is sufficient to prove that the injuries were intentionally or knowingly inflicted, even when defendant testifies he did not intend to injure the victim.' And the child in Ripley had nowhere near the injuries Julie Grace had.

"Counsel talks about how it is involuntary manslaughter and we provided Your Honor with cases on that, it is not involuntary. Crucial distinction in the case law is one between giving the instruction arriving at the involuntary verdict which all the cases Counsel cited go toward instruction, and all the cases we gave, toward looking at what the ultimate verdict is. And when the court's looking at these things, they look at what the acts were, not what the defendant's self-serving statements were. It is found in Bartaugh, Bracket, Howry, Vic Edwards, Givens, Daniels, Reed, Terrell. Bracket and eleven other cases tell us to look at the size and relative strength of the victim and defendant, especially Givens, which was the bike messenger case. They look at what the prior acts were, and they gave a lesser included instruction, and the courts looked to see if it was still murder and it was.

"Julie Grace was pretty weak. She was too weak. She had no muscle mass. Her doctor testified she was almost in a constant state of drunkenness except when he had beaten her so bad she couldn't get another drink.

"Counsel also cited the Burnettes case, which I think is important. That was a case out of this building in front of Judge Salone, and it was basically a felony murder, home invasion and what happened was Judge Salone found the defendant guilty of home invasion, and he found the defendant guilty of involuntary manslaughter. The court sent back the involuntary manslaughter, basically saying that lesser included couldn't stand, based on the evidence. And as a result, basically the person in Burnette got away with a free homicide. Actually, it was murder because he found him guilty of the home invasion.

"In this case, there has been some talk about provocation and it would be the same thing here, Judge. Defense has been very skillful in raising these issues without arguing them. And maybe you might want to think about a second degree on this case, but I would implore you not to because by finding this defendant guilty of second degree, it would be a slow acquittal because the Appellate Court would do the same thing they did in Burnette. It is not involuntary. It is not second degree. There is no self-defense here.

"Self-defense requires force be used against the defendant and the defendant actively and selectively believed danger existed. That is how you get to second degree, by showing self-defense. There is no force against his defendant. He, by his admission on the stand and by his statement in the video, he's the one who goes to Julie. She comes out and tells him to turn the stereo down and he doesn't want to take that. She's not being in line. He engines and he becomes the initial aggressor. There is no eminent danger because we know from the medical examiner that she is no threat to him. There is no unlawful force being used against him, and I think it is important to point out in the video he says he pushed her on the bed first, then she came at him, probably trying to get away.

"But it is three years later, he adds, oh no, she came out. She started slapping me. It is nonsense. It is not to be believed. The only words that she used was to tell him to turn the stereo down and that doesn't give you self-defense. Case after case says self-defense does not protect your wounded pride.

"Judge, this defendant, what he committed on that day, was first degree murder. It was first degree murder based on the severity of the injuries, based on the differentials in size, strength, gender, damage. It was first degree murder based on the severity of the injuries and whether or not it took her 3 days to die, whether or not, when she is not able to make any type of contact with anybody.

"Did Counsel mention there is phone records there? Well, they brought in the store manager. Where are the other people who talked to Julie Grace if this is their defense?"

"Objection Judge," exclaimed Mr. Breen. "We have no burden."

"Sustained," replied the judge. "You can't shift the burden of proof, State. Listen to my statement. Unless you show some type of exclusive control over witnesses you are shifting the burden, so stop it right now."

"Judge, it is irrelevant," said Mr. Groth. "The phone records regarding whether there is no activity on the phone that day, because there is no preponderance of evidence about who was making those calls. There is no evidence about what the condition of the person was. Kenya Moore came in and testified that Julie sounded drunk. The delivery boy who we didn't have any control about, is not here, there a"

"Excuse me," interrupted Mr. Breen. "That is absolutely inaccurate. The name of the grocery store and the circumstances were given to them before yesterday, Your Honor."

"When were they given to them?" asked Judge Gaughan.

"I don't know," answered Mr. Breen. "Why don't you tell us when you got the receipt from"

"Thursday or Friday, three days ago," replied Mr. Groth.

"Well, he certainly would have been entitled to a continuance if he thought it was necessary," said the judge. "Go ahead."

Mr. Groth continued. "The person who can testify about her condition isn't here. Mr. Iwamuro testified about how her condition was on the phone which was consistent with Dr. Arangelovich. There is also two phone calls made there, the ten minutes and two minutes which is consistent with somebody being a little confused, a little bit disoriented."

"Mr. Groth, that is a stretch," commented the judge. "Let's move on. You've got one minute."

"Judge," replied Mr. Groth, "I am asking you to find this defendant guilty of what it is, what he did, which is first degree murder."

"Thank you," said Judge Gaughan. "Ladies and gentlemen I am going to go into chambers, review the evidence and come up with my decision. I know this is very stressful and this is very, very emotional for the families involved for both Ms. Julie Grace and Mr. Thompson. When I come out and I'm going to say what my findings are, I do not want any emotional outbreaks. Disrupt my court and you will be arrested and put in jail for direct contempt.

"So what I want you to do is look into your heart. If you feel that you can handle this emotionally, you're more than welcome to stay and I want you to stay. If you feel that you might break out in emotional yelling or screaming or disruptions of court, I'd ask you to leave this court and I will have deputies up here."

The judge exited the courtroom and a short recess was taken. In approximately fifteen minutes, the judge returned and said, "Court's back in session. Please remain seated."

I knew we were just moments away from hearing George's verdict. I kept praying he would pronounce George guilty of first-degree murder. Even though there was no verdict tough enough to relieve the pain George had inflicted upon me and my family, I couldn't bear the thought of him being awarded a lesser verdict. My stomach was in knots as I waited for the judge to speak.

CHAPTER 14
THE VERDICT

"I've listened to the arguments, paid attention to the evidence, watched the demeanor of the witnesses as they testified, and reviewed my notes and the evidence in this case. It is a basic principal of law that the burden of proof is on the State, but if the defendant takes the stand or the defense puts on evidence, then all of the evidence must be reviewed and the burden of proof is still on the State. So, using these factors and evaluating the facts and the evidence and arriving at that and applying the law, first, I have to make some statements about some of the evidence.

"As to the video statement taken by the Assistant State's Attorney, the statement was ten minutes long. There was very little detail asked by the assistant state's attorney about what happened from Saturday night to Tuesday morning. There was quite a bit of leading questions in there and which is a little shocking, too, is that when the state's attorney was asked to show, was shown a photograph that he used in the video-taped statement, he said that he couldn't identify the dresser, that Mr. Thompson had stated was a dresser in the statement. He said, also, that Mr. Thompson had pushed Julie from behind and that wasn't in the statement. Even after he took the statement, he went and approved charges. So this is a very tragic case.

"I also have to look at the factors involved, that the death occurred of Julie Grace on May 20th, 2003, and there wasn't a cause of death arrived at that time until July, a couple of months later in 2003.

"Then there is the testimony of the manager from the Pottash Grocery Store. Certainly he was an independent witness and his credibility was there, and his testimony was clear and convincing that on the night of Sunday, a day after approximately 22 hours later from the incident, Julie placed an order of 29 items, and a lot of these were concerning food, as pointed out by the defense. One was vodka and the other one was concerning cigarettes, and the fact that Julie didn't smoke but she was ordering cigarettes for Mr. Thompson.

"So combining all of this, and my heart goes out to the families, all right, the only verdict I can reach or finding I can reach is that Mr. Thompson is guilty of involuntary manslaughter, and he is guilty of the violation of the order of protection."

After a brief discussion between the attorneys and the judge regarding post-trial motions and a sentencing date, Mr. Groth asked, "Judge, did you enter a finding on the felony domestic battery, as well?"

"There is a finding of not guilty," answered the judge.

A continuance was taken to June 15th, 2006.

The verdict was in. Glenn and I couldn't believe our ears. Involuntary manslaughter! Unbelievable! We were devastated. In our minds, Judge Gaughan was rendering merely a slap on the hands to a cold murderer. How could he do this to my Julie? Where was the justice for Julie?

How could the assistant state's attorney allow this to happen? As we sat through the trial, Glenn and I were concerned about the way Julie was being portrayed, but our only hope was that Mr. Groth would eventually produce some convincing evidence to convict George of first degree-murder. But he never did, and why didn't he? We asked ourselves this over and over again. Why didn't he bring the doorman of Julie's building in to testify that because of George's abusive nature the condo association had banned him from the building unless he was escorted by Julie?

Why did Mr. Groth have Dr. Arangelovich testify instead of the doctor that personally performed the autopsy, Dr. An? Dr. An would have been able to provide the facts per his personal observation, and, unlike Dr. Arangelovich, he would have been a more convincing witness than Dr. Arangelovich, since she had nothing to do with the autopsy.

Why didn't Mr. Groth ask Corazon Cruz about all the times she heard Julie's screams and calls for help but failed to call the police?

Why didn't Mr. Groth call credible witnesses that had known and worked with Julie for many years and who had witnessed the physical abuse subjected upon her by George Thompson? Why didn't he ask Julie's best friend, Julie Starsiak, to testify?

What about George's previous employer? Why was he not called to testify? What was the reason George got fired? Could it be because he was fighting at work and beat up a co-worker? And what about his previous landlord? Why wasn't he called to testify regarding George's violent behavior when he destroyed his apartment and had to be evicted? And speaking of apartments, why didn't Mr. Groth produce witnesses who had visited Julie's apartment on numerous occasions who could testify that its appearance on May 20th, 2003 was not typical of how it normally looked? Julie kept a nice, neat apartment and would never have allowed it to look the way it did when the police found it on the day she died.

What about other women who were abused victims of George? They were out there, and Mr. Groth knew who they were. Why didn't he subpoena them to testify?

Why didn't Mr. Groth question George as to why he stayed with Julie if she was so abusive to him and because of her alcohol problem if he was so frustrated because he had to babysit her all the time? Why would anyone stay under those circumstances? Could it be because she was providing him with a very good lifestyle, supporting him, and even making his truck payments?

Also, why didn't he bring in any witnesses that could have attested to Julie's physical condition a few weeks prior to her death? There is no way she could have physically gone up against George and harmed him in any way. She was much too frail.

Why didn't the assistant state's attorney bring in witnesses that could attest to George's crack cocaine habit?

Why didn't Mr. Groth question a medical expert who could have provided credible testimony regarding head trauma injuries and the episodes the body experiences before succumbing?

Mr. Groth and the state's attorney's office had so many opportunities to prove George had taken terrible advantage of Julie's warmhearted nature, and the only thing she did wrong was became a victim of his selfish, noncaring, abusive ways. Saddened, disheartened, and frustrated by the whole ordeal, Glenn and I were determined to let the world know just how badly the Illinois court system had let us down and how it unfairly allows the misrepresentation of innocent victims of murderers by twisting the evidence and discrediting an individual who would have never caused harm to anyone under any circumstances.

At the onset of the trial, Glenn and I were very amazed when we learned that the accused has all the rights, and the victims and/or their families basically have none. After all, George was the only one allowed to decide whether it would be a bench trial or a jury trial. Is that fair? Why don't the victims have any say? Also, why is the accused allowed to choose the attorney to represent them while the victim is forced to take whomever the state's attorney's office appoints?

Because of the liberal Illinois court system, the court and the attorney of the accused turned a victim of domestic violence into her own murderer while the assistant state attorney sat back and watched. It was obvious Julie had been

217

tried and convicted before her accuser's trial ever began. Unfortunately, the only thing Julie was guilty of was caring too much for people and allowing someone as evil as George into her heart and home, someone who was there merely for his own personal needs and gratification. He expected Julie to provide him with a nice home, food, alcohol, cigarettes, and drugs, and pay all his bills. His way of thanking her for all she did was to rob her of her gold jewelry and other valuable items and mentally and physically torture and abuse her when he didn't get his way.

Yes, it was no secret that Julie had a drinking problem, but alcohol did not kill her, George Thompson did. The toxicology reports clearly stated there was no alcohol in her system when she died. However, the photos show the horrible beating which caused her untimely death. That's why her death certificate states the cause of death as homicide. Nowhere does it make any reference to alcoholism. That's because no amount of alcohol could have been responsible for causing the horrible wounds and bruises to Julie's body. The real truth is that George, in one of his violent rages, beat my daughter close to death, and because he didn't want to go back to jail, sat for three days and watched her die a slow, painful death. Only a vicious animal would do such a cruel and inhumane thing. Julie died not because she was an alcoholic. She died because she was a warm, caring person who was too trusting of everyone, especially George Thompson.

Deeply upset with the judge's verdict, Glenn and I left the courtroom, made our way to the airport and got on a plane to fly back to Florida. Tormented by the trial's result, we knew we were not going to quietly accept the judge's outrageous miscarriage of justice without speaking our minds. On June 15th, we were determined we were going to speak out for Julie since she was unable to tell her side of the story. George Thompson was supposed to have been on trial for Julie's murder. Instead, during the course of the trial, George somehow became the victim of Julie's supposed abuse, and her death was a result of her own acts and not anyone else's.

Eager to tell the court Julie's story, Glenn and I worked diligently on our victim impact statements, as that was the only way we were going to be able to get in front of the courtroom and speak out for Julie.

Although the judge had scheduled the continuance for June 15th, 2006, it was postponed and rescheduled to June 29th, 2006.

CHAPTER 15
GEORGE'S SENTENCING

When the date of the continuance finally arrived, Glenn and I once again made a trip from Florida to Chicago. On the morning of June 29th, we entered the courtroom and were prepared for the day's activities, which would eventually result in the sentencing of George Thompson. Prior to returning to Chicago, our impact statements had been written and submitted for review per Illinois judicial requirements. Glenn and I could hardly wait to tell the court Julie's side of the story so everyone would know she was a wonderful, caring person and not the abusive alcoholic she had been portrayed to be. Even though we knew our statements would have little impact on George's sentencing as the judge had already decided his fate, Glenn and I could not sit idly by without looking Julie's killer in the eye and letting him know that although he had fooled the judge, he hadn't fooled us.

When Glenn and I walked into the courtroom, it was filled with news reporters, just as it had been throughout the trial. All were there to hear George's sentencing and then promptly report in the daily news the final results of the trial.

Judge Gaughan opened the court just as he had done in the past. Mr. Groth advised him that Glenn and I were going to present our impact statements. Mr. Breen strongly objected and said Illinois law did not allow victim impact statements to be made. Also, the judge appeared to be in a hurry to get the day's procedures wrapped up as soon as possible and felt there was no need nor was there time for Glenn and me to speak. Since there was confusion among the attorneys and the judge, Judge Gaughan called a recess and Mr. Groth, and Mr. Breen and he went into the judge's chambers to discuss whether the Illinois judicial system allowed impact statements to be made.

Everyone in the courtroom waited several hours for the court to reconvene. Glenn and I became more and more frustrated and impatient as the day went on. We were very anxious to speak, and why Mr. Breen and Judge Gaughan were so against it was very puzzling to us. We knew our rights, and I sincerely believe they were trying to frustrate us through their stall tactics, and they hoped we would just give up and leave. But that was not the case. No amount of stalling they could ever do would keep Glenn and me silent.

After waiting for what seemed like an eternity, the attorneys and judge finally emerged from the judge's chamber. The judge announced that Glenn and I would be allowed to speak to the court and read our impact statements. Without hesitation, I walked up to the front of the courtroom.

Nervously, I began, "Your Honor, I need your patience and understanding. I am the mother of Julie Grace. She did not come into this world easy. She and I almost died during childbirth. I did not know if I had a boy or a girl for two days. The doctor came in the room and said, you have a baby girl. You have a million dollar family. I already had a little boy, Glenn. He was four years old. My family was complete. Julie and Glenn meant everything to us.

"Let me tell you about Julie. I loved having a daughter. When Julie was a little girl she had pretty naturally curly hair. Every day I would brush each little curl around my fingers. Her long hair was so beautiful. She would say to me, Mom, I love you and I like you. Julie was a good child and always fun and loving. She set high goals. She was a good student, full of life and energy. She loved life and loved to be with people. She enjoyed ballet, piano, and music. She liked sports. She was a competitive swimmer and won many ribbons and medals. She would volunteer at the local hospital as a candy striper. Julie completed her life guard training from the American Red Cross. At fourteen years old, Julie worked as life guard at the local community pool. She rescued a boy who did not know how to swim and had sunk to the bottom of the pool. She saved his life by performing CPR.

"She grew up to be a beautiful woman and I was proud of her when she left for college. After Julie graduated from Taylorville High School in 1980, she continued her education at Southern Illinois University. She majored in public relations. Julie was very involved in college. She was a member of a sorority. She was also the runner-up for homecoming queen. Julie came home occasionally for weekends and holidays. When she came home, she would often spend her weekend taking care of a disabled eighty-five-year-old lady named Vivian, who could not walk. She would give up her entire weekend and would even spend the night with her. Often she would pick a bouquet of wild flowers for her, read to her, sing to her and take her food. Julie loved helping others. I have a letter that Julie wrote to Vivian when Julie was in Washington doing her internship. Julie always took time out of her busy schedule to remember people like Vivian who were alone and forgotten. Many times during the holidays Julie would volunteer to serve food to the homeless at the Salvation Army. During the winter, if Julie saw a child on the street that was cold, she would give that child her own hat and wrap the child with her scarf and do without herself."

Mr. Breen became very agitated by my statements and continuously interrupted and objected to almost everything I said. Needless to say, this was quite rude and disruptive and made it very difficult for me to read my statement. I finally looked at the judge and said, "I need your patience and understanding. May I please read my statement?"

Judge Gaughan looked and Mr. Breen and said, "Leave her alone." He instructed him to remain quiet and allow me to speak.

Reluctantly, Mr. Breen held his tongue while I continued.

"As Julie was nearing her college degree, she had to do an internship. So, she started to write and call her senators and congressmen to ask about possible internships. I will never forget the day that she got her letter in the mail from Senator Alan Dixon, letting her know that she had been chosen as one of his interns. I cannot begin to tell you the excitement on Julie's face when she received that letter. She had worked so hard and we were so proud. Her hard work was starting to pay off.

"After Julie completed her internship, she started working for Senator Paul Simon. While working in Washington, she brought home a special surprise for my birthday. She had gone to many famous senators and congressmen with their photos and had each one write me a personal happy birthday message with their autograph. I remember the smile she had on her face when I looked at those photographs. She was so proud of what she had done.

"After Washington, her interests turned to politics and she moved to Chicago to work on the Mondale presidential campaign. Later, she worked for the Illinois Attorney General and Illinois Department of Tourism.

"Her dream came true in 1991, when she was offered a job with *TIME* magazine. I was very excited and proud but also worried because I knew she would be traveling a lot and would sometimes be doing interviews in some dangerous places.

"She was working around the clock but loving it. Soon *TIME* magazine was calling her every time there was a natural disaster, gruesome murder, school shooting, or any other dramatic story. She covered the Columbine school shootings, the Jonesboro school shootings, the standoff at Roby Ridge, the OJ Simpson murder trial and many other murder stories. So many times she was planning to come home or already home for a holiday and she would get a call from *TIME* telling her they needed her to cover a story. She was getting praise, awards, and promotions for her reporting. Julie was living her dream and I was so proud of her.

"On the morning of May 20th, 2003, my husband, Duard, and I heard the phone ring and I thought Julie was calling. Julie and I usually started our day out talking. However, this time it was a detective on the phone with the most dreadful news I could have ever imagined. Julie and I had been talking and making plans for her move to Florida. Instead, the detective told me that Julie was dead.

"Soon after that call we got another call from one of Julie's friends. She told us that Thompson had called her on Sunday and said that Julie is real, real sick and needs a doctor but Thompson said he was afraid to call because Julie was in bad shape and he was afraid that he would go back to jail. Julie's friend told him to go to a phone booth, not give his name and call 911 for help. If he would have called, then Julie would have lived. Instead, he let her die.

"When I heard that Julie had been killed, I could not stop crying. The detective asked to speak with my husband because I could not speak because I was crying so hard. I felt paralyzed. I could not even walk. My legs would not move. It seemed like a nightmare where I could wake up the next morning and everything would be okay. But it was not a nightmare. Julie was dead. I could not bring myself to say those words for a year after her death. I cannot describe the loss. To my husband and me, it felt like a big black hole in our hearts. We had two children that we loved so much, Glenn and Julie, who were the most important things in our lives. It was unbelievable to us that Julie had been murdered.

"My husband and I were faced with the task we felt that we just could not do, arrange a memorial service for our baby daughter, Julie. At that time, we could not think or make decisions. We felt completely out of it. Fortunately, Julie had so many wonderful friends to help us through this horrible ordeal. One close friend, Lisa, met us at the airport, took us into her home and looked after us. Another close friend, Thom, took it upon himself to make all the arrangements for her memorial service. We received countless offers of help and support from Julie's many friends.

"Your Honor, my husband and I went to the funeral home to make final arrangements for Julie. We wanted to see our baby daughter one last time, to hold her hand and kiss her beautiful face. We wanted to tell her that we loved her and that we will meet again in heaven. But the mortician would not let us see her. He said we see all kinds of people who have been victims of accidents, burns, gunshot wounds and most of the time family can spend time with their loved ones and we encourage it. He said, 'Mr. and Mrs. Grace, your daughter has been too badly battered and beaten. You would not recognize her and it would be just too painful.' The mortician also told us that we would have to have someone to identify Julie's body. So Julie's doctor of many years, Dr. Footy, was kind enough to take time from his busy schedule to come in to identify Julie's body. I asked the mortician for a locket of Julie's hair. We never had a chance to tell our darling daughter goodbye.

"It is hard to describe the sense of loss I felt. I go to bed with it on my mind and get up with it on my mind. It never goes away. Your Honor, Julie's murder has left such a void in my heart, my life and my family. This wound that has cut me so deep to the heart that only death will give me peace. I am tormented in my sleep with my daughter's screams, the beatings, the torture, and her pain and all her suffering. I know she was beaten to death. The pain never goes away and I ask why. I wish so much for the phone to ring and it would be my Julie and I could hear her say, 'Mom, I love you' and tell me, 'Don't worry. Everything is all right.'

"Thompson not only killed Julie, he killed her dad, my husband, Duard Grace. Before Julie's death, he was in good health and enjoyed traveling. After she was murdered, I remember something that he said over and over again, 'How could someone beat Julie and let her lay there without getting help?' I can't imagine how Thompson can be so cruel. He would cry all night long. He could not eat or sleep. He would walk the floors all night long. When he would sleep, he would have nightmares. Her dad and I could barely bring ourselves to think of how she must have suffered. She was lying there on the floor suffering, vomiting blood and bleeding from the mouth and ears. She had no food, no water, no medicine and no one to help her to the bathroom. His heart just could not stand up to it. He lived only eighteen months after Julie's death. He died of the grief of knowing how Julie had suffered.

"Julie was always doing special little things for people. Right before Thompson killed Julie, she had told me that she had just bought two bathing suits for her little baby nephew, Matthew. She wanted to be the first person to get her little nephew a bathing suit. She never made it back to Florida to give Matthew his bathing suits. She never got to see him or hold him again. She was murdered.

"Every day I ask myself, how could someone so beautiful, so kind, so thoughtful, so giving, and so successful wind up with such a cruel, selfish loser like George Thompson. Thompson took Julie's kindness, goodness and her money and he returned it with cruelty and pain. Julie was always taking in strays and taking care of them. This time, she took in a two-legged stray and he killed her. Even with an animal in pain we would get help. But my Julie wasn't treated even as good as an animal. He left Julie to die and no punishment can be great enough. There are not enough tears to make my pain go away.

"When the detective called with the news that Julie was dead, I knew immediately that Thompson had killed her because Julie and I talked every single day. Sometime we would talk two, three, or more times per day. We would talk for hours and Julie would tell me everything. I knew of all the times that Thompson had beaten her because she told me about them, often the same day that he beat her. I was afraid for Julie that Thompson was going to kill her.

"I remember several times after Thompson beat her up, Julie would have him arrested. Sometimes she would have to go to the hospital because he had beaten her so badly. Julie told me that Thompson would call from jail, collect, often every few minutes begging her to get him out of jail and to take him back. Julie had huge telephone bills. I know because I would be on the phone with her when his calls came in. Julie had call waiting and she would say, 'That's Kenneth calling.' I saw the five to six hundred dollar phone bills with all of Thompson's collect calls on it.

"Thompson was not paying a penny to be there in Julie's apartment. He did not have a dollar to his name. Julie was paying for everything including his food, clothing, and spending money. Julie was also making Thompson's five hundred dollar a month truck payment payable to Thompson's stepfather. Julie was also paying Thompson's legal fees because he had destroyed a rented condo in the suburbs. Thompson was regularly getting parking fines that Julie, of course, would have to pay. Finally, Julie even had to pay for replacing the two plate glass windows that Thompson threw barstools through. I have copies of the checks. Thompson repaid her kindness with stealing everything he could get his hands on to support his cocaine habit along with any other drug he could get.

"Julie told me that Thompson would promise never to hit her, choke her, or pull hair out again. He would promise to quit using crack cocaine and go to anger management class. When she told me that, here is what I said to Julie. I said, 'Julie, a guy who goes and sets firecrackers off in a high school and is expelled, and then beats up his last girlfriend who only escapes by crawling through a window, and then goes to work and beats up a fellow at work and gets fired, and then after his landlord asks him to move out of his apartment because he is not paying his rent goes on a rampage and destroys the place, Julie this guy is never, never going to change. He is so violent and dangerous. You have to get away from him.'

"Julie went through hell. I cannot imagine the pain and suffering she went through. Since we were talking every day, I felt like I was going through that hell with her, but I know it was nothing compared to the torture that he was putting her through. She told me about how he pulled out her hair by the handful and she said, 'Mom, it hurt so bad.' She told me about the time he hit her in the mouth and she had to go to the dentist. Her mouth was swollen and hurting so bad that she could only drink liquids. She told me about the time when he was going after her with a knife. That is when he cut her wrist. She was protecting herself. He was going to stab her. She told me about the time he punched her in the face and broke her nose.

"One time Julie called me crying saying that she was all bruised up and could hardly move and her dog, Bronte, was in an animal hospital and might not live. She told me that Thompson pushed her and Bronte out of his moving truck. I was on the telephone with her when he threw a year's supply of her contacts down the garbage chute so she could not see. I was on the phone talking to Julie the first time he threw a metal bar stool through a twentieth floor plate glass window. I never heard so much glass shatter in my life. I was so scared and upset. I could not imagine anyone doing something that awful. He could have killed several people including moms, dads and children.

"One time Julie came to Florida after Thompson had tried to suffocate her. She told me about how he had tried to choke her to death. She escaped by running out into the street with only a sheet around her because he took her clothes. She said that some guys stopped to help her and they called 911 and had Thompson arrested. That is when she got the order of protection against him. I saw her badly bruised chin and neck where he had choked her.

"Julie had Thompson arrested April 22nd, 2003, for threatening her with the telephone and beating her up. Thompson broke the order of protection. Thompson was supposed to serve a six-month sentence. But Thompson asked the judge if he could come back and start serving his sentence on June 1st, 2003. He told the judge he had something to take care of. The judge agreed to release Thompson. Previously Thompson had told Julie if I can't have you, no one will. Thompson went right back to Julie's condo. Several days later, he gave her the worst beating ever. He punched her in the eyeball. She screamed out in pain as he beat her. He beat her in the face and under the breast. He beat her arms, legs, back and thighs. He beat her until she collapsed on the floor. He did nothing to help, but just watched her until she was close to death and turning blue before he called 911. Julie should not have been murdered in her own home. Julie should have felt safe in her own home.

"Everyone in Julie's building was afraid of Thompson. The doorman of Julie's building, an older man, told me that one time Thompson walked by him, spit in his face and cussed him. He said that he had not done anything wrong, just opened the door for Thompson. He told me that he is the meanest guy that I have ever seen, nothing but a walking devil. One of Julie's friends told me that the condo association held a special meeting where they tried to ban Thompson from coming in the building. Since Julie owned the condo, they could only require that Julie had to escort him into the building. He was not allowed to be in the elevator alone.

"Thompson swore to tell the truth on the witness stand. He said that the hair that he pulled out from Julie's head might have been his hair. Thompson knew that was Julie's hair. He will lie and say anything, especially if he is caught. Thompson did not think one thing about lying on the witness stand. It is just another lie to try to see if he can get away with beating and murdering Julie. Thompson has no heart and is a coward. I heard Thompson get up on that witness stand, lie and say he was Julie's babysitter. Would you want a monster like that for your babysitter?

"Everyone was afraid for Julie and knew that Thompson was so violent and dangerous. They were afraid for her life. Her doctor, a police detective, the neighbors, her friends, the doorman, and even the man who replaced the second plate glass window that Thompson threw a barstool through, all warned Julie that her life was in danger. I know, because I talked with all of these people. Instead, she listened to Thompson and all his lies and promises to change.

"Your Honor, George Thompson murdered my only daughter at the age of forty-one. Julie did not die from drinking. Even though Thompson said they had been drinking, he lied. According to Northwestern Hospital records, at the time she died there was no alcohol in her body. She did not die of a diseased liver or kidney infection. She died from a terrible beating from George Thompson. If he had not beaten her that night, she would still be alive. If he had called 911 earlier like Julie's friend told him, she would still be alive. But he did kill her.

"A couple of weeks ago I called Northwestern Hospital and Julie's insurance company, The Hartford, to discuss their records of Julie's death. I also reread the medical examiner's report. They all listed the same cause of death, homicide. It was Thompson's last brutal beating that killed Julie.

"Julie is dead. We cannot bring her back, Thompson saw to that. But we can protect other women so they will not suffer like Julie suffered. As long as Thompson is behind bars, there will not be another mother in front of a judge describing the pain of her loss because George Thompson murdered her daughter."

There, I had said what I had to say. Now it was Glenn's turn. As I stepped down, Glenn made his way to the witness stand.

"Your Honor, I am Glenn Grace, the brother of Julie Grace. On May 20th, 2003, my sister died as a direct result of a beating that she received from George Thompson. I would like to talk about the impact that this criminal act has had upon my life, beginning with several comments about aspects of the trial that have had an impact on me."

Just like my impact statement, Glenn's words didn't bode well with the defense attorney. Without delay, Mr. Breen began rudely interrupting Glenn, and he objected to almost every sentence that came out of Glenn's mouth. Although the judge did not order Mr. Breen to remain silent as he did with me, his interruptions didn't stop Glenn, who was determined he was going to read his entire statement no matter how long it took and no matter how many times Mr. Breen objected.

"First, the defense's argument that my sister died because of poor health due to alcoholism, has a major problem. The defense attorney has a law degree not a medical degree. He is an attorney, not a medical doctor and cannot competently advance medical theories or explanations. Where was the defense's forensic medical expert? My bet is he could not find one to support his theory. However, two medical doctors from the Coroner's office did examine the case. They both ruled that my sister's death was a homicide. Their medical finding was that George Thompson killed Julie.

"The defense also argued that my sister's death was an inevitable tragedy that was somehow destined to occur whenever two alcoholics get together. That idea is simply not true. The vast majority of alcoholic men do not beat their wives and girlfriends to death. Rather, if you want to find a group of men that better describes George Thompson, then you should look at men that frequently beat women. Chronic domestic violence toward women, not chronic drinking is what predicts whether a man will kill his wife or girlfriend. George Thompson killed Julie not because he drank but because he would viciously beat Julie whenever he got angry with her.

"The defense's argument of a mutually abusive relationship and that George Thompson was defending himself from my sister is absurd. There was an incredible physical difference between Thompson and Julie in strength. I saw Julie about a few months before she died. She was weak and frail. I remember that I was worried about Julie holding my infant son. I was afraid that she might drop him because she was so weak. George Thompson is an ironworker. He is a very strong man. He could have easily held her by the wrists or pinned her to the floor. He could have simply walked out the door. Julie certainly could not have stopped him. Instead, he chose to beat my sister brutally. And that is what he did. He beat her many, many times until he finally killed her.

"Other than Thompson, the defense had only a single witness that said my sister called in a delivery list to a local market the day after George Thompson had beaten her. The defense attorney made a big deal of the issue that Julie did not call for help at this time but instead, called in a grocery order. If she did make that call, the defense is ignoring the fact that my sister was in a progressively worsening mental state due to brain injury. The testimony of the medical examiner described Julie's brain damage as getting progressively worse every day after Thompson had initially beaten her. In the past when Julie thought she needed to go to the hospital, she always went. Because of that beating by Thompson, my sister did not have the ability, insight, or judgment to appreciate the fact that she was dying and needed to call for help. Julie did not want to die. If she had known that she was dying she would have called.

"Finally, I would like to speak about the defense's strategy of blaming my sister for her own death. The defense talked endlessly about Julie's alcohol abuse as if she was on trial not Thompson, the man who killed her. This despicable strategy of blaming the victim is not just factually wrong, it is morally wrong. According to the defense, Julie is to blame because of her drinking problem. According to the defense, Julie is to blame because she did not call an ambulance in time. People with mental or substance abuse problems do not deserve to be killed just because they have problems. Someone who murders a person with a diseased liver is still guilty even though people with diseased livers are easier to kill. My sister had a problem with alcohol that did cause problems with her health. However, there is only one person to blame for Julie's death, the man who beat her to death, George Thompson.

"When I met George Thompson, he initially made a positive impression as a polite guy with a pleasant manner. I noticed that he was quite muscular and had a very strong grip when we shook hands. My sister had initially described him as a guy with an alcohol problem who she met in rehab. Later, through accounts of his behavior by Julie and her friends, I learned that Thompson's initial positive impression was a superficial facade masking a selfish, exploitive, cruel man with an explosive temper. He liked to drink but alcohol was the least of his addiction problems. His drug of choice was really crack cocaine. After Thompson moved in with my sister, he soon quit working. Julie still had a regular income and she began supporting him as well as his crack cocaine habit. Thompson stole every piece of gold jewelry that Julie had collected to buy crack except for one piece that my mother had urged her to put into a safety deposit box knowing Thompson would steal it.

"Thompson was clearly a parasite exploiting my sister for money and her comfortable Lincoln Park apartment lifestyle. My mother has many copies of checks written for Thompson and his stepfather. The worst began after Thompson soon revealed his vicious temper and began to batter my sister on a regular basis. The many trial witnesses attested to cruelness of his beating and these do not include the many beatings that went unreported. At the same time, Thompson became increasingly intimidating and threatening to both Julie and to employees and residents of the Lincoln Park condominium where Julie lived. Twice, in a rage, Thompson threw a barstool through Julie's twentieth floor plate glass apartment window unconcerned that it might kill or injure someone walking below.

"My sister did have a problem with alcohol. Of course, all of us have problems. We all have good and bad times in our lives. Usually there are people there to help us when we are down. Unfortunately, sometimes there also are people who can recognize that we are having problems and see this as an opportunity to exploit us. When Julie was down, she met many good and kind people who tried to help her overcome her problems. Unfortunately, she also met someone very bad, George Thompson who saw a golden opportunity to exploit someone who was down and needed help.

"My sister had lost her way but she could have found her way back. She could have overcome her alcohol problem and started fresh again, perhaps in journalism or perhaps in a completely different area. She could have made a new life for herself. You might ask, how often do people really do that? How often do people quit drinking and turn their life around? The answer is every single day hundreds, if not thousands of times every single day. All these individuals had what was stolen from Julie, an opportunity for a second chance. I am certain that Julie would have eventually turned her life around and gone on to resume a successful and happy life. For me, the most tragic loss that Julie suffered is that when Thompson killed her, he robbed Julie of her opportunity for a second chance.

"I am very proud of my sister, Julie. She leaves a legacy of many honors and accomplishments. Julie was a gifted writer who reported on and/or co-wrote over one hundred news stories for *TIME* magazine. I could talk for hours describing her many important new stories but I will single out just one. In 1994, she reported on the *TIME* cover story entitled, 'The Short Silent Life of Robert Yummy Sandifer: So Young to Kill, So Young to Die.' Inside the issue was a special 'To Our Readers' column from *TIME* that featured a quote from Julie that illustrated the dramatic impact of reporting on this intense story. It begins, 'Grace was particularly shaken by the interviews she did with Robert's former neighbors. It's depressing to hear them talk about murder as if it's an everyday thing,' she says. 'And it's just as heartbreaking to talk to 10 and 11-year-olds who do not expect to live past 19. As I was leaving Yummy's block, a woman called out to me, when are you coming back? You've gotten to be my friend. Sometimes stories get to you; this one left my stomach in knots.' This quote really shows the empathy and compassion that Julie had for people not only in her reporting but also for people she met in her daily life.

"Prior to becoming a reporter, Julie was also involved in public service through her work in government as well as assisting in many political campaigns. Outgoing and friendly throughout her life, Julie made many close friends, all of who were deeply saddened by her tragic death. Upon her death, the Illinois House of Representatives and the Chicago City Council presented our family with resolutions honoring Julie's life and achievements.

"And what are the legacy and achievements of the man that killed Julie, George Thompson? Thompson has only a legacy of violence, selfishness and cruelty. The highlights of his life include domestic violence, drug abuse, felony destruction of property and killing my sister. His only accomplishment has been to bring pain and misery into the lives of others.

"When George Thompson killed my sister, he devastated my entire family. I am the proud father of two boys, ages three and a half and two. Julie was able to see and hold my oldest son, Matthew, as an infant, but she never got a chance to see my younger son, Michael. My two sons will never know their Aunt Julie. What a terrible loss for them and for my sister.

"Julie's murder has been particularly devastating for my mother. Since Thompson killed Julie, she has become deeply despondent and grieves her loss every day. She has filled her house with Julie's pictures, awards, and honors to memorialize Julie's life. She cannot talk about Julie without bursting into tears. Worst of all, she blames herself for Julie's death saying I should have called the police when Thompson told me to get off the phone. If I had, she would still be alive. I try to remind her that there is only one person responsible for Julie's death, George Thompson.

"Julie's death was extremely hard on my father, Duard Grace. He loved Julie so much that he could not stand the grief of her loss. I can still remember how he used to sing songs to her as a little girl and she would laugh aloud. During the year and a half after Julie was killed, my father seemed to age twenty years. I visited my parents often during this time and it would seem like every time I saw him he looked much older, like he was aging in fast forward. My father died of a heart attack at the age of seventy-four, a year and a half after Julie died. Your Honor, my father was a good man. He took good care of his family and was always there for us. He spent nearly forty years working in the Illinois school system, first as a teacher, later as a principal and finally as a school psychologist. He worked hard trying to help children with problems and to make a living for his family. My dad did not deserve to spend his last eighteen months of life depressed and grieving over Julie's murder.

"I was shocked and deeply saddened by my sister's death but what I find particularly disturbing is how she suffered during the last months of her life. I had heard about the terrible beatings by Thompson and the final beating that resulted in a slow, miserable death over three days. Hearing the graphic testimony about the beatings from the witnesses at this trial has been particularly painful for me. I have not looked at the photographs of her abused body and never plan to look at them. However, people who have viewed the photographs have been shocked at how brutally and severely Thompson beat Julie.

"Often my mind will drift to thoughts and memories of Julie. I try to remember happier times like when we would go for a run together along Lincoln Park laughing and joking the whole time. Inevitably, thoughts of her abuse and suffering creep in. It is hard for me to think about Julie without thinking about those awful beatings that she took from Thompson. I try to tell myself that she is in a place now where she is no longer suffering; where she is no longer feeling the pain of those terrible punches and kicks to her body and has no more fear of Thompson's terrifying rage.

"My sister was an extremely generous person. She was always giving people gifts and presents. If a friend saw something in her apartment that he or she liked, Julie would often just give it to them. Julie never met a stranger. She was extremely outgoing and made friendships everywhere she went. She was friendly and generous with everyone and did not seem to ask herself if this is a good or bad person, can this person be trusted? Julie trusted everyone. Unfortunately, she trusted Thompson, invited him into her life and thought that she could help him. Instead, he betrayed that trust and used her, beat her, and killed her.

"Your Honor, my sister and I were born in Ingalls Memorial Hospital in Harvey, Illinois. Even though we spent our early childhood years in suburban Country Club Hills we actually grew up in a small farming town in central Illinois called Taylorville. If you want to travel to Taylorville sometime, you will have to get off the interstate highway and take a two-lane highway. What you will see on your trip is miles and miles of cornfields and soybean fields as far as the eye can see.

"Growing up in Taylorville in the 1960's and 70's was probably much different than it is today. We would ride our bicycles all over town without the slightest fear. There was almost no crime and many people did not bother to lock their doors or even take their keys out of their cars. We never saw a homeless person until one time when my parents were shocked to find Julie giving all of her money to a homeless man who was out begging on the street.

"Julie graduated from Southern Illinois University and then later made Chicago her home for the rest of her life. She loved Chicago. However, even after twenty years of living in Chicago, Julie was still just a small town girl from Taylorville. Judge Gaughan, my sister could not tell the difference between a devil and an angel if they were sitting right beside each other. But I can and George Thompson is a devil.

"I can tell you that George Thompson is an evil man who beat my sister and will beat other women in the future. He is a killer who murdered my sister and will murder another woman in the future. During the trial, Thompson showed no remorse and expressed no regrets. Rather, he frequently expressed his contempt for Julie and showed absolutely no compassion for her suffering. He simply blamed Julie as the reason he beat her and blamed Julie as the reason he killed her. Blaming the victim is common among domestic violence perpetrators and one of the reasons they keep repeating their abuse.

"Three years ago, not long after washing my sister's blood from his hands, Thompson sat down with police and confessed on videotape to beating Julie to death. Just three years later, I watched Thompson, confident and cocky get on the witness stand, lie and try to take back his confession. Thompson took absolutely no responsibility for his behavior. He has obviously learned nothing from this experience. Instead, in his criminal arrogance he feels emboldened that he can lie and manipulate himself out of any jam and get away with anything, including murder. Thompson will, of course, quickly return to his life of drug abuse and violence and he certainly will abuse women again. Past behavior is by far the best predictor of future behavior and this would predict that George Thompson will resume using crack cocaine. He will resume his violent behavior. He will beat another woman and he will kill another woman.

"Your Honor, I am worried about Thompson's future victims, the women that he will batter after he is released. But I know that every day that he is incarcerated, none of these women will be brutally beaten, punched, and kicked until they die of brain damage and pneumonia like my sister Julie. Finally, as long as Thompson remains behind bars, no brother will have to endure the misery of losing his sister and then have to come to court to watch George Thompson and his defense attorney blame his sister as the reason that Thompson beat her to death."

CHAPTER 16

WHAT WAS THE JUDGE THINKING?

Glenn and I did the best we could to make it clear to the court that Julie was a victim of a horrible domestic violence altercation and, as a result, was murdered. She did not die from alcohol abuse; she was murdered. Alcoholism contributed to her body's frail condition, but ultimately the blows she sustained from George were the direct cause of her death. In other words, if George had not beaten her she would still be alive. Even though the judge had already reduced the first degree murder charge to involuntary manslaughter, our only hope was that Glenn's and my words in our impact statements would cause the judge to at least give George as tough a manslaughter sentence as possible. Again, Glenn's and my idea of what seemed to be the obvious course of action for the judge to take was soon dispelled when Judge Gaughan handed down George's sentence of seven and a half years. Since he had already been incarcerated three years, the maximum time he had left to spend in jail was four and a half years.

Although I'm sure there are some who will agree that Judge Gaughan's verdict was the correct verdict for George, Glenn and I will always believe that justice for Julie was not served. As a result, we were once again very upset, mad, and heartbroken, but it was over. The judge's decision was final, and there was nothing more we could do. It's unfortunate, but based on government statistics, many domestic violence cases end up just as Julie's did, and because they do, it's not uncommon to see repeat offenders back in the courtroom time and time again.

There's no doubt in my mind that domestic violence killed my Julie, and, unfortunately, it will continue to kill others. It's a real shame that my beautiful daughter, with such an outgoing and caring personality, got deceived and taken advantage of by someone as evil and heartless as George Thompson. Why did it have to happen to Julie, and why does it continue to happen to other defenseless women? Why did Julie get involved with someone like George? What causes other women to do the same? Julie wasn't raised in a home where there was ever any physical abuse displayed on her or anyone else. She was raised to be kind and giving to others and to look for the good in everyone. She had never been exposed to any form of domestic violence, so why would she become involved with someone who chose to use and abuse her and was an expert at making her believe that she was the cause of all the abuse inflicted upon her?

Although I had several unanswered questions regarding why Julie did what she did, there was one thing I definitely knew the answer to, and that was that the Illinois judicial system had failed me, Julie's dad, and Glenn, but worse yet, it had failed Julie. How anyone could possibly imply that Julie had not suffered a violent death by the hand of George Thompson is irresponsible and unjustifiable as far as I'm concerned. Although it's impossible for me to be objective, the Illinois Department of Public Health, an objective third party, provides insight into what happened and what caused Julie to be a victim. According to information provided by this agency, "Domestic violence, or intimate partner violence, occurs when one person causes physical or psychological harm to a current or former intimate partner. It includes all acts of violence within the context of family or intimate relationships."

In addition, the Illinois Department of Public Health reports, "Besides the obvious physical injuries, domestic violence can lead to depression, anxiety, panic attacks, substance abuse, and post-traumatic stress disorder."

The Department provides a list of traits of domestic violence abusers. They include:

1. Someone who physically hurts, such as kicks, pushes, chokes or punches his/her partner or ex-partner.
2. Partner uses the threat of hurting victim or members of victim's family to get victim to do something.
3. Partner destroys victim's property or things victim cares about.
4. Partner tries to keep victim from seeing their family or doing other things that are important to victim.
5. Victim feels they are being controlled or isolated by their partner. Partner tries to control money, transportation, activities, or social contacts.
6. Partner forces victim to have sex when victim may not want to.
7. Partner is jealous and always questioning whether victim is faithful.

8. Partner regularly blames victim for things that he/she cannot control or for his/her violent outbursts.
9. Partner regularly insults victim.
10. Victim often becomes afraid of their partner or of going home and consequently, the victim feels unsafe.

The Illinois Department of Public Health warns, "There are other signs of domestic violence that observers might see in a relative or friend who is in an abusive relationship. They include:

- Being prone to 'accidents' or being repeatedly injured
- Having injuries that could not be caused unintentionally or that do not match the story of what happened to cause them
- Having injuries on many different parts of the body, such as the face, throat, neck, chest, abdomen, or genitals
- Having bruises, burns or wounds that are shaped like teeth, hands, belts, cigarette tips or that look like the injured person has a glove or sock on (from having a hand or foot placed in boiling water)
- Having wounds in various stages of healing
- Often seeking medical help or, conversely, waiting to seek or not seeking medical help even for serious injuries
- Showing signs of depression
- Using alcohol or other drugs
- Attempting suicide."

Domestic violence killed my Julie, and, unfortunately, it will continue to kill others. The National Coalition Against Domestic Violence (NCADV) reports that, "One in every four women will experience domestic violence in her lifetime. An estimated 1.3 million women are victims of physical assault by an intimate partner each year. 85% of domestic violence victims are women. Historically, females have been most often victimized by someone they know. Females who are 24-25 years of age are at the greatest risk of nonfatal intimate partner violence. Most cases of domestic violence are never reported to the police."

In addition, NCADV information shows that, "Almost one-third of female homicide victims that are reported in police records are killed by an intimate partner. In 70-80% of intimate partner homicides, no matter which partner was killed, the man physically abused the woman before the murder. Less than one-fifth of victims reporting an injury from intimate partner violence sought medical treatment following the injury. Domestic violence is one of the most chronically underreported crimes. Approximately 20% of the 1.5 million people who experience intimate partner violence annually obtain civil protection orders. Approximately one-half of the orders obtained by women against intimate partners who physically assaulted them were violated."

In determining the guilt or innocence of George Thompson, one would have to wonder what Judge Gaughan was thinking. To rule that George was not guilty of first-degree murder but guilty only of manslaughter, I ask again, what was Judge Gaughan thinking? After all, the trial was held in the state of Illinois, so one would expect the court system to base rulings upon facts provided by its own state-run governmental agencies. However, it's obvious that is not the case. At least it wasn't in Julie's case.

To be specific, the traits of a domestic violence abuser (as stated by the Illinois Department of Public Health), were exhibited on numerous occasions by George Thompson during the time he knew Julie. Although these were brought out during the trial, Judge Gaughan either failed to or was unwilling to believe there was any correlation between George's abusive treatment and Julie's untimely death.

However, anyone who reviews and analyzes the facts will find that on numerous occasions George physically hurt, such as kicked, pushed, choked, or punched Julie. This was clearly stated or implied by several witnesses who testified that they had visually seen the physical abuse George imposed upon Julie.

George had no problem abusing animals, another trait of a domestic violence abuser. This was displayed when he threw Julie and Bronte out of his moving truck and caused great harm to both of them. Bronte almost died of her injuries, but fortunately, she survived. However, as was typical of George, he never showed any remorse for causing harm and endangering the lives of both Bronte and Julie.

Also, George had no problem destroying Julie's personal property and her prized possessions. That was discussed several times during the trial by witnesses who had seen the destruction caused by George merely because he was upset with Julie, and he wanted to punish her for whatever caused him to be so distraught. After all, it was her fault that she would not allow him to control her every move or because he was jealous of someone Julie had seen that day. The incident when I was talking to Julie on the phone and George threw her contacts away signifies his way of punishing her because he didn't want her to talk to me. It made him even more upset when she refused to hang up the phone.

Another characteristic of a domestic violence abuser that got a lot of attention in the trial is the one where George regularly blamed Julie for things that she could not control, such as her alcohol addiction. In George's testimony, he implied Julie was the cause of his violent outbursts. Because she would drink, he had to be her "babysitter," and he got tired of taking care of her. His reasoning for throwing a barstool through the plate-glass window, I'm sure, was because Julie had upset him so badly that she forced him to cause physical harm/destruction to anything or anyone around him.

Other things that were frequently discussed during the trial by George as well as some of the witnesses, were the physical signs that Julie was a victim of domestic violence. These included testimony regarding how Julie was prone to accidents or being repeatedly injured. Julie's autopsy photos and reports showed extensive injuries on many different parts of her body. George tried to say her injuries were due to her fall and hitting her head on a table. However, medical experts testified that the injuries found on the majority of her body could not have been the result of her falling, as they did not match the story of what George said caused them. Even though the defense attorney did a good job of twisting the testimonies of medical experts to make it sound as if alcoholism was the main cause of Julie's death, after reviewing the facts and crime scene photos, any rational person would conclude that alcohol did not kill Julie, and George Thompson did. But because the defense attorney was able to portray Julie as a chronic alcoholic, and that's what ultimately caused her death, one would have to assume the judge felt that George just happened to be an innocent bystander whose only crime was not getting her medical help before she was close to death. Furthermore, he did nothing more than try to take care of Julie and protect her from herself, and that is the reason for the involuntary manslaughter verdict and not first-degree murder.

Additional facts from the Mid-Valley Women's Crisis Service, which Judge Gaughan either was unaware of or refused to acknowledge, were, "Despite what many people believe, domestic violence is not due to the abuser's loss of control over his behavior. In fact, violence is a deliberate choice made by the abuser in order to take control over his wife or partner. If you ask an abused woman, 'Can he stop when the phone rings or the police come to the door,' she will say, 'yes.' Most often when the police show up, he is looking calm, cool and collected and she is the one who may look hysterical. If he were truly 'out of control' he would not be able to stop himself when it is to his advantage to do so. The abuser very often escalates from pushing and shoving to hitting in places where the bruises and marks will not show. If he were 'out of control' or 'in a rage' he would not be able to direct or limit where his kicks or punches land."

It was brought out in the witnesses' testimonies that George remained calm whenever police came after one of his abusive incidents where he caused harm to Julie and her property. He allowed himself to be taken into custody without incident and in the process (according to him), made light of the situation, even cracking jokes about Julie and the incident while he was being hauled off to jail. At no time did he appear to be "out of control." George exhibited this same trait throughout the trial, as he always remained very cool and calm and never showed any type of remorse for Julie's death.

Not only does George fit the mold of an abuser, Julie had the traits of someone who was a victim. Again, the judge either failed to have knowledge of these traits (as outlined by the Illinois Department of Public Health), or else he chose to ignore them. After all, the defense's main argument was that Julie ultimately died because she was a chronic alcoholic. The fact that her body was battered and bruised so badly that the mortician said it was the worst he'd ever seen and refused to allow Duard and me to identify her, would cause most any other reasonable person to deduce that Julie's death was not ultimately caused from her alcohol addiction. Coincidentally, some of the effects of domestic violence on victims include substance abuse, depression, and anxiety. Granted, Julie had these conditions prior to meeting George, but if he was truly her "babysitter" (like he said he was) and looking out for her best interests, he would have tried to seek help for her so she could have received the proper treatment for her problems. He would have insisted she move to Florida to be with her parents, as that would have been the best thing for her. Instead, he took advantage of her time and time again, causing her addiction to get worse instead of better.

When someone finds herself or himself in an abusive situation, the Illinois Department of Public Health recommends the victim leave the abusive partner. However, the agency warns, "Leaving an abuser can be dangerous. In order to do it as safely as possible you should plan ahead." This is what Julie was doing. She was moving to Florida to be with her family and make a new start for herself. Why she felt compelled to tell her neighbor she was moving is one question that will never be answered. The second unanswered question is, how did George find out?

On July 3rd, 2006, George Thompson was sentenced to seven years and five months in jail. As previously mentioned, because he had already served three years in jail prior to the trial and subsequent sentencing, he was left with approximately four and a half more years in jail. However, under Illinois State Law, George was required to serve only one-half, or three years, eight months and fifteen days of the eighty-nine month sentence he received, making his release date May 26th, 2007, only ten months and twenty-three days after his sentencing date. Again, where was the justice for Julie? The Illinois court system failed my family and society one more time and allowed a murderer to go free long before he should have.

I don't know where George is today, but I am fearful Julie will not be his last victim. I sincerely hope and pray he hasn't charmed his way into the life of some other non-suspecting woman. I certainly don't want anyone else to suffer from his abuse or become another statistic of domestic violence, nor do

I want any parent to endure the never-ending emotional pain and suffering of losing their child in such a brutal manner.

My Julie's gone, but her legacy will never die. She will always be remembered by her family and friends as a beautiful, compassionate woman who loved life and loved everyone in it. Every day when I stare at her picture on my dining room wall, and I see her beautiful brown eyes and her warm smile looking back at me, it's difficult for me to accept that she's no longer with me. However, I find comfort in knowing she's safe and will never suffer from the cruel acts of anyone ever again.

Julie Ruth Grace
1962–2004

Reference List

Domestic Violence and Abuse. Helpguide.org. Database online at www.helpguide.org.

Domestic Violence Facts. National Coalition Against Domestic Violence. Database online at www.publicpolicy@ncadv.org.

Domestic Violence Warning Signs of an Abuser. Mid-Valley Women's Crisis Service. Database online at www.mvwcs.com.

Facts about Domestic Violence. Illinois Department of Public Health. Database online at www.idph.state.il.us

State of Illinois County of Cook, Circuit Court of Cook County; County Department–Criminal Division, C.S.R. 84-1194. The People of the State of Illinois vs. George Thompson: 05 CR 13087. Hearing Dates: May 11, 12, 15 & 16, 2006.